NATIVE NATIONS
The Survival of Fourth World Peoples

2nd Edition

Edited by
Sharlotte Neely

JCharlton
PUBLISHING Ltd.
3104 30th Ave., Suite 228
Vernon, BC V1T 9M9

www.jcharltonpublishing.com

JCharlton Publishing Ltd.
3104 30th Ave., Suite 228
Vernon, BC Canada
V1T-9M9

www.jcharltonpublishing.com

Cover photo © Stamatoyoshi.
Map of the Fourth World © Sharlotte Neely.
Author photo, back cover, © Katie Englert.

Library and Archives Canada Cataloguing in Publication

Native nations : the survival of fourth world peoples / edited by Sharlotte Neely. -- 2nd edition.

Includes bibliographical references and index.
ISBN 978-1-926476-17-9 (softcover)

1. Indigenous peoples. I. Neely, Sharlotte, 1948-, editor

GN380.N38 2017   305.8   C2017-902213-X

This book is dedicated with gratitude to my granddaughter
Quinn Donnelly
and to my mother-in-law
Mary Stauber Donnelly.

Map of the Fourth World

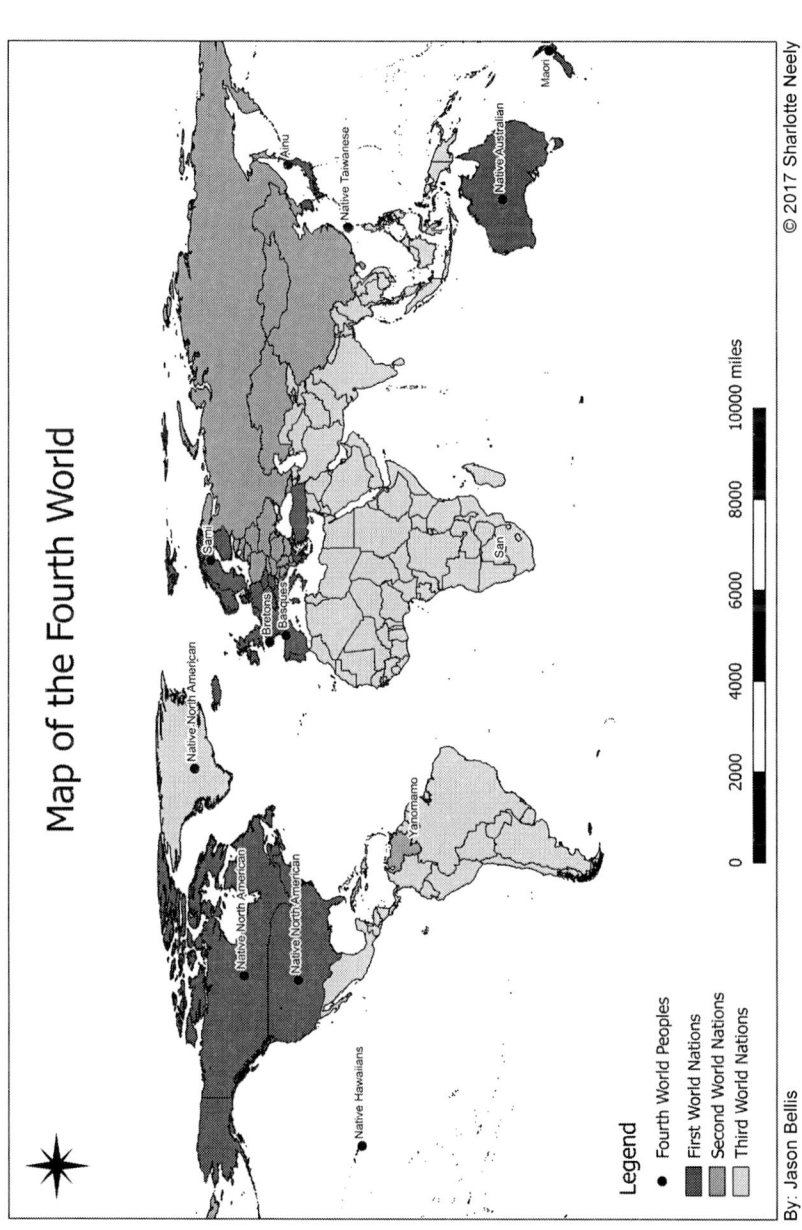

Legend

- Fourth World Peoples

First World Nations

Second World Nations

Third World Nations

Maori

Native Australian

Ainu

Native Taiwanese

Sami

Bretons

Basques

San

Native North American

Yanomamo

Native North American

Native North American

Native Hawaiians

0   2000   4000   6000   8000   10000 miles

By: Jason Bellis

Table of Contents

PART I

Overview

Introduction

Sharlotte Neely

Northern Kentucky University

*I*ndigenous minorities—Fourth World Peoples—continue to exist in some of the wealthiest, most modern nations on earth. Despite acculturating to some degree, these Native groups have survived with their unique ethnic identities and many of their cultural traditions intact.

In recent years the phrase "Fourth World" has been used in at least three, sometimes overlapping, ways. Sometimes the term has been used to mean the poorest of the Third World countries where the First World refers to wealthier democratic nations often aligned with the West, the Second World refers to one-time or current communist nations previously aligned with the former Soviet Union, and the Third World refers to politically non-aligned, poorer, usually non-Western, nations. In other cases "Fourth World" has been used to refer to the world's unrecognized, non-sovereign, "wannabe nations" like Tibet, Kurdistan, Palestine, Catalonia, Euskal Herria, the Kingdom of Hawaii, or so many others that would like to carve their territory out of one or more recognized nations. (Most recently, South Sudan has actually made the transition from wannabe nation to sovereign nation.) Finally, "Fourth World" can refer to the surviving, Indigenous (Native, Aboriginal) minorities within the wealthier First World nations. That is the meaning of "Fourth World" in this book.

Here nine anthropologists, one linguist, one historian, one geographer, and one political scientist focus on nine groups of Fourth World Peoples within twelve First World nations and, for comparison, one Indigenous group in a Second World nation and one in four Third World nations. All are compared and contrasted in regard to their strategies for survival.

Within the First World:
- Native North Americans within the USA, Canada, and Greenland (Denmark)
- Native Australians
- Native Hawaiians of the USA
- Māori of New Zealand
- Ainu of Japan
- Taiwanese Aborigines
- Sámi of Norway, Sweden, and Finland
- Basques of Spain and France
- Bretons of France

Within the Second World:
- Yanomami of Venezuela

Within the Third World:
- San of Botswana, Namibia, South Africa, and Zimbabwe.

This list of Indigenous Peoples, while representative, is not exhaustive and could, for example, also include additional groups within First World nations like the Ryukyuans of Okinawa (Japan), Torres Strait Islanders of Australia, the Chamorros of Guam (the USA), Samaritans of Israel, and the Scots and Welsh in the United Kingdom and within Second and Third World nations the Ainu, Sami, and Tungus of Russia; Mosuo of China; Semang of Malaysia; Andaman Islanders of India; Baka of central Africa; Hadza of Tanzania; and various Native American groups throughout Latin America.

Studies of groups such as Fourth World Peoples were especially encouraged by the illustrious anthropologist Fredrik Barth (1969) in his classic book, *Ethnic Groups and Boundaries*, when he noted that not all ethnic groups succumb to acculturation despite great pressure to do so. Because Fourth World Peoples exist within prosperous, modern, democratic First World nations, they have opportunities—and problems—not afforded Indigenous minorities in less well off countries. The World Bank estimates that worldwide there are about 300 million Indigenous people. This study, however, focuses on Native minorities within First World nations and offers a unique opportunity to compare and contrast the success of ten Fourth World Peoples and even the possibility of affecting government policies aimed at assisting in the survival of Indigenous peoples.

The nine Fourth World Peoples considered here are diverse. "At contact" some, like the Aborigines of Australia, were nomadic foragers; others, like the Sámi and Basques survived on domesticated animals or plants; and others, like Native Hawaiians and the Bretons, lived within complex chiefdoms that soon developed into sovereign states. Various individual Native North American groups fall into all three of those categories. Of the Fourth World Peoples considered here, many were the only peoples in their territories for thousands, and often tens of thousands, of years, before later peoples invaded their lands. Today, most Fourth World Peoples comprise less than 5%--sometimes much less than 5%--of their particular nation's population. The major exception is the Māori of New Zealand who are more than 15% of their nation's population and increasing in number and percentage. Of the Fourth World examples examined here, only the Ainu of Japan live in a country without a European heritage. The Natives of Taiwan were dominated by both Asian (China and Japan) and European (the Netherlands and Spain) nations.

All the Indigenous groups here have concerns about preserving their traditional values, languages, sacred lands, festivals, art, music, foods, clothing styles, and other aspects of their culture. All went through periods where their nations attempted to assimilate them, often by forcing their children to be educated at boarding schools far from home and by suppressing their Native languages. Many encompass a great deal of linguistic and other diversity. For example, there are nine surviving Sámi languages, more than two-dozen Native Taiwanese languages, hundreds of Australian Aboriginal languages, and hundreds of Native American languages. There are more than one hundred Māori groups. Some, like the Ainu, Basques, and Bretons, have even had their claims of being Indigenous challenged. All desire some degree of sovereignty within their modern nations. Here at the beginning of the 21st Century, all have achieved some level of appreciation within their nations, even if only because of their tourism appeal.

What makes a people Indigenous? For anyone who is Native-born to a place, especially if descended from generations of Native-born people, one's homeland has special meaning, and there is the feeling of "always" having been there. Many of my own ancestors came from various parts of Europe, but so long ago that Europe does not feel like my homeland. My homeland is the United States, and it does not seem less my homeland because a majority of my ancestors were not Native Americans. Native Americans have been in what is now the United States for a much longer period of time than European or other Americans. In fact, for the entire time period humans have been in North America, for more than 95% of that time, the only people here were Native Americans. But science informs us that even Native Americans were not always here.

The science of genetics tells us through DNA evidence that truly modern humans like ourselves evolved probably somewhere along the borders of the present-day nations of Botswana, Namibia, and South Africa about 200,000 years ago (Henn, 2016). The science of paleontology tells us through fossil evidence that shortly after that time some truly modern humans had spread to an area along the Omo River in Ethiopia. The most direct descendants of these first modern humans are probably the San ("Bushmen") people who still live in southern Africa. From that point 200,000 years ago, humans eventually spread over Africa and out of Africa to all the continents on earth. Perhaps as long ago as 80,000 years, a few hundred people successfully left Africa for Asia. Modern humans probably arrived in Australia 60,000 years ago and in Europe 40,000 years ago. By 30,000 years ago modern humans were poised to enter the Americas. The last big migration into new lands began only about 5,000 years ago when the Polynesians began spreading into the islands of the Pacific, and the very last place to which modern humans finally spread was probably New Zealand when the Polynesian ancestors of the Māori arrived mere centuries ago.

Groups of people have displaced other groups of people all over the world and throughout human history. Some would argue that the current influx of Muslim refugees from the Middle East into Europe is just the beginning of one group of people, Europeans, being displaced by another. Most of us are descended from both the displaced and the displacers. One need not limit examples to people of European descent displacing Native Americans or other Indigenous Peoples. The Swat Valley, within the "tribal" region of Pakistan, for example, has had a succession of groups migrating in and displacing the previous inhabitants. At one time most of the people in the Swat Valley were Buddhists. But they were displaced by Hindus. And they were displaced by waves of Muslims. The Dilazak people were displaced by the Swati who were in turn displaced by the Yusufzai (Barth, 1965). Who are the truly Indigenous people of the Swat Valley? The first humans in the Swat Valley may have gone extinct in prehistoric times, migrated out of the valley, or their genes may still flow through the bodies of the present inhabitants, some more than others. Many groups in the Swat Valley feel like they are the "real" Natives.

While one can make the argument that Indigenousness is relative, that does not diminish issues around the world of who the "real" Natives of a homeland are. The United Nations, World Bank, International Labor Organization (ILO), and European Union are just a few of the groups who have attempted to define who are Indigenous and what Aboriginal rights should include. The European Union, for example, recognizes the Sámi, but not the Bretons or Basques, as Aboriginal. The struggle between Jews and Muslims, each claiming to be the "real" Indigenous people of Israel, is only the most prominent example of such "Native" conflicts.

No matter how long a group has lived in a particular homeland, there always seems to be another group who has been there longer. In the southwestern United States, for example, Latino Americans claim primacy over Anglo Americans when they point to the Mexican American War's (1846-1848) aftermath and invoke the popular phrase that "we didn't cross the border, the border crossed us." Meanwhile, Native Americans from Texas to California point out how much longer than both Latino and Anglo Americans they have been Natives of the American Southwest. And, finally, Native American groups like the Hopi point out how much longer they have been in the Southwest than Native American groups like the Navajo.

Genocide, as in the former Yugoslavia, is the result of one group of people trying to assert their rights over another to a commonly claimed homeland. Perceptions of Indigenousness are at the heart of many world conflicts. These conflicts are not little issues. The fate of Israel, for example, the only predominantly Jewish state on the planet, may hinge on peoples' perceptions about Indigenousness.

Nevertheless, there are within many of the planet's First World nations, ethnic minorities who have been in those homelands for a much longer period of time than the present majority. That time depth marks them as Indigenous. No longer feeling much of a threat from these Fourth World Peoples, most First World nations have ceased overbearing attempts to abolish their identities and fully assimilate these people.

This tolerance, however, does have its limits. Only two of the twelve First World countries included in this book, Norway and Denmark, have, for example, signed onto the ILO's Indigenous and Tribal Peoples Convention of 1989. The others are reluctant to do so mostly because the ILO Convention would require them to defend Aboriginal land ownership. Sweden, for example, wishes to discourage large-scale reindeer herding by the Sámi so that traditional pasturelands can become government or private property.

In a similar vein, when the United Nations voted in 2007 on whether or not to adopt the Declaration on the Rights of Indigenous Peoples, four countries voted against adoption. Those four nations, Australia, Canada, New Zealand, and the United States, all had Fourth World Peoples within their borders. One of several issues addressed by the document is land inhabited by Indigenous Peoples. (It should be pointed out that all four countries did later endorse the declaration, Australia in 2009 and the other three in 2010.)

Has limited tolerance developed out of the realization of how small a minority and how little a threat most of these Indigenous Peoples are? Or, is something more noble going on? Have people learned to be less ethnocentric and more appreciative of diversity? Or, have these Indigenous minorities taken on these First World nations and, to some degree, won their right to exist? What strategies have these small ethnic groups used to survive? How have they "won" when winning should have been impossible? Why are they still here?

These are just a few of the questions considered in the following chapters. Some of the chapters' authors are themselves Fourth World Peoples; all are academics of the highest order. I thank each one of them for sharing their expertise, and I thank Northern Kentucky University anthropology alumnus Jason Bellis for the map of Fourth World Peoples.

References

Barth, Fredrik. (ed.).
1969. *Ethnic Groups and Boundaries*. Prospect Heights, IL: Waveland Press.

Barth, Fredrik.
1965. *Political Leadership among Swat Pathans*. New York: Humanities Press.

Henn, Brenna.
2016. "The Origins of Modern Humans in Africa." *Symposium at the Center for Academic Research and Training in Anthropology*, University of California at San Diego. April 2016.

PART II

Indigenous Peoples in the Developed
First World: Fourth World Peoples

Native North Americans of the USA, Canada, and Greenland (Denmark)

Mark Q. Sutton

California State University, Bakersfield

For centuries, Euro-Americans have viewed Native North Americans as inferior, second-class citizens with a dispensable culture. However, in the last few decades, the attitudes of non-Native people have shifted, and Native Peoples have won some important legal battles and have gained some political power. As a result, a revival of Native culture is taking place, with Native groups reasserting their sovereignty and regaining some rights related to land, water, hunting, fishing, mineral resources, and religion (Champagne, 2007a; Jorgensen, 2007).

Nevertheless, many stereotypical views of Native life and culture remain. Many still see Native North Americans as people of a romantic past, rather than as members of contemporary cultures. Government agencies and other groups continue to perceive Native people as children incapable of making their own decisions. Coupled with this ethnocentric view is the general Western belief that Native thought and science are inferior.

Today, Native North Americans are confronted by a myriad of problems and issues. They are struggling to regain their land, dignity, and freedom, and to recast their public and political identities. Compared to the United States national average, Native Peoples earn about 25% less, have double the poverty rate, almost double the unemployment rate, are 2.5 times more likely to be the victim of a violent crime (including hate crimes [Perry, 2008]), have a 32% higher homicide rate, 25% higher infant mortality, 2.4 years lower life expectancy, 51% higher rate of death by alcohol, 62% higher suicide rate, a 50.6% higher dropout rate from high school, and are about 50% less likely to earn a Bachelor's degree (Schaap, 2010, p. 377). These and other problems have prompted a movement to the cities, where communities of Native people have taken root. In 2000, some two-thirds of the Native people in the United States lived in cities (Fixico, 2000), where they experienced problems of ethnocentrism, poor health care, unemployment, and loss of identity.

Native political activity has generally focused on the plight of Native peoples as a whole, rather than problems of specific groups. This has led to the formation of a pan-Native identity; both the non-Native public and some Native people themselves, particularly those living in cities, have often adopted this view of Native people as essentially one large group, combining diverse heritages. One by-product of this phenomenon is the idea of a "generic Indian" as seen in the stereotypical Plains Indian costume featured at many events, in the blending of ceremonies, dances, and songs from different traditions, and in the adoption of these generic traits by non-Natives. Yet at the same time, many groups have retained and revitalized their individual identities, have begun teaching traditional language and knowledge, have opened cultural centers, and are attempting to gain control of their own lives.

Despite the large number of issues that face contemporary Native Peoples and the considerable literature that exists on those issues (Barker, 2009; Champagne, 1999, 2007a; Christie, 2005; Johnson, 1999; Thornton, 1998), the space here permits only a brief treatment. The major topics include sovereignty and decolonization, preservation of traditions, economic development, climate change, and expression.

A Brief History of Government Policies Toward Native North Americans
Native Policies of the United States

Control of the lands south of Canada and west of the Mississippi passed to the newly created United States after 1783. Much has been written about the policies of the U.S. government toward Native Americans, with a comprehensive treatment being provided by Finkelman and Garrison (2009; also see Deloria, 1992; Hirschfelder & de Montaño, 1993, p. 8–35; Iverson, 1998). Fewer accounts are available about the impacts of the policies of the individual states towards Native Peoples (Corntassel & Witmer, 2008; Rosen, 2007).

Early in its history, the United States considered Native groups to be sovereign nations, though not *foreign* nations, and signed more than 400 treaties with various Native Peoples (Fixico, 2008). Many of these agreements were ratified in good faith by the respective governments, only to be broken by aggression by white settlers or, less often, by young Native men (Deloria, 1988; Prucha, 1994, p. 17–18). By the 1830s, Native groups within the boundaries of the United States were considered to be *domestic, dependent* nations. By 1871, most groups without treaties had been militarily subdued, so treaties were no longer sought. Thus, Native political units evolved from sovereign to dependent status in relation to the U.S. government, occupying an ambiguous place in the political and cultural life of the United States—and this peculiar state of affairs exists to this day.

In 1775, the United States created several Indian Commissions, mostly in an effort to obtain Indian military assistance during the Revolutionary War. The U.S. government also recognized the 1763 Proclamation Line (a boundary set by the British to prevent the westward expansion of settlers) but this was ignored by the settlers themselves and when settlers ventured beyond that line and came into conflict with Native groups, the U.S. government felt obligated to protect the settlers. Thus, settlement and conflict continued moving west.

In 1781, the Indian Department was created to manage Native Peoples. Its initial placement within the War Department provides some clue as to its real mission. In 1824, the name of the agency was changed to the Bureau of Indian Affairs (BIA) (Porter, 1988). The BIA became an independent agency in 1834 and was transferred to the newly created Department of the Interior in 1849. Initially, the goal of the BIA was to maintain good relations with sovereign Native groups in order to obtain land and promote trade.

The BIA is still the principal federal agency that interacts with Native peoples in the United States. Today, the BIA has four primary responsibilities: (1) education of Native Peoples; (2) providing other governmental services to Native groups (e.g., law enforcement and health services); (3) management of the 56.2 million acres held in trust for various Native nations; and (4) fostering Native self-determination. Not until 1970 was an Indian appointed as the director of the BIA.

Manifest Destiny

As European settlers continued to push westward, an idea evolved to justify the displacement of Native Peoples and the confiscation of their lands. Known as *manifest destiny*, it gave Euro-Americans a seemingly noble duty: to tame the wild lands of the west and to bring "civilization" to its Native inhabitants. The idea gained momentum with the acquisition of the Oregon Territory in 1846 and of California and the American Southwest in 1848.

In the new territories, the west coast was colonized first, due partly to the California Gold Rush. Two new American population centers, the west coast and the region east of the Mississippi, were formed, with "Indian Country"— the Plains, Rockies, and Great Basin—lying between them. Many agreements between the government and Native groups were made to create transportation corridors for wagon trails and railroads between the Mississippi River and California/Oregon. As these treaties were broken, considerable hostility between white settlers and Native groups ensued, setting the stage for the famous Indian Wars of the west.

Removal and Reservations

While the early U.S. Indian policy might be characterized as one of moderation (although actual events tell a somewhat different story), after the War of 1812, the policy changed to removal and segregation, formalized with the Indian Removal Act of 1830. Most of the Indians in the southeastern United States were forced, some at bayonet point, to walk to various reservations that had been established in what is now Oklahoma, collectively known as "Indian Territory." Thousands of men, women, and children died in a series of "trails of tears." Oklahoma essentially became the "dumping ground" for many disparate Indian groups, most of them separated from their homelands and economic bases. In 1904, the Indian occupants of Indian Territory petitioned Congress to admit the territory to the Union as an "Indian State," but their petition was rejected. Oklahoma was admitted to the Union in 1907.

In 1865, the U.S. government decided that all Natives would be put on reservations. Over the next few years, a series of reservations was created on the Plains, this time located in the homelands of the affected Native Peoples, and a number of large groups moved to these reservations. The government attempted to provide for these groups, but many of the politically appointed Indian agents prevented much of the money and supplies from getting to the Natives. Due to this corruption and greed, starvation became a serious concern, so some people left the reservations to find food. The government perceived these actions as "uprisings," which they often quelled through bloodshed. Other Natives revolted at the poor treatment through raiding and warfare. Finally recognizing the corruption of Indian agents, the government appointed religious organizations—presumed to have higher morals—to administer the reservations and Indian payments through the Board of Indian Commissioners. This also failed, and the plight of the Natives worsened.

The Military Solution

Throughout the history of contact between Native Peoples and Euro-Americans, the Natives were almost always the ones defending their lands and lifeways. When provoked, Native groups often responded, and numerous military confrontations ensued. Many Native groups possessed substantial military power and were adept at small-scale warfare. Small-scale conflict between armed settlers and Native Americans was a constant feature of the frontier. Large-scale warfare between Indians and the U.S. Army (or with the British prior to 1783) was uncommon and pitched battles were rare. Man for man, the Indians were more than a match for any European or American military force; however, the Indians lacked a sufficient number of modern weapons and were not able to sustain a dedicated force in the field for years on end.

In 1867, the United States instituted a "Peace Policy," forming the Indian Peace Commission to try to stop the incessant warfare. To the U.S., peace meant the defeat and submission of the Natives, and a central component of the Peace Policy was to impose peace on the Native Peoples by force if necessary. It was decided that the best way to obtain peace was to exterminate the Native populations, although many Americans were opposed to that policy. While the Natives were not exterminated, the ruthless pursuit, defeat, incarceration, and mistreatment of Native Peoples crushed their resistance, thereby achieving "peace."

Assimilation

As of the early nineteenth century, many believed that Native Peoples were on the verge of extinction and that the survivors should be assimilated. Beginning in the 1870s, government policy began to shift from segregating Natives on reservations to attempting to assimilate (i.e., "civilize") them into mainstream society. Thought to be a humane solution to the "problem," it was to be accomplished through educating Native children (i.e., forced acculturation at boarding schools run by Christian missionaries), converting them to Christianity, and transforming Native economies to farming (many Indian economies were already based on farming, but this was ignored).

It was reasoned that if the Natives became civilized, they would no longer require all of the lands of the reservations. Whites generally considered the Natives to have too much land already and proposals were made to parcel out reservation lands to individuals so that the Natives could be property owners, like whites. Thus in 1887, the Dawes Act (or General Allotment Act) was passed to break up communally owned reservation land and to allot parcels to individual Natives (including women) as private property, although some reservation land was exempted due to earlier treaties. The allotments were made in 40- to 360-acre parcels, depending on the quality of the land. The "surplus" land could then be sold to whites, with the money, in theory, being used to help the Natives. The Dawes Act also made citizens of those Natives who received an allotment and moved away from their reservations. (It was not until 1924 that all Natives in the U.S. were finally granted citizenship and the right to vote.)

Individual ownership of land meant that the owners had to pay property taxes, which most Native people could not afford. As such, the government held the allotments in trust, tax-exempt and nontransferable, for 25 years. Much reservation land was never allotted and remained in tribal hands. Many of these provisions were later changed, resulting in a further loss of Native lands to whites. In some cases, the government used their own definition of "Indian" to deny lands to individuals so that less land would be allotted (Doerfler, 2009). The legacy of the Dawes Act is still confronting the tribes today (Ruppel, 2008).

After 1877, schools were established to educate Native children, some on reservations and others at boarding schools (Reyhner & Elder, 2004). Frequently, Native children were forcibly removed from their families, taken to boarding schools, and "educated" either to "become white" (DeJong, 1993) or to serve as domestic help for white families. They were often punished severely if they spoke their Native languages or observed their traditional customs. This practice continued until the 1960s, when boarding schools were finally phased out in favor of local public schools.

The Indian New Deal

As the U.S. gained a New Deal during the presidency of Franklin D. Roosevelt, so did Native groups. Roosevelt appointed a new director of the BIA, John Collier, who initiated sweeping reforms in the BIA and major changes in policy (Philp, 1977), moving away from assimilation and toward cultural pluralism (partly based on a 1928 report that was highly critical of Indian policies). Many of these reforms were passed into law with the Indian Reorganization Act of 1934. With this Act, the allotment system was ended and unsold reservation lands were returned to federally recognized tribes. In addition, efforts were made to purchase land to "close up" the allotments and restore the land base. Groups were then allowed to organize tribal governments to manage their own affairs, albeit to a limited extent.

World War II provided an opportunity for many Natives to participate in American society, including work in war industries and in the military. Some 25,000 Native people joined the military and fought overseas. In fact, Native people have fought for the U.S. in every war in its history. Patriotism and the chance to earn battle honors were incentives to join. The general movement of Native people to the cities was accelerated by those seeking jobs in war industries and by the return of war veterans, eventually setting the stage for more politically sophisticated Native activism.

Beginning in the 1940s, the U.S. government initiated the Termination

Policy to end the recognition—including status and rights—of some Native groups, to eliminate their reservations, and to move them into white society. The National Congress of American Indians (NCAI) was formed in 1944 in response to those efforts and to protect the rights of Native Peoples, including Native Alaskans. The NCAI was instrumental in a number of successes, including health and environmental issues, and after 1958, the government ceased its efforts to terminate tribal governments. In the 1960s and 1970s, the civil rights movement and the war on poverty provided some funding and programs to help many Natives.

In 1968, the American Indian Movement (AIM) was founded to promote Indian rights (Smith & Warrior, 1997). The mission of AIM was to force the U.S. government and people to listen to and to act on Native rights, and it was felt that only militant action, which would attract media coverage, could effectively communicate their message. Among AIM's first actions was the occupation of Alcatraz in San Francisco Bay, beginning in October 1969 and lasted until June 1971 (Johnson, 2008), at which time it was forcibly ended by the U.S. government. This event, which was widely reported, was designed to publicize the loss of Native lands and to raise awareness among the non-Indian public. Every Thanksgiving Day, AIM holds a ceremony on Alcatraz to commemorate the 1969 occupation and to symbolize the loss of Native lands. In 1972, members of AIM seized the headquarters of the BIA in Washington, D.C., for seven days to publicize the mismanagement of Native lands by the BIA.

Then, in early 1973, some 200 armed AIM members occupied Wounded Knee Creek, the site of the 1890 massacre of several hundred Sioux by the U.S. Army. The FBI surrounded Wounded Knee, initiating a tense 71-day standoff that ended in the deaths of several people and the imprisonment of some AIM members. The occupation accomplished little to change U.S. policy at the time but did result in considerable publicity for the Indian cause. After Wounded Knee, AIM lost its momentum—partly due to disagreements among the leadership and partly because several leaders were imprisoned—and is no longer a major force in Native politics. Beginning in the mid-1990s, efforts have been initiated to revitalize AIM.

The establishment of the National Council on Indian Opportunity and the passage of the American Indian Civil Rights Act, both in 1968, brought about better legal protection for an outline of Native legal rights (Pevar, 1997). In 1970, the BIA changed its basic policy from managing Native Peoples to serving them. Beginning in the early 1970s, Native Peoples began to campaign more actively for their rights and a revitalization of their cultures. As a result of these efforts, Congress passed the Indian Self-Determination and Education Assistance Act (1975), the American Indian Religious Freedom Act (1978), the Indian Gaming Regulatory Act (1988), and the Native American Graves Protection and Repatriation Act (NAGPRA). These new legal rights allowed a number of groups to sue some states for the loss of their lands, and many have won substantial monetary damages.

Each U.S. administration has had a different set of priorities regarding Indian policy, from general neglect to active self-determination. Today, there are some 310 federal Indian reservations in the U.S. (including pueblos and rancherias; see Tiller (2005) for a profile of each) and the federal government holds some 56 million acres of land in trust. There are also a few additional reservations that have been set up by individual states, mostly in the east. In early 2010, the U.S. and Canada signed a Memorandum of Understanding to better communicate about Indigenous and northern issues, and in December 2010, the U.S. government finally endorsed the 2007 United Nations Declaration on the Rights of Indigenous Peoples.

Native Policies of Canada

Canada became independent from Britain in 1867, and subsequently developed their own policies regarding Aboriginal Peoples. Native Peoples in Canada probably endured the Euro-American invasion better than those in the U.S., as Canada had far fewer Euro-American immigrants and much less development and the British were a little more sympathetic to their needs. Nonetheless, problems remained. Slavery was not outlawed in Canada until 1834, and Natives were the primary slaves.

In 1867, the Office of Indian Affairs was established within the office of the Secretary of State, was moved to the new Department of the Interior in 1873, was renamed the Department of Indian Affairs in 1880, and in 1966 was renamed the Department of Indian and Northern Affairs. The Canadian government established a system of Native boarding schools similar to that of the U.S., called the Canadian Residential School System.

Between 1871 and 1921, the Canadian government signed 11 major treaties with Native groups, who were moved to reserves where the government was to protect and support them. The Indian Act of 1876 was passed to manage Native Peoples, although it did not apply to Inuit groups until after 1939, when the Canadian Supreme Court ruled that the Inuit should be considered Indians and be under the jurisdiction of the government (the Inuit were finally recognized as a distinctive group of Canadian aboriginals under the Constitution Act of 1982). The Indian Act of 1876 designated Indians as either Status Indians formally recognized with treaty rights, or Non-Status Indians who, for some reason, had lost or given up their status. The Indian Act of 1876 also denied Native groups the right to practice their social and religious customs. To enforce the ban on religious activities, the government confiscated religious paraphernalia from a number of groups, particularly on the Northwest Coast (Cole, 1985). The Indian Act of 1876 (repealed in 1969) remains the measure most emblematic of the mistreatment of Native people by Canada. An attempt to pass a new Native policy, the First Nations Governance Act, failed in 2004.

In 1888, Canada passed a law similar to the U.S. Dawes Act of 1887 with the intent of breaking up reserve lands through an allotment policy. Native people had very little power to stop it, but the loss of land was not as severe as it was in the U.S.

An alliance of Northwest Coast groups won a small land claims case against the Canadian government in 1927, which prompted Canada to pass a law forbidding all collective Native political action. However, in reevaluating its policies in the 1940s, the Canadian government passed the Indian Act of 1951. In this Act, Native people were granted citizenship and local voting rights (although they could not vote in national elections until 1960), were allowed to practice their religions, and could pursue claims against the government. Also, Native groups on reserves, usually called "bands," were expected to establish councils to make decisions that related to the bands. Nevertheless, many of these decisions were subject to approval by the Canadian government.

Canadian Native groups made several attempts to organize, such as in 1919 with the short-lived League of Indians in Canada, followed by the North American Indian Brotherhood in the late 1940s, by the National Indian Council in 1961, and finally by the National Indian Brotherhood (NIB) in 1968, the latter of which evolved into the Assembly of First Nations, a group that is still active.

In 1969, the Canadian government repealed the Indian Act of 1876 and attempted to break up the reserves in a move similar to the failed U.S. Termination Policy (see above). This caused the politically dormant Canadian Native Peoples to unite, protest, and make demands, forcing the government both to abandon its termination policy and to repeal the 1927 law against Native political activity. The Native groups went to court to have their treaty provisions honored and won some victories. In 1974, the government set up the Office of Native Claims. In the past few decades, a number of land claims have been settled with various Native groups, resulting in the formation and enlargement of reserves, special rights to land use, and cash payments.

Comprehensive Land Claim Settlements have recently been signed with a number of groups (Bone, 1992: Table 10.1; also see Crowe, 1991). These include agreements with the James Bay Cree in 1975 (Niezen, 1998), the Nisga'a in 1998, and the Nuu-chah-nulth in 2001 (although this agreement is not yet in effect). In a 1999 agreement with the Inuit, the Northwest Territory was divided and the eastern part was designated as a new Canadian territory, called Nunavut and governed by the Inuit (Kulchyski, 2005). Three other Inuit "settlement regions," Inuvialuit, Nunavik, and Nunatsiavut, had already been recognized in northern Canada, and together with Nunavut, they form "Inuit Nunangat" (in essence, Inuit territory, including land, water, and ice).

Another group, the Métis, are considered the "third aboriginal group" in Canada, recognized by Canada in 1982. The Métis are the descendants of European fur traders and their Indian (usually Cree) wives (Peterson & Brown, 2001). Over the centuries, the Canadian Métis (there are also some Métis in the U.S.) developed their own cultural identity and speak a distinct language (Michif, a mixture of Cree and French) as well as French and English. In 1983, the Métis in Canada formed their own governments within the provinces, but a national government has not been recognized.

In 2008, the Canadian government apologized to its Native people for their policy of assimilation and the treatment of children in Indian schools, although a colonial "settler" mentality persists in the treatment of Canada's Native populations (Barker, 2009). Nevertheless, in November 2010, the Canadian government endorsed the 2007 United Nations Declaration on the Rights of Indigenous Peoples.

As of 2006 (the most recent census in Canada), there were about 1,173,000 Native people living in Canada, including 50,500 Inuit, 390,000 Métis, and 698,000 First Nations Indians. They are organized in some 615 recognized bands representing about 50 nations (e.g., tribes), living on some 2,240 reserves (similar to reservations in the U.S. but generally smaller). The reserves are held in trust by the Canadian government.

Native Policies in Greenland

Greenland has a unique history of relations between Native Americans and Europeans. The Norse established several colonies in Greenland in A.D. 982, the Inuit entered the area about A.D. 1200, and by A.D. 1400 the Norse had abandoned Greenland. It is possible that the Inuit pushed the Norse out by force, or that the climate became too cold (the Little Ice Age) for Norse agriculture, or that the Norse left due to a loss of trading opportunities (Diamond, 2011; Dugmore et al., 2007). Whatever the case, only the Inuit occupied Greenland when the Norse left. After A.D. 1380, Denmark and Norway were a combined kingdom and no one in that government knew that the Norse settlements had been abandoned. Thus, Greenland continued to be considered a colony. In 1721, not having heard from their Greenland colony for centuries, an expedition was sent to investigate. Discovering no Norse colony, the Danes/Norwegians established a new one. Denmark split from Norway in 1814 and took control of the Greenland colony. While the colony was essentially a trade station that had little impact on the Inuit (Petersen, 1995), the Inuit view that land was communal was interpreted by the Danes as meaning all land belonged to the crown, effectively establishing colonial rule. The colony was administered by Danish civil servants.

Greenland became a "country" controlled by Denmark in 1953, technically ending colonial rule although Danish administrative control continued. Modernization of the economy and infrastructure changes began, and hunting and fishing became less common. While this certainly impacted traditional Inuit lives, health care, education, and housing were improved. This "Danization" transformed Greenland into a modern country but resulted in a major increase in the role of Denmark in Inuit lives, making Greenland even more "colonial" than before (Petersen, 1995, p. 121).

In 2009, Greenland became an autonomous country. (Greenland, the Faroe Islands, and Denmark form the three autonomous nations within the Kingdom of Denmark.) Nevertheless, the Danish government has retained responsibility for Greenland's foreign affairs, security, and financial policy, partly due to the view that Inuit were not capable of doing it themselves. This colonial view persists to this day and has been accepted by many of the Greenland Inuit themselves, making it even more difficult to decolonialize the government (Petersen, 1995). Greenland is still dependent on Denmark for support, receiving more than 60% of its annual budget as a block grant from Denmark, reinforcing the "colonial" economy.

Nevertheless, the Inuit now dominate internal politics in Greenland as the Prime Minister and most of the members of parliament are Inuit. Greenlandic (an Eskimoan language) is the official language. In 2010, there were about 45,000 Inuit or mixed Inuits/Danes in Greenland.

Sovereignty and Decolonization

Prior to contact, Native groups were sovereign and independent political entities, making their own decisions and managing their own affairs. Upon contact with the European powers, many groups established government-to-government relations, each recognizing the other as a sovereign nation. This sovereignty was confirmed by treaty, was upheld by court decisions, and has never been extinguished. However, in actual practice, the independent status of Native nations rapidly changed to that of dependent nations and Native Peoples lost control of their land, lives, livelihoods, and identities.

The reaffirmation of sovereignty remains a major issue as Native Peoples strive to assert control over their own lives and regain political and economic independence (Cobb & Fowler, 2007; Den Ouden & O'Brien, 2013). Nevertheless, in the U.S., tribes remain dependent nations, although in 1994 President Clinton issued an Executive Memorandum directing government agencies to cooperate on a government-to-government basis with federally recognized tribes.

Decolonization, or the restoration of Native control over their own lives, is a related major issue. In the U.S., the BIA has considerable control over Native life, although Native groups do have some control, such as legal jurisdiction over most matters, including tribal police forces and court systems. Being "colonized," Native Peoples on reservations must deal with multiple levels of sovereignty and political interaction (Biolsi, 2005), including (1) tribal members on reservations, (2) co-managers of off-reservation sacred sites and other resources, (3) "national Indigenous space" off the reservation, and (4) "hybrid" political space in which Native people exercise rights of dual citizenship in the reservation and host country and as citizens in a multicultural society. Many groups want to abolish the BIA, but at a minimum, they want the authority to act on their own behalf on their own lands. The imposition of Christianity on Native groups is also an agent of colonialism, suppressing Native religions.

The establishment of the new Canadian Territory of Nunavut governed by the Inuit in 1999 seems to be a major step forward in the establishment of

Native sovereignty. However, the 2008 summit of Arctic Rim States (e.g., Canada, Norway, Russia, and the U.S.) that dealt with issues of Native sovereignty excluded Native Arctic Peoples. This exclusion was due, at least in part, to tensions between Arctic Peoples and the other governments regarding curbs on Native hunting and fishing. For example, in 2009, the European Union (EU) banned the importation of seal products (e.g., skins and oil) but under pressure from the Danes, exempted the Inuit. In 2009, Native groups from Alaska, Canada, Greenland, and Russia proposed and adopted the "Circumpolar Inuit Declaration on Arctic Sovereignty" detailing their views on issues of self-determination.

Tribal Recognition and Ethnic Identity
In the U.S. (and Canada), a Native group must be "recognized" by the federal government in order to receive benefits from the government. Only federally recognized tribes can have reservations, open casinos, and apply for BIA funding, among other benefits. To be federally recognized, a tribe must demonstrate that they have existed as a distinct community from historical times; have membership criteria (usually blood quantum); have political influence over its members; and have a membership that consists of individuals who descend from a historical Indian tribe and who are not enrolled in any other tribe. The desire for benefits has prompted many groups to apply for federal recognition. However, some groups do not want federal recognition since it would create a dependency on the BIA.

It can be very difficult to obtain federal recognition and the applications of some groups have been pending for decades; as of 2008, the applications of approximately 250 Native groups were in process. The difficult issue is often one of demonstrating a community from historical times. With so much discrimination and government interference, many members of groups have moved away and lost contact with other tribal members, thus fragmenting the community to the point that the BIA does not consider them distinct entities.

For example, the Lumbee in North Carolina have been recognized as an Indian tribe by the state government since 1885 but have been unable to achieve federal recognition. The issue seems to be primarily tied to federal rules about blood quantum since the Lumbee are multicultural with considerable European and African-American "blood" (Lowery, 2009). In 1956, the federal government recognized the Lumbee as Native Americans but not as a formal tribe. Most recently, federal legislation to grant recognition to the Lumbee was finally approved by the House of Representative in 2009 but as of 2013 is still awaiting Senate action.

Self Determination
Self-determination is at the heart of decolonization. This can include regaining complete independence and sovereignty. For example, Greenland is moving toward independence from Denmark (and the EU) and the separatist Inuit

Ataqatigiit party won a near majority in the Greenlandic legislature in 2009. This drama has yet to be played out. In the U.S., the Mohawk—following their traditional role in the decision-making process in the Iroquois League—are now taking the lead in Haudenosaunee resurgence (Landsman, 1988). They are working to rebuild the league and seeking recognition by international organizations, including the United Nations. They have issued their own passports for use in travel between the U.S. and Canada, a right set forth in a 1794 treaty between the U.S. and Britain. Finally, as discussed above, the Inuit have gained some level of self-determination in their control of the new Canadian Territory of Nunavut.

Self-determination is generally associated with people that have a land base, such as a reservation or reserve. However, many – if not most – Native people, some 67% in the U.S. (Fixico, 2000) and 50% in Canada (Christie, 2005), now live in cities and face a different set of issues regarding self-determination, such as ethnocentrism, poor health care, unemployment, and a loss of identity (Christie, 2005). One coping mechanism is the adoption of a pan-Indian identity.

Land Claims and Settlements

A major issue for Native Americans has always been the loss of Native lands (Clark & Powell, 2008). Much land was ceded by treaty early on and vast tracts of other land were taken through other means, many of which were illegal. If the Native Peoples resisted militarily, they were forcibly removed. Others fought the actions in court, but found little justice. As the years went by, ownership of Native lands by non-Natives became entrenched.

In 1946, the U.S. government formed the Indian Claims Commission to consider land claims (although claims against the original 13 states were to be handled in state courts). Treaties signed by states after the adoption of the U.S. Constitution were deemed invalid (once part of the U.S., states have no authority to sign treaties) and claims originating from those treaties had to be heard in federal court. The Indian Claims Commission has heard many cases and has decided in favor of Native groups in numerous instances. In 1971, a comprehensive settlement, known as the Alaska Native Claims Settlement Act (ANCSA) was reached with Native groups in Alaska and 44,000,000 acres were returned to Native groups, along with a cash payment of $962 million, and a royalty of $500 million on mineral rights.

The Canadian government is also attempting to settle Native claims. As noted above, Canada has signed several Comprehensive Land Claim Settlements. However, not all of these efforts have worked out well. In late 1978, the government of Alberta built an all-weather road through the territory of the Lubicon Lake Cree, claimed ownership of Cree lands, threatened the Cree with eviction, and leased portions of the land for oil exploration and logging (Martin-Hill, 2008). The Lubicon Lake Cree filed suit, lost, and were ordered to pay the oil company's legal expenses. As a result of that decision, the Lubicon

Lake Cree organized a boycott of the 1988 Winter Olympics in Calgary and gained the support of Amnesty International. The United Nations Committee on Human Rights found Canada in violation of Article 27 of the International Covenant on Civil and Political Rights and has repeatedly called on Canada to correct the situation. The Lubicon Lake Cree, now forced to subsist on welfare, are still waiting.

In some cases, tribes with money from either casino profits or settlements from the government have begun buying back land with their own money. This is an issue for some states who stand to lose the tax revenue when land is transferred from private (and so taxable) to tribal ownership where states have no jurisdiction.

In other cases, Native groups own the land that non-Natives live on. In one example, the entire city of Salamanca in western New York was built on lands leased from the Haudenosaunee in the late nineteenth century. The leases were for 99 years, at very low rates. Frequently, the lease payments were never made, and the land was bought and sold without consideration of the leases. Many people bought houses unaware that the land was leased. When the leases began to expire, residents feared that the Indians would expel them. However, the Indians preferred to renegotiate the leases at fair market value, although this angered many residents as well. Much of the land on which the city of Palm Springs in California sits was also leased from the Indians, who are now poised to make a nice profit.

Control of the Past
Interpretations of Native cultures are often dominated by Western science, which often does not include Native perspectives (Smith, 2010; Watkins, 2000, 2005). To some, this is a colonial, even racist, mechanism designed to control Native Peoples (Echo-Hawk & Zimmerman, 2006) and that even the excavation of Native archaeological sites is "colonial" (Martinez, 2006).

Museums are a good example of this idea of control. In many cases, Native materials are displayed within the same museums that display rocks and animals, perpetuating the stereotype that Native Peoples are of nature and not humanity. In one case, an Indian man visited a museum only to find the skeleton of his grandfather on display. On the plus side, these attitudes are changing.

In 2004, the National Museum of the American Indian (NMAI) opened in Washington D.C., with materials and displays designed by Native Americans rather than non-Native anthropologists, although this has also had its problems and issues (Spruce & Thrasher, 2008). A major goal of the NMAI is to challenge the commonly held stereotypes of American Indian history and culture (Lonetree, 2006). Nevertheless, issue remains regarding the exhibition of identities in museums and other places of cultural tourism, such as a focus on male roles (Martinez, 2012).

NAGPRA

A very important and emotional issue to Native Peoples is the return of the remains of their dead ancestors that had been collected over the last several hundred years by museums and universities. In 1990, Congress passed the Native American Graves Protection and Repatriation Act (NAGPRA), requiring federal agencies and institutions receiving federal funding to inventory their collections for any human remains (e.g., skeletons) and associated funerary objects and other sacred objects, to identify the tribal affiliation of those materials, to notify the identified tribes, and to repatriate the materials if requested by the tribes. Materials whose affiliations cannot be determined would remain in the collections pending further review, although some unaffiliated remains have been reburied under the "Return to the Earth Project." NAGPRA further requires that if human remains or scared objects are accidentally unearthed, such as during construction, the appropriate Native American groups will be consulted.

A number of states have since passed similar laws, although Iowa passed its burial law in 1976, much earlier than the NAGPRA legislation. While NAGPRA provides for the study of remains prior to their repatriation, many researchers have argued that the remains are too important to science to rebury. To many Native Peoples, the issues are religion (reclaiming their dead), politics (the return of their heritage), and empowerment (ownership and interpretation of the past) (Bordewich, 1996, p. 162–184; Schweninger, 2009). Most archaeologists understand and agree with these issues (Killion, 2008). A similar law in Israel is more restrictive that NAGPRA.

However, problems remain. In 1996, a skeleton was discovered on federal land near Kennewick, Washington, and became a major test case for the study of remains under NAGPRA. The Kennewick skeleton had a very different morphology than other Native American remains, was dated to about 9,300 years ago, and was thought to represent a population of people that may have been unrelated to contemporary Native Americans (e.g., an early and separate migration into North America). The skeleton was claimed by local tribes and was due to be repatriated by the U.S. government. A group of archaeologists sued, claiming the skeleton was not affiliated with the local tribes, should not be reburied, and should be studied. In 2004, the court agreed with the archaeologists and the skeleton was studied (Owsley & Jantz, 2014). In 2005, a bill to amend NAGPRA to make it easier for tribes to claim unaffiliated remains was introduced but it was not passed. However, in 2010, that change was codified as a rule under NAGPRA. Information on the Kennewick issue can be found in Burke et al. (2008), Chatters (2001), Owsley and Jantz (2001, 2014), and Thomas (2000a), and additional information on the various issues involved with NAGPRA can be found in Fine-Dare (2002), Mayes (2010), Peregoy (1999), and Swidler et al. (1997).

Native American Historians, Anthropologists, and Archaeologists

Anthropologists are now keenly aware of the issues surrounding the control of the past and there is a new emphasis on including Indigenous views in interpretation and in directly involving more Indigenous Peoples in research. Collaborative efforts between archaeologists and Indigenous Peoples are now much more common and are generating additional understanding of the past (and the present) (Atalay, 2008; Bruchac et al., 2010; Colwell-Chanthaphonh, 2012; Colwell-Chanthaphonh & Ferguson, 2007; Phillips & Allen, 2011; Smith, 2012). Additionally, in order to have a greater voice, a number of Native American groups in the U.S. have established their own archaeological management programs (Stapp & Burney, 2002; Two Bears, 2006) and founded their own museums, both to exercise sovereignty over the material remains of their past and to present their own interpretations of it.

More Indigenous people have become anthropologists but this has its challenges. Indigenous scholars receive training in a different (i.e., Western) thought system (Mihesuah & Wilson, 2004) and they must be both a "scientist" and a member of a community that may view archaeology as a colonial enterprise. Native American history is also an issue. Mainstream American history appears to sustain old stereotypes of Native Americans (Hurtado, 2008) and recent times have seen the development of Native American Studies programs at many universities (Kidwell, 2009; Larson, 2009), often with Native American scholars as faculty. Such programs help to focus the issues and can play a political role within many tribes (Champagne, 2007b).

Health and Welfare

The availability of health care is a continuing problem to many Native Americans. Many Native communities do not have health facilities, and few doctors choose to work on reservations or in isolated Native communities. In addition, many Native people have major health problems such as diabetes (Sievers & Fisher, 1981), and there is a high incidence of HIV among Native women, due both to poverty and associated risky social behaviors (Vernon & Thurman, 2009).

The greatest health problem facing Native Americans is alcohol (May, 1999). After the Prohibition Act was repealed in 1933, alcohol was still banned on reservations. In 1953, it became legal to sell alcohol on reservations, but most reservations still do not permit it. Nonetheless, a great number of Native people have an alcohol problem and alcohol-related crime and death rates among Native people are much higher than those of the general population. In addition, Native infants are more likely to be affected by fetal alcohol syndrome than non-Native infants, treatment of alcohol-related illness consumes some 70% of the BIA health budget, and the emotional health and cultural productivity of Native people due to alcohol are greatly impacted. It seems that a major cause of alcoholism is despair rooted in the experience of discrimination, lack of economic opportunity, and loss of culture. In 2012, the Oglala

Sioux sued a major beer maker in Federal court, claiming they knowingly contributed to the tribe's alcohol problems. The suit was later dismissed.

Associated issues include mental health (Nebelkopf & Phillips, 2004), substance abuse, homelessness, and special needs individuals. Access to specialized health care to address these issues is very sparse, although some traditional healers are now helping to deal with these problems.

Preservation of Tradition

Basic to any identity is religion and language, and their retention is a critical issue. Other traditions are also important, particularly if they are appropriated and misused. In some sense, many Native people identify with both a pan-Indian "tradition" with generalized practices and a specific tribal or group tradition. The various practices in each can get conflated and so be confusing.

Religion

Native religion and healing are integral to any culture or to a cultural revival (Irwin, 2008; O'Brien, 2008). Probably in recognition of this, both the U.S. and Canada early on sought to control, restrict, and eliminate Native religious practices and freedom due to bias against and fear of these practices. This was reinforced by missionaries who attempted to convert Native people to other religions, mostly Christianity. In the nineteenth and early twentieth centuries, Native people in white schools and on reservations were actively discouraged from practicing traditional religious rites. After the early twentieth century, government restrictions became less severe but continued to hamper the practice of Native religions.

Within the past few decades, Congress has passed several Acts, including the American Indian Religious Freedom Act of 1978 and the Religious Freedom Restoration Act of 1994, to ensure that Native Americans could freely practice their religions. These Acts have not halted prejudice and discrimination, or the continuation of missionary work among Native Peoples, but they at least prevent the federal government from legally interfering with Native religions.

An example of the difficulties in practicing Native religions is the use of peyote. In the late nineteenth century, some Native Peoples in the Southwest, the Plains, and the Great Basin began to use peyote, a small cactus that grows in Mexico, in their religious ceremonies. Peyote is a mild hallucinogen but is not narcotic. Use of this substance spread quickly as a means of communicating with the supernatural world. A number of states eventually banned peyote, and in response the Native American Church (NAC) was established in 1918 with the ingestion of peyote as a central practice (Stewart, 1987).

By the 1940s, most state laws dealing with peyote had been repealed but federal officials often broke up peyote ceremonies as illegal drug parties. In 1959, California banned peyote, and in 1962 three Indians using it were arrested. These men were convicted, but the California Supreme Court overturned their convictions on the basis of religious freedom. Federal drug laws subsequently exempted peyote use by members of the NAC, a right upheld by the U.S. Supreme Court in 1990. However, to legally use peyote, one has to be a member of the NAC and membership is strictly regulated by the church to prevent abuse. The NAC has some 250,000 members from many different tribes (Smith & Snake, 1997).

Education and Language Revitalization
The delivery of education by nation states to Indigenous populations is a problem all over the world, and North America is no exception (Abu-Saad & Champagne, 2006).

Formal education was once conducted by the BIA in boarding schools, taught in a foreign language (English) in unfamiliar settings (away from home and family), and was quite traumatic (Fear-Segal, 2007). The transmission of education by Native groups to their own people is a sovereignty issue (McCarty, 2002) and the availability of education remains a concern (Ward, 2005).

Historically, Native people have had a very high dropout rate; the rate of high school completion is much lower than that of the rest of the U.S. population. However, some progress is being made and a great effort is being undertaken to increase the number of Natives attending four-year universities. Part of that effort is making education more accessible. Within the past several decades, many groups have established their own school systems and a number of community colleges have been established on reservations, along with a number of accredited four-year colleges. Increased availability of scholarships is allowing more Native people to attend other colleges and universities as well.

Of the many hundreds of Native languages that once existed in North America, many are no longer spoken, resulting in a substantial loss of history, traditional knowledge, and ethnic identity. Many of the languages were lost as the result of intentional policies to extinguish them, such as in Indian boarding schools. The preservation of Indigenous languages is now a worldwide issue and numerous efforts are underway to record and catalogue Native languages (Frawley et al., 2002) and to revitalize them (Kroskrity & Field, 2009; McDermott, 2014; Reyhner, 2005).

In 1990, Congress passed the Native American Languages Act, making it U.S. policy to preserve Native languages and to provide funds to tribes and educational organizations for programs of language retention. Progress is being made and a number of conferences on language conservation and revival have been held, including the 2009 National Native Language Revitalization Summit held at the National Museum of the American Indian and the 1st International Conference on Language Documentation and Conservation held at the University of Hawai'i in 2009.

Intellectual Property
All cultures acquire and categorize knowledge about their environment, and

many hold specialized knowledge relating to medicine, religion, and other fields. The practical applications of traditional knowledge and wisdom have attracted ecological scientists as well as anthropologists (Ford & Martinez, 2000). However, intellectual property rights remain an issue in regard to this knowledge (Brush & Stabinsky, 1996; Posey, 2001).

It has been argued that Native knowledge is being stolen without compensation to the holder of the knowledge, a sort of copyright or patent infringement. Many see this as an extension of Western colonial practices and a further exploitation of Native Peoples. Ways to deal with this issue, such as extending "copyright laws" to include unwritten traditions, are being proposed (Laird, 2002).

Use and Misuse of Native Traditions and Icons

Native American activists have long objected to the use of Native American images and icons in the dominant culture (Hemmer, 2008; Johansen, 2007, p. 143-181; Spindel, 2000). Of note has been the use of Natives as mascots by schools and sports teams. Some have argued that the use of such mascots further exploits Native Americans and that, as many other mascots are animals, their use equates them with animals (Deloria, 1995). Debate on this issue has continued and by 2010, most schools had dropped the use of Native mascots (the Florida State Seminoles, which has formal permission from the Seminole Tribe of Florida, is a notable exception).

However, a few professional teams continue to resist changing their mascots, citing a loss of revenue from the sales of team gear with the logos. Notable among these teams are the Washington Redskins (Native people understandably object to the derogatory name), Cleveland Indians (the derogatory mascot, Chief Wahoo), and Atlanta Braves (the Tomahawk Chop). Some legal actions have been undertaken but have been unsuccessful. For example, the Washington Redskins were sued in 1998 over the use of the "Redskin" trademark. The team lost the initial ruling in 1999 but it was overturned in 2009, meaning the team can continue to use the trademark. Some members of Congress had petitioned the National Football League to force a name change but in 2013, Commissioner Roger Goodell refused. California banned the use of "Redskins" as school mascots in 2015 and in 2016, a federal judge ordered the cancellation of the team's trademark registration. The team is appealing. However, a Washington Post poll conducted in 2016 showed that most Native Americans were not offended by the name.

Others have argued that the use of Native names conveys a healthy spirit of competitiveness. In that vein, the U.S. military continues to name many of its weapons after Native groups or individuals, partly to convey a "warrior image" (e.g., Cheyenne, Kiowa, Apache, and Blackhawk helicopters and tomahawk missiles). In addition, the military continues to refer to enemy-occupied territory as "Indian Country."

Native names are also used in many commercial endeavors, such as the Jeep

Cherokee, the Pontiac automobile (now defunct), and the Winnebago recreational vehicle. Further, hundreds of places, including 28 states (e.g., North Dakota, South Dakota, Kansas, Missouri, Alabama, Delaware, Illinois), many cities (e.g., Wichita, Miami, Ottawa, Detroit, Seattle), and numerous other localities, are named for Native American locations, icons, and persons.

Some members of the 1960s U.S. counterculture adopted "Indian ideals," viewing Native Peoples as the original ecologists, at peace and living in harmony with their environment. This general trend continues today with the adoption of Indian ideals and views by "New Age" enthusiasts. However, the New Age movement can be seen as further exploitation of Native Americans by people interested in their ceremonies and crafts but not so much in the Natives themselves (Aldred, 2000; Deloria, 1995), and many Native people object to this (Jenkins, 2004).

Economic Development

Many Native groups were initially placed on reservation lands that whites thought to be of little value, often leaving them isolated and with few resources. For a very long time, the government retained control so that Native peoples had no way to develop their own economies. In the last few decades, tribes have achieved a much greater role in this development, although not without restrictions.

For many decades, reservations on the northern Plains were so isolated and devoid of resources that very little development was possible. There were too few people to support very many casinos, too few tourists, and very few jobs. It has recently been realized that the northern Plains, which are among the windiest places in North America, are perfect for wind farms and plans are underway to develop this resource. In addition, massive reserves of natural gas have been found there, almost ensuring development.

Natural Resources

Among the most basic of natural resources for Native Peoples are the plants and animals upon which they have depended for millennia. Access to game animals, fish, and plant resources is a critical issue and many treaties guaranteed the rights of Native groups for fishing, hunting, and gathering. In many instances, these rights have been ignored and are now being reclaimed. For example, Indian fishing rights in Washington were reaffirmed in the 1974 Boldt decision and upheld by the U.S. Supreme Court in 1979 (Cohen, 1986), over the protests of non-Indians.

In 1987, the Chippewa won a court decision granting them the right to hunt and gather any resource within their territory without regard to state regulations. This had been affirmed by treaty in the nineteenth century but was subsequently ignored by the state government. This ruling, opposed by many non-Indians, set a precedent for other such suits.

In another example, since 2002, the Asubpeeschoseewagong First Nation in northwestern Ontario has been fighting the clear-cutting of forests on what they consider to be their traditional lands (Willow, 2009). The issue appears to be less about the logging itself and more about a lack of Aboriginal rights to the land and involvement in the process. This can be viewed as a continuation of Canadian colonialism, with the government imposing its will on a subjugated people.

The U.S. government, along with some state governments, is beginning to become more sensitive to Native needs and wishes. For example, the U.S. Forest Service and U.S. Park Service have granted special permission to some Native groups to gather traditional materials from areas normally closed to such activities. In addition, standard Forest Service practices have been changed to accommodate Native lifeways, such as halting the poisoning of pandora moths so that the Owens Valley Paiute can continue to collect the caterpillars.

In other cases, problems persist. The hunting of seals and whales was curtailed by the EU and World Trade Organization (WTO) based on animal rights issues, but this caused a problem in traditional Inuit economies. Canada authorizes a seal hunt each year (the 2012 quota was 400,000 animals), but the ban on the importation of seal products showed that the EU and WTO lacked an understanding of traditional practices and wished to impose their values on Indigenous Peoples. The Inuit were exempted from this ban in 2009.

Other natural resources are also of concern. Most Native land (some 56.2 million acres) is held in trust by the U.S. government, and it was often the government, not the tribes, that negotiated leases with the various mining companies. In many cases, the leases were exceedingly favorable to the companies, with very small royalties paid to the tribes (Grinde & Johansen, 1995). More recently, many tribes have hired and/or trained their own legal staffs and are fighting such exploitation in court. In 1975, 25 tribes with coal, oil, or gas reserves (including groups from the Plains, Southwest, Northwest, and Great Basin) formed the Council of Energy Resource Tribes (CERT) to better control the exploitation of resources on the reservations. In 2009, the Federal Government agreed to pay a number of tribes $1.4 billion in back royalties for use of their land and another $2 billion to buy back land, but the agreement must still be approved by Congress.

Gaming

One of the better known economic developments on Native lands is "Indian Casinos." In 1979, the Seminole Tribe of Florida opened a high-stakes bingo parlor on their reservation, which was immediately shut down by the County Sheriff. The Seminole sued in court and won. In 1980, the Cabazon tribe in California opened a casino, and it too was quickly shut down. In 1987, the tribe sued in federal court and won. The ruling was appealed and eventually reached the U.S. Supreme Court, which ruled in favor of the Indians. As a result, Congress passed the Indian Gaming Regulatory Act of 1988 to encourage tribal self-sufficiency, as well as to provide regulation for gaming on their lands

(Rand & Light, 2006). The National Indian Gaming Commission was established as the federal agency responsible for the regulation of Indian gaming. Nevertheless, each tribe must have an agreement with their state to operate a casino (Corntassel & Witmer, 2008) and additional federal legislation was passed in 2006 to tighten control and permit greater local participation. However, the passage of the federal and state laws governing Indian gaming may have eroded the sovereignty of the tribes (Ackerman & Bunch, 2012, p. 65).

One of the largest casinos in the world is the Foxwoods Casino in eastern Connecticut that opened in 1992 and is owned and operated by the Mashantucket Pequot tribe. It grosses more than one billion dollars a year and has allowed the tribe to establish health, police, fire, and educational services, as well as to buy back some of their traditional lands (Anthes, 2008). The state of Connecticut originally objected to the establishment of the casino, but finally acquiesced when it was agreed that the state would be given a share of the gross (about $75 million a year).

As of 2012, at least 240 tribes (including two Alaska villages) operate some 400 gaming facilities in 28 states and have taken in more than 26.7 billion dollars (Ackerman & Bunch, 2012, p. 50). Many casinos are very profitable, while others are less so, and a few have failed. Gaming provides some 636,000 jobs (including casino employees, support jobs, and related jobs (Schaap, 2010, p. 369)), many held by non-Indians, and the federal government and various states collect billions in taxes. Many tribes do not have casinos, and their members often continue to live in poverty.

Tourism
In addition to casinos, many tribes are implementing tourism programs (Bunten, 2010; Lew & Van Otten, 1998). The attractions include natural scenery within a number of reservations, archaeological sites (Thomas, 2000b), famous battlefields (e.g., Little Bighorn), and Indian towns themselves. In some cases, the large numbers of non-Native tourists will sometimes hinder normal life in a town, forcing the Indians to close the town to tourists for certain periods so they can conduct their ceremonies.

Climate Change
Probably the most pressing climate issue to Native people in North America is the warming of the Arctic (Johansen, 2007, p. 279-286; McBeath & Shepro, 2007; Wassillie, 2015). For example, rising sea levels are causing increased coastal erosion and inundation that threatens the destruction of traditional villages and cemeteries. The reduction in sea ice has resulted in changing types and numbers of animals available, such as the decline in seal populations that has impacted the food sources for both people and polar bears.

The reduction in sea ice has had other consequences. The exploration of oil and gas is ironically much easier and an intense competition to find and exploit these resources by the U.S., Canada, Russia, and Denmark, all of which have vast territories in the Arctic, is now beginning. In addition, the fabled "Northwest Passage" may finally be viable at least part of the year, opening the sea-lanes for commerce. All of this development will greatly impact Arctic Peoples and biosystems (Anderson, 2009).

Native Peoples in the Arctic are responding in part with the use of new hunting technologies (boats and all-terrain vehicles) and safety equipment (for unstable sea ice and melting permafrost). Further, traditional properties are being moved to higher ground, although the relocation of traditional burial grounds is a difficult emotional and logistical endeavor.

Expression

Expressive art and literature has always been a part of Native culture. Contemporary Native art can be found in a number of media, including painting (Anthes, 2006), sculpture in stone and wood (e.g., totem poles), pottery (some potters are very famous and their pots sell for thousands of dollars), textiles (e.g., Navajo blankets), basketry, and jewelry. In the past, such materials were not typically considered quality art, but this has changed and many Native artists are now seen as among the best in the world. Photography is also a medium in which Native Peoples preserve their identity (Williams, 2014).

There is an increasing body of Native American literature and a presence of Native American views in other literature (Crozier-Hogle & Wilson, 1997). While there have always been Native American authors, the publication of the Pulitzer Prize winning *House Made of Dawn* by N. Scott Momaday (1968) brought Native American writing into the mainstream and opened the door for other authors, such as Leslie Silko (1977) and Paula Gunn Allen (1997, 2010). Some Native American literature is cathartic, such as tales of abuse in boarding schools (McKegney, 2007), expression of feelings on general issues (Moore 2003; Owings 2011), and to communicate Native viewpoints of their own cultures (Lobo et al., 2009; Swann, 2004). However, writing in English as a second language can be difficult (Weaver et al., 2006).

The Future

After more than 500 years of oppression, Native North Americans are beginning to recover their place on this continent and the prospects for their future seems good. The strides made in the last few decades in regaining their rights are certain to be built upon, and there is little prospect of repealing those gains. Both sovereignty and identity are being regained, although there is little potential for the creation of fully independent Native nations (Greenland may prove to be an exception). Education has greatly improved and some groups have initiated special programs to save their languages. The ability of Native groups to practice their religions appears to have been restored. Resolutions to the rights for lands, water, and resources are moving more slowly and there is still much to be done in this area.

Among Fourth World Peoples, Native North Americans are moving in the right direction. Despite the very checkered history of U.S. and Canadian Indian policies, these governments have spent many tens of billions of dollars to help their Aboriginal inhabitants, a record no other nation can match.

References

Abu-Saad, Ismael, and Duane Champagne. (eds.).
2006. *Indigenous Education and Impowerment: International Perspectives.*
Lanham, MD: AltaMira Press.

Ackerman, William V., and Rick L. Bunch.
2012. A Comparative Analysis of Indian Gaming in the United States.
American Indian Quarterly 36(1), 50-74.

Aldred, Lisa.
2000. Plastic Shamans and Astroturf Sundances: New Age
Commercialization of Native American Spirituality. *American Indian
Quarterly* 24(3), 329–352.

Allen, Paula Gunn.
1997. *Life Is a Fatal Disease: Collected Poems 1962–1995.* Albuquerque: West
End Press.

Allen, Paula Gunn.
2010. America the Beautiful: Last Poems. Albuquerque: West End Press.
Anderson, Alun M. 2009. *After the Ice: Life, Death, and Geopolitics in the New
Arctic.* New York: Smithsonian Books.

Anthes, Bill.
2006. *Native Moderns: American Indian Painting: 1940-1960.* Durham: Duke
University Press.

Anthes, Bill.
2008. Learning from Foxwoods: Visualizing the Mashantucket Pequot Tribal
Nation. *American Indian Quarterly* 32(2), 204–218.

Atalay, Sonya.
2008. Multivocality and Indigenous Archaeologies. In *Evaluating Multiple
Narratives: Beyond Nationalist, Colonialist, Imperialist Archaeologies.* Junko
Habu, Clare Fawcett, and John M. Matsunaga, eds, pp. 29-44. New York:
Springer.

Barker, Adam J.
2009. The Contemporary Reality of Canadian Imperialism: Settler
Colonialism and the Hybrid Colonial State. *American Indian Quarterly* 33(3),
325–351.

Biolsi, Thomas.
2005. Imagined Geographies: Sovereignty, Indigenous Space, and American Indian Struggle. *American Ethnologist* 32(2), 239–259.

Bone, Robert M.
1992. *The Geography of the Canadian North: Issues and Challenges*. Toronto: Oxford University Press.

Bordewich, Fergus M.
1996. *Killing the White Man's Indian: Reinventing Native Americans at the End of the Twentieth Century*. New York: Doubleday.

Braun, Sebastian Felix.
2008. *Buffalo Inc: American Indians and Economic Development*. Norman: University of Oklahoma Press.

Bruchac, Margaret, Siobhan Hart, and H. Martin Wobst. (eds.).
2010. *Indigenous Archaeologies: A Reader on Decolonization*. Walnut Creek, CA: Left Coast Press.

Brush, Stephen B., and D. Stabinsky. (eds.).
1996. *Intellectual Property Rights and Indigenous Knowledge*. Washington: Island Press.

Bunten, Alexis Celeste.
2010. More Like Ourselves. *American Indian Quarterly* 34(3), 285–311.

Burke, Heather, Claire Smith, Dorothy Lippert, Joe Watkins, and Larry Zimmerman (eds.).
2008. *Kennewick Man: Perspectives on the Ancient One*. Walnut Creek, CA: Left Coast Press.

Champagne, Duane. (ed.).
1999. *Contemporary Native American Cultural Issues*. Walnut Creek, CA: AltaMira Press.

Champagne, Duane.
2007a. *Social Change and Cultural Continuity among Native Nations*. Lanham, MD: AltaMira Press.

Champagne, Duane.
2007b. In Search of Theory and Method in American Indian Studies. *American Indian Quarterly* 31(3), 353–372.

Chatters, James C.
2001. *Ancient Encounters: Kennewick Man and the First Americans*. New York: Simon and Schuster.

Christie, Gordon.
2005. Challenges to Urban Aboriginal Governance. In *Reconfiguring Aboriginal-State Relations*, Michael Murphy, ed., pp. 93–115. Montreal: McGill-Queen's University Press.

Cobb,http://www.amazon.com/Beyond-Red-Power-American-Indigenous/dp/1930618867/ref=pd_sim_b_4 - # Daniel M., and Loretta Fowler.
2007. *Beyond Red Power: American Indian Politics and Activism Since 1900*. Santa Fe: School for Advanced Research Press.

Colwell-Chanthaphonh, Chip.
2012. Archaeology and Indigenous Collaboration. In *Archaeological Theory Today* (2nd ed.). Ian Hodder, ed, pp. 267–291. Cambridge: Polity Press.

Colwell-Chanthaphonh, Chip, and T. J. Ferguson.
2007. *Collaboration in Archaeological Practice: Engaging Descendant Communities*. Walnut Creek, CA: AltaMira Press.

Cohen, Fay G.
1986. *Treaties on Trial: The Continuing Controversy over Northwest Indian Fishing Rights*. Seattle: University of Washington Press.

Corntassel, Jeff, and Richard C. Witmer II.
2008. *Forced Federalism: Contemporary Challenges to Indigenous Nationhood*. Norman: University of Oklahoma Press.

Crowe, Keith J.
1991. *A History of the Original Peoples of Northern Canada*. Montreal: McGill-Queen's University Press.

Crozier-Hogle, Lois, and Darryl Babe Wilson.
1997. *Surviving in Two Worlds: Contemporary Native American Voices*. Austin: University of Texas Press.

DeJong, David H.
1993. *Promises of the Past: A History of Indian Education in the United States*. Golden, CO: North American Press.

Deloria, Vine, Jr.
1988. *Custer Died for Your Sins: An Indian Manifesto*. Norman: University of Oklahoma Press.

Deloria, Vine, Jr. (ed.).
1992. *American Indian Policy in the Twentieth Century*. Norman: University of Oklahoma Press.

Deloria, Vine, Jr.
1995. *Red Earth, White Lies: Native Americans and the Myth of Scientific Fact*. New York: Scribner.

Den Ouden, Amy E., and Jean M. O'Brien. (eds.).
2013. *Recognition, Sovereignty Struggles, and Indigenous Rights in the United States: A Sourcebook*. Chapel Hill: University of North Carolina Press.

Diamond, Jared.
2011. *Collapse: How Societies Choose to Fail or Succeed* (revised ed.). New York: Penguin.

Doerfler, Jill.
2009. An Anishinaabe Tribalography: Investigating and Interweaving Conceptions of Identity during the 1910s on the White Earth Reservation. *American Indian Quarterly* 33(3), 295–324.

Dugmore, Andrew J., Christian Keller, and Thomas H. McGovern.
2007. Norse Greenland Settlement: Reflections on Climate Change, Trade, and the Contrasting Fates of Human Settlements in the North Atlantic Islands. *Arctic Anthropology* 44(1), 12–36.

Echo-Hawk, Roger C., and Larry J. Zimmerman.
2006. Beyond Racism: Some Opinions About Racialism and American Archaeology. *American Indian Quarterly* 30(3/4), 461–485.

Fear-Segal, Jacqueline.
2007. *White Man's Club: Schools, Race, and the Struggle of Indian Acculturation*. Lincoln: University of Nebraska Press.

Fine-Dare, Kathleen S.
2002. *Grave Injustice: The American Indian Repatriation Movement and NAGPRA*. Lincoln: University of Nebraska Press.

Finkelman Paul, and Tim Alan Garrison. (eds.).
2009. *Encyclopedia of United States Indian Policy and Law* (2 vols.).
Washington, D.C.: CQ Press.

Fixico, Donald L. (ed.).
2008. *Treaties with American Indians: An Encyclopedia of Rights, Conflicts, and Sovereignty* (3 vols.). Santa Barbara: ABC-CLIO.

Fixico, Donald L.
2000. *The Urban Indian Experience in America.* Albuquerque: University of New Mexico Press.

Ford, Jesse, and Dennis Martinez. (eds.).
2000. Traditional Ecological Knowledge, Ecosystem Science, and Resource Management. *Special Section, Ecological Applications* 10(5), 1249-1340.

Frawley, William, Kenneth Hill, and Pamela Munro. (eds.).
2002. *Making Dictionaries: Preserving Indigenous Languages of the Americas.* Berkeley: University of California Press.

Grinde, Donald A., and Bruce E. Johansen.
1995. *Ecocide of Native America: Environmental Destruction of Indian Lands and Peoples.* Santa Fe: Clear Light Publishers.

Hemmer, Joseph J., Jr.
2008. Exploitation of American Indian Symbols: A First Amendment Analysis. *American Indian Quarterly* 32(2), 121–140.

Hirschfelder, Arlene, and Martha Kreipe de Montaño.
1993. *The Native American Almanac: A Portrait of Native America Today.* New York: Macmillan.

Hurtado, Albert L. (ed.).
2008. *Reflections on American Indian History: Honoring the Past, Building a Future.* Norman: University of Oklahoma Press.

Irwin, Lee.
2008. *Coming Down from Above: Prophecy, Resistance, and Renewal in Native American Religions.* Norman: University of Oklahoma Press.

Iverson, Peter.
1998. *"We Are Still Here": American Indians in the Twentieth Century.* Wheeling, IL: Harlan Davidson, Inc.

Jenkins, Philip.
2004. *Dream Catchers: How Mainstream America Discovered Native Spirituality*. New York: Oxford University Press.

Johansen, Bruce E.
2007. *The Praeger Handbook on Contemporary Issues in Native America* (2 vols.). Westport CT: Praeger.

Johnson, Troy R. (ed.).
1999. *Contemporary Native American Political Issues*. Walnut Creek, CA: AltaMira Press.

Johnson, Troy R.
2008. *The American Indian Occupation of Alcatraz Island: Red Power and Self-Determination*. Lincoln: University of Nebraska Press.

Kidwell, Clara Sue.
2009. American Indian Studies: Intellectual Naval Gazing or Academic Discipline? *American Indian Quarterly* 33(1), 1–17.

Killion, Thomas W.
2008. *Opening Archaeology: Repatriation's Impact on Contemporary Research and Practice*. Santa Fe: School for Advanced Research.

Kroskrity Paul V., and Margaret C. Field. (eds.).
2009. *Native American Language Ideologies: Beliefs, Practices, and Struggles in Indian Country*. Tucson : University of Arizona Press.

Kulchyski, Peter K.
2005. *Like the Sound of a Drum: Aboriginal Cultural Politics in Denendeh and Nunavut*. Winnipeg: University of Manitoba Press.

Laird, Sarah A. (ed.).
2002. *Biodiversity and Traditional Knowledge: Equitable Partnerships in Practice*. London: Earthscan.

Landsman, Gail H.
1988. *Sovereignty and Symbol: Indian-White Conflict at Ganienkeh*. Albuquerque: University of New Mexico Press.

Larson, Sidner.
2009. Contemporary American Indian Studies. *American Indian Quarterly* 33(1), 18–32.

Lew, Alan A., and George A. Van Otten. (eds.).
1998. *Tourism and Gaming on American Indian Lands*. New York: Cognizant Communication Corporation.

Lobo, Susan, Steve Talbot, and Traci L. Morris.
2009. *Native American Voices: A Reader* (3rd ed.). New York: Prentice Hall.

Lonetree, Amy.
2006. Missed Opportunities: Reflections on the NMAI. *American Indian Quarterly* 30(3/4), 632–645.

Lowery, Malinda Maynor.
2009. Telling Our Own Stories: Lumbee History and the Federal Acknowledgement Process. *American Indian Quarterly* 33(4), 499–522.

Martinez, Desireé Reneé.
2006. Overcoming Hindrances to Our Enduring Responsibility to the Ancestors: Protecting Traditional Cultural Places. *American Indian Quarterly* 30(3/4), 486–503.

Martinez, Doreen E.
2012. Wrong Directions and New Maps of Voice, Representation, and Engagement: Theorizing Cultural Tourism, Indigenous Commodities, and the Intelligence of Participation. *American Indian Quarterly* 36(4), 545-573.

Martin-Hill, Dawn.
2008. *The Lubicon Lake Nation: Indigenous Knowledge and Power*. Toronto: University of Toronto Press.

May, Philip A.
1999. The Epidemiology of Alcohol Abuse Among American Indians: The Mythical and Real Properties. In *Contemporary Native American Cultural Issues*, Duane Champagne, ed., pp. 227–244. Walnut Creek, CA: AltaMira Press.

Mayes, Arion T.
2010. These Bones Are Read: The Science and Politics of Ancient America. *American Indian Quarterly* 34(2), 131–156.

McBeath, Jerry, and Carl E. Shepro.
2007. The Effects of Environmental Change on an Arctic Community: Evaluation Using Local Cultural Perceptions. *American Indian Quarterly* 31(1), 44–65.

McCarty, Teresa L.
2002. *A Place to Be Navajo: Rough Rock and the Struggle for Self-Determination in Indigenous Schooling*. Mahwah, NJ: Lawrence Erlbaum Associates.

McDermott, Brian.
2014. Language Healers: Revitalizing Languages, Reclaiming Identities. *Cultural Survival Quarterly* 38(1), 18-19.

McKegney, Sam.
2007. *Magic Weapons: Aboriginal Writers Remaking Community After Residential School*. Winnipeg: University of Manitoba Press.

Mihesuah, Devon A., and Angels Wilson. (eds.).
2004. *Indigenizing the Academy: Transforming Scholarship and Empowering Communities*. Lincoln: University of Nebraska Press.

Momaday, N. Scott.
1968. *House Made of Dawn*. New York: Harper and Row.

Moore, MariJo.
2003. *Genocide of the Mind: New Native American Writing*. New York: Thunder's Mouth Press/Nation Books.

Nagel, Joane.
1996. *American Indian Ethnic Renewal: Red Power and the Resurgence of Identity and Culture*. New York: Oxford University Press.

Nebelkopf, Ethan, and Mary Phillips. (eds.).
2004. *Healing and Mental Health for Native Americans: Speaking in Red*. Walnut Creek, CA; AltaMira Press.

Niezen, Ronald.
1998. *Defending the Land: Sovereignty and Forest Life in James Bay Cree Society*. Boston: Allyn and Bacon.

O'Brien, Suzanne J. Crawford. (ed.).
2008. *Religion and Healing in Native America: Pathways for Renewal*. Westport, CT: Praeger Publishers.

Owings, Alison.
2011. *Indian Voices: Listening to Native Americans*. New Brunswick, N.J.: Rutgers University Press

Owsley, Douglas W., and Richard L. Jantz.
2001. Archaeological Politics and Public Interest in Paleoamerican Studies: Lessons from Gordon Creek Woman and Kennewick Man. *American Antiquity* 66(4), 565–575.

Owsley, Douglas W., and Richard L. Jantz.
2014. *Kennewick Man: The Scientific Investigation of an Ancient American Skeleton*. College Station: Texas A&M University Press.

Perdue, Theda, and Michael D. Green.
2007. *The Cherokee Nation and the Trail of Tears*. New York: Viking.

Perry, Barbara.
2008. *Silent Victims: Hate Crimes against Native Americans*. Tucson: University of Arizona Press.

Petersen, Robert.
1995. Colonialism as Seen from a Former Colonized Area. *Arctic Anthropology* 32(2), 118–126.

Peterson, Jacqueline, and Jennifer S. H. Brown. (eds.).
2001. *Being and Becoming Métis in North America*. St. Paul: Minnesota Historical Society Press.

Pevar, Stephen L.
1997. *The Rights of American Indians and Their Tribes: American Civil Liberties Union, Handbooks for Young Americans*. New York: Puffin Books.

Peregoy, Robert M.
1999. Nebraska's Landmark Repatriation Law: A Study of Cross-Cultural Conflict and Resolution. In *Contemporary Native American Political Issues*, Troy R. Johnson, ed., pp. 229–274. Walnut Creek, CA: AltaMira Press.

Phillips, Caroline, and Harry Allen. (eds.).
2011. *Bridging the Divide: Indigenous Communities and Archaeology into the 21st Century*. Walnut Creek, CA: Left Coast Press.

Philp, Kenneth R.
1977. *John Collier's Crusade for Indian Reform, 1920–1954*. Tucson: University of Arizona Press.

Porter, Frank W., III.
1988. *The Bureau of Indian Affairs*. New York: Chelsea House Publishers.

Posey, Darrell Addison.
2001. Intellectual Property Rights and the Sacred Balance: Some Spiritual Consequences from the Commercialization of Traditional Resources. In *Indigenous Traditions and Ecology: The Interbeing of Cosmology and Community*, John A. Grom, ed., pp. 3-23. Cambridge: Harvard University Press.

Prucha, Francis Paul.
1994. *American Indian Treaties: The History of a Political Anomaly*. Berkeley: University of California Press.

Rand, Kathryn R. L., and Steven Andrew Light.
2006. *Indian Gaming Law and Policy*. Durham: Carolina Academic Press.

Reyhner, Jon Allan.
2005. *Education and Language Restoration: Assimilation Versus Cultural Survival*. New York: Chelsea House Publishers.

Reyhner, Jon Allan, and Jeanne Eder.
2004. *American Indian Education: A History*. Norman: University of Oklahoma Press.

Rosen, Deborah A.
2007. *American Indians and State Law: Sovereignty, Race, and Citizenship, 1790-1880*. Lincoln: University of Nebraska Press.

Ruppel, Kristin T.
2008. *Unearthing Indian Land: Living with the Legacies of Allotment*. Tucson: University of Arizona Press.

Schaap, James I.
2010. The Growth of the Native American Gaming Industry: What Has the Past Provided, and What Does the Future Hold? *American Indian Quarterly* 34(3), 365–389.

Schweninger, Lee.
2009. "Lost and Lonesome": Literary Reflections on Museums and the Roles of Relics. *American Indian Quarterly* 33(2), 169–199.

Sievers, Maurice L., and Jeffrey R. Fisher.
1981. Diseases of North American Indians. In *Biocultural Aspects of Disease*, Henry Rothschild, ed., pp. 191–252. New York: Academic Press.

Silko, Leslie M.
1977. *Ceremony*. New York: Viking Press.

Smith, Claire. (ed.).
2010. *Indigenous Archaeologies*. London: Routledge.

Smith, Huston, and Reuben Snake. (eds.).
1997. *One Nation Under God: The Triumph of the Native American Church*.
Santa Fe, Clear Light Publishers.

Smith, Linda Tuhiwai.
2012. *Decolonizing Methodologies: Research and Indigenous Peoples* (2nd ed.).
London: Zed Books.

Smith, Paul Chaat, and Robert Allen Warrior.
1997. *Like a Hurricane: The American Indian Movement from Alcatraz to
Wounded Knee*. New York: The New Press.

Spindel, Carol.
2000. *Dancing at Halftime: Sports and the Controversy over American Indian
Mascots*. New York: New York University Press.

Spruce, Duane Blue, and Tanya Thrasher.
2008. *The Land Has Memory: Indigenous Knowledge, Native Landscapes,
and the National Museum of the American Indian*. Chapel Hill: University of
North Carolina Press.

Stapp, Darby C., and Michael S. Burney.
2002. *Tribal Cultural Resource Management: The Full Circle to Stewardship*.
Walnut Creek, CA: AltaMira Press.

Stewart, Omer C.
1987. *Peyote Religion: A History*. Norman: University of Oklahoma Press.

Swann, Brian. (ed.).
2004. *Voices from Four Directions: Contemporary Translations of the Native
Literatures of North America*. Lincoln: University of Nebraska Press.

Swidler, Nina, Kurt E. Dongoske, Roger Anyon, and Alan S. Downer. (eds.).
1997. *Native Americans and Archaeologists: Stepping Stones to Common
Ground*. Walnut Creek, CA: AltaMira Press.

Thomas, David Hurst.
2000a. *Skull Wars: Kennewick Man, Archaeology, and the Battle for Native American Identity*. New York: Basic Books.

Thomas, David Hurst.
2000b. *Exploring Native North America*. New York: Oxford University Press.

Thornton, Russell. (ed.).
1998. Studying Native America: Problems and Prospects. Madison: University of Wisconsin Press.

Tiller, Veronica E. Velarde.
2005. *Tiller's Guide to Indian Country: Economic Profiles of American Indian Reservations*. Albuquerque: BowArrow Publishing Company.

Two Bears, Davina R.
2006. Navajo Archaeologist Is Not an Oxymoron: A Tribal Archaeologist's Experience. *American Indian Quarterly* 30(3/4), 381–387.

Vernon, Irene S., and Pamela Jumper Thurman.
2009. Native American Women and HIV/AIDS: Building Healthier Communities. *American Indian Quarterly* 33(3), 352–372.

Ward, Carol J.
2005. *Native Americans in the School System: Family, Community, and Academic Achievement*. Lanham, MD: AltaMira Press.

Williams, Kristen.
2014. Reimagining Native America: Matika Wilbur's "Project 562." *Cultural Survival Quarterly* 38(2), 6–7.

Wassillie, Katya.
2015. On Thin Ice: Subsistence Walrus Hunting and the Adaptation to a Changing Climate in Alaska. *Cultural Survival Quarterly* 39(3), 8–9.

Watkins, Joe.
2000. *American Indian Values and Scientific Practice*. Walnut Creek, CA: AltaMira Press.

Watkins, Joe.
2005. Through Wary Eyes: Indigenous Perspectives on Archaeology. *Annual Review of Anthropology* 34, 429–449.

Weaver, Jace, Craig S. Womack, and Robert Warrior.
2006. *American Indian Literary Nationalism*. Albuquerque: University of New Mexico Press.

Willow, Anna J.
2009. Clear-Cutting and Colonialism: The Ethnopolitical Dynamics of Indigenous Environmental Activism in Northwestern Ontario. *Ethnohistory* 56(1), 35–67.

Native Australians

Robert Tonkinson

University of Western Australia

*A*ustralia is home to two Indigenous minorities, comprising about 2.5% of the total population. They are the Torres Strait Islanders, people of coastal northeast Queensland and offshore islands, who number about 60,000. Most are Melanesians (Papua New Guinea lies very close, to the north) but there has also been significant presence of Pacific Islanders, Japanese, and others. The Aborigines, who are the subject of this essay, are present across the entire continent and many of its adjacent islands.[1]

The ancestors of the Aborigines arrived on the Australian continent about 60,000 years ago. Recent mitochondrial DNA evidence indicates that they are a genetically distinct group, not closely related to the peoples of neighboring lands. This suggests a long period of isolation, which ended when visits from what is now Indonesia began in the 16th century to some coastal areas in the north of the continent. These seasonal visits left few traces, material, or cultural. About 150 years later, British explorers "discovered" Australia and soon established colonies there. For more than 99% of the time humans have inhabited Australia, the only people there were Aborigines. Estimates of the continent's population before contact vary between 300,000 and one million. Given their great length of tenure on the continent, it was inevitable that population densities, subsistence patterns, and economies would have changed, yet an undeniable homogeneity remained. Many shared features were a consequence of the Aborigines' mode of adaptation, since nomadic societies everywhere are integrated largely via webs of kinship, marriage, and systems of exchange.

Aboriginal societies represent possibly the world's longest continuous hunter-gatherer adaptation. Their ancestors successfully peopled an entire continent, despite the absence of domesticable plants and animals.[2] Australia is predominantly arid, so it is very likely that population densities were generally low, with small dispersed groups the norm. Although nomadic, the Aborigines were notable for very strong attachments to their home countries. An estimated 220 different languages were spoken, indicating that Aboriginal identity was, at base, strongly localized.

Social Organization

The Aboriginal subsistence economy rested on a largely gender-based division of labor: women and children gathered vegetable foods and hunted small animals, while men hunted larger animals, such as kangaroos, crocodiles, and emus. Seniority and gender were key differentiating criteria, and wisdom and respect accrued with age. The concerns of mature males predominated, espe-

---

1. Word limits preclude discussion of the Torres Strait Islanders in this overview. For an excellent introduction to Indigenous Australia, see *The Little Red Yellow Black Book*. Canberra: Aboriginal Studies Press.
2. The dingo arrived only a few thousand years ago, and was never fully domesticated.

cially in the vital matter of religion, since they claimed primary responsibility for the cultural reproduction of society. Their societies were characteristically small in scale, 'familistic', kinship-based, and broadly egalitarian. People travelled in small groups or bands, and lived in a world of kin; strangers could not interact until formal introductions were completed. Each kinship term, "mother", "son", etc., encoded a set of expected behaviors and responsibilities. Wider groupings also existed; in fact, Aboriginal societies were unique in the complexity of their social category systems. These groupings (moieties, sections, and subsections) overlaid and complemented kinship systems. They were activated for certain purposes, most often connected with ritual and during major rites of passage, but were irrelevant to getting a living.

Aboriginal people today continue to use kin terms in addressing and referring to others, with all of whom some feeling of mutual obligation and responsibility ideally exists. Because hunter-gatherer societies lacked formal institutions of social control, heavy reliance was placed on individual self-regulation and kin-based enforcement of rules, when required. Traditionally, for every punisher there was a protector (in different situations, key kin, such as a male's elder brother or female's elder sister, could be both), for every critic, a defender, and so on. Children were free to give voice to their emotions and test the limits of their environment, unless they were putting themselves in danger. Yet with the onset of adolescence, and without a word from any elder, their demeanor would become typically shy, more serious, and low-keyed. This transition into responsible adulthood was generally smooth, and for males entailed a lengthy process of initiation. A deeply imbued sense of shame/embarrassment lies at the heart of individual self-control. Verbal shaming would normally be sufficient to subdue high emotions and bring an end to verbal and physical conflict. Today, throughout most of Australia, terms like "shame job" are commonly invoked to reproach antisocial behaviors.

An estimated 500 or so "tribes" existed at the time of the British invasion, but this label is problematic, since these larger entities could not be mobilized economically or politically as unified on-the-ground groups; in Australia, such functions were the concern of smaller units, the most visible being the band. Varying in size, it typically had a core of closely related people. When other groups were encountered and available food and water resources were sufficient, this larger grouping might remain together for a while. In the Western Desert, for example, people would have spent about 95% of their time in a band. Its "range", the circuit normally covered by a band in its quest for food, typically overlapped to a certain extent with those of its various neighbors. The band, however, was in no way coterminous with "society". Powerful bonds, for example of kinship, friendship, marriage, dialect, exchange relationships, and shared religious responsibilities, continually focused people's attention outwards, to a larger body of culturally similar others.

This larger society (akin perhaps to the tribe or a number of neighboring tribes) was realized, in large part, by periodic gatherings at a pre-arranged venue, one with sufficient water and food resources to support a large group for a week or two. These "big meetings" are still very important in the lives of many remote-dwelling Aboriginal people. They include dispute settlement, initiation of males, performance of rituals, exchange of sacred and mundane knowledge and information, items of material culture and other lore, arrangement of betrothals, and planning for future meetings. The highlight of the social calendar, such gatherings are exciting occasions, providing a context for formal introductions to previously unmet kin, and heightened emotions generated by ritual performances, gossip, and romance. The public settlement of outstanding disputes was an essential preliminary, after which conflict was strictly forbidden. Across the continent, these gatherings were an integral element of Aboriginal society.

Traditional Worldview

The Aboriginal cosmic order comprises human society, the plant and animal world, the physical environment, and the spiritual realm. Two key symbols of society, the Dreaming (or Dreamtime) and the Law, underpinned Aboriginal worldviews. Orderly social life was based on obedience to the dictates of a body of rules said to have been instituted by ancestral beings in the creative epoch, "the Dreaming" – a complex concept embracing past, present, and future. Today, in remote areas, Aborigines commonly talk of "the Law" in reference to this blueprint for life. The Law is all-encompassing: a body of jural rules and moral evaluations of customary and socially sanctioned behavior patterns, attributable to the dictates of the creative ancestral beings. The Law spelled out which Dreaming behaviors were to be emulated or avoided. If someone transgresses, people must punish the offender. Even where spiritual sanctions existed, human agents are in most cases essential for carrying them out. In remote Australia, the great power believed to reside in sacred objects and in certain songs, dances, and localities is considered extremely dangerous for some sections of the society. For example, should women somehow see such objects or trespass into men's sacred areas, they would sicken and die.

Broadly, the Dreaming explains how things came to be as they are, and the Law specifies how life is to be lived. The Dreaming is a timeless "everywhen"[3] that embraces past, present, and future and is still part of the lived reality of most remote-dwelling Aborigines. The concept shares certain characteristics across the continent. In the Western Desert, for example, it is said that eons ago, beyond human memory, large and beautifully decorated humanoid beings (but also possessing various animal characteristics) came ashore on a featureless, empty continent, which they proceeded to populate with hu-

---

3. This most apt term was coined by the great scholar of Aboriginal religion, anthropologist W.E.H. Stanner

manity, flora and fauna. The traveller ancestral beings whose extensive tracks crisscross the land were widely known because their associated rituals were performed regionally. There were also many localized creative beings, whose exploits are commemorated among much smaller groups of people. All, however, possessed superhuman magical powers; they hunted, gathered, met up and exchanged religious objects, rituals, and knowledge. Some were prone to excessive behaviors, and their implicit motto could be rendered as: "Don't imitate all that we've done; act according to the Law that we have given you". Prominent or distinctive shapes and features in the landscape inspired much mythology; for example, a salt-lake brought into being by the tears of an ancestral woman, a watercourse carved out by a giant python, or a granite outcrop comprising large oval boulders, the metamorphosed eggs of an emu ancestor. For Aboriginal people, the landscape is alive with possibilities.

Eventually grown old and weary from their superhuman efforts and weighed down by their splendid body decorations, sacred paraphernalia and weapons, the creative beings lay down and "died". They then metamorphosed into stones, other natural features, or celestial bodies, before, as indestructible spirits, they withdrew forever into the spiritual realm, somewhere in the cosmos. Left behind on earth, however, was the powerful "life essence" contained in their bodies and in everything they possessed and touched. It animated all life forms, yet its power remains undiminished. The withdrawn creative beings and their associated spirits, some of which act as vital intermediaries between human and spiritual realms, were believed to display a keen interest in earthly activities. The Law spelled out which Dreaming behaviors were to be emulated or avoided. Even where spiritual sanctions existed, human agents were in most cases essential for enforcing them. The great power believed to reside in sacred objects and in certain songs, dances, and localities was considered extremely dangerous to all but the initiated.

Besides acknowledging the superior powers of creative beings, Aborigines recognized human social hierarchy: males and the elderly were generally accorded higher status and enjoyed greater rights than females and the young. Despite these differences, there was no such hierarchy of creative beings. Though unreachable in the course of everyday mundane activities, they or their spirit-being messengers were amenable to contact during altered states of consciousness, through reverie, rituals, dreams, and so on. Aborigines' strong sense of security was grounded in their encyclopedic environmental knowledge. Their ordained responsibility was to nurture the country and its resources, and perform the rituals necessary to maintain the seasonal cycle and continuing fertility of flora and fauna.

The intimate relationship between humans and nature was expressed and affirmed in totemic beliefs. Totemism posits a unity of substance or flesh between individuals (and members of groups), plant and animal species and other elements of the natural environment. Multiple and enduring totemic associations link individuals to the Dreaming powers. For example, among Western

Desert people, conception totemism gives every individual a unique story of his or her transition from spirit-child to human, linking them to place, spirits, and other humans, and back into the Dreaming itself. It may be that Aboriginal identity is notably strong because of these multiple groundings. Yet despite their highly symbiotic relationship with nature, Aborigines saw themselves as unique and distinct from it.

Today, with the great majority of Aboriginal people living in large rural towns or the major cities, knowledge of the Law and the Dreaming is most likely to be acquired through their elders and from books and other media, such as television. Yet this distancing from lived tradition does not diminish people's pride in the cultural achievements of their ancestors. In remote regions, the Dreaming and the Law remain part of most Aboriginal people's lived reality and, together with kin and country, are essential components of their identity and distinctiveness.

Brief History of Contact

British colonization began in 1788, then progressed rapidly in some parts of the continent, especially along the coast and in areas suited to farming, and more slowly elsewhere. There is abundant historical evidence of huge Aboriginal depopulation post-1788, brought about initially by introduced diseases and warfare, and later by the pernicious effects of exclusion, removal from country, marginalization, inadequate medical care – and other negative factors that endure to this day. The early administrators, guards, and settlers arrived with convicts and so had no need of Aboriginal labor. They tended to judge the Indigenes by what they lacked rather than what they had achieved. They equated the Aboriginal people's failure to till the soil with parasitism, evidencing a lower form of humanity. Also, Europeans equated nomadism with the absence of private property, making it easy for them to rationalize their usurpation of Aboriginal land. In a tragic irony, a people who were steeped in religion were seen as "almost wholly devoid of religious susceptibilities", as one European observer put it.[4]

The Australian frontier was highly masculine, thought not to be a fit place for European women. Many white men formed liaisons of various kinds, but mostly fleeting, with Aboriginal women, which gave rise to people of mixed descent. They were nurtured in their mother's society, and in time came to greatly outnumbered those with full Aboriginal ancestry in southern and eastern Australia. In Tasmania, disruption and dispossession accelerated the decimation of the Aborigines, and the few survivors were taken to islands in Bass Strait. The alienation of land for agriculture and animal husbandry neces-

---

4. Norwegian adventurer, Carl Lumholz, who did fieldwork in 1882-3 among North Queensland Aborigines

sitated fences, which upset the movement of wild animals and compromised the Aboriginal hunting economy. With the disappearance of native species, Aborigines began killing sheep and cattle, leading to violent retaliation. The homesteaders had superior weaponry, but were sometimes prey to dawn raids, which quickly led to "treacherous" being attached to the label "Natives". For decades, a form of guerrilla warfare obtained along a frontier that was not controlled, and there were notable massacres of Aborigines by Whites. Survivors either came under the "civilizing" influence of missions, or were left to fend for themselves as beggars in fringe settlements near towns. Still others remained in camps or on pastoral and cattle properties, where they became the nucleus of a labor force. Aboriginal people did not take to Christianity initially, and most of the early missions in eastern Australia failed. One possible reason for this was an Aboriginal social fabric so thoroughly permeated by religion that nomadism itself can be understood as a religious act, carried out in emulation of the activities of ancestral creative beings.

Government Policies
European impacts have varied in intensity and outcomes, and the frontier of first contacts with the invaders lasted into the 1970s in the desert. They were earliest and most pronounced over much of the southwestern, southeastern, and mid-eastern areas of the continent, causing an attenuation in traditional Aboriginal life there. Many Aborigines were attracted to, or forced into, fringe settlements, which became "tribally" and linguistically mixed communities. In the early decades of settlement, increasing numbers of colonists, particularly town-dwellers of a humanitarian persuasion, were becoming sufficiently disturbed by frontier violence to petition the authorities in England to take ameliorative action before physical extinction occurred. Between 1856 and 1911, the Australian colonies enacted laws concerning the care and protection of Aborigines, many of whom were moved to "reserves" and given food and clothing to "smooth the dying pillow", because they were widely assumed to be doomed.

Numerous reserves were created to serve as a buffer between Aborigines and Europeans, and under Aboriginal Protection Acts people who lived on them were wards of the state. Protection Board members were their legal guardians and exercised virtually complete power over reserve dwellers. Some reserves were like prisons, with inmates needing permission to leave or return, and staff controlled inmates' money. In some, children were removed from their parents and put into dormitories. Physical punishment was sometimes severe, and people could be jailed for minor transgressions. Conditions on Christian missions varied considerably. They assumed a significant role in education, health, and pastoral care, and for adults, at least, offered greater freedoms than many reserves. Over time, missionaries and government welfare agents raised the level of humane treatment. During the last sixty years, many missionaries have withdrawn, and Aboriginal people now administer their own communities. As in the wider society, evangelical sects have grown in popularity among Aborigines, many of whom are practising Christians. Today, governmental instrumentalities have responsibility for many of the educational, vocational, and health services, and work closely with community councils and other Indigenous representative bodies.

By the 1930s, the many paternalistic and restrictive laws passed by colonial and state authorities had been gradually dismantled. The Commonwealth Government had the power to legislate on behalf of Indigenous Australians, and in 1939 it announced a policy of assimilation, abandoning the notion of biological absorption in favor of citizenship rights and equality of opportunity. After World War II, a period of unprecedented growth and improvement in material circumstances and wealth bypassed Aboriginal people. Through the 1960s White Australians became increasingly concerned about this neglect. Various organisations devoted to giving Aboriginal people a "fair go" sprang up. In the same period, political protest and resistance movements arose, led in most cases by urban Aboriginal activists, who drew attention to racism and neglect and agitated for the development of pan-Aboriginal unity.

In the remote regions of central and northern Australia, Aboriginal people retain a significant tradition-orientation despite strong Westernizing influence on lifestyle and diet. These Aborigines live much as they had before, and continue to enjoy hunting and gathering, but with vehicles, guns, and iron tools. Continuities with the past have remained important in the values and behaviors surrounding kinship and social relations, and in recent decades there has been a strong emphasis on cultural revival, particularly in southeastern Australia. Forced adaptation entailed impoverishment, both material and cultural, and left a legacy of passive but determined opposition by Aboriginal people to cultural absorption by the invaders. An important milestone was the referendum of 1967, when the nation's populace voted 91% in favor of including Aborigines in the Census and enabling the Commonwealth to make laws for Indigenous Australians. This may not sound like much, but the Referendum's symbolic impact on Aboriginal and non-Aboriginal Australians was considerable.

In the 1970s, positive self-management policies emerged, promoting Indigenous community and land councils, and creating service organizations. Yet inequalities persisted and Aboriginal health was declining rapidly. Despite many setbacks and criticisms about financial mismanagement, directed at Indigenous organizations by sections of the public, there was a notable increase in Indigenous control over resources. On Australia Day, 1972, in a brilliant political coup, activists set up a "Tent Embassy" (representing a displaced nation), opposite the federal parliament in Canberra. The protesters demanded land rights, compensation, protection of heritage, and full statehood for the Northern Territory. The "Embassy" remains to this day, as a constant reminder of unfinished business.

The mid-1990s saw the rise of the One Nation Party, whose leader's racist pronouncements, including attacks on Aborigines, failed to draw comment from the then Prime Minister, despite being played up by the media. One Nation's failure to thrive was perhaps related to the nation's growing multiculturalism, which doesn't sit well with xenophobia. By 2000, the conservative federal government began taking a tougher line on Indigenous affairs. It disbanded ATSIC (the Aboriginal and Torres Strait Islander Commission), the national Indigenous elected representative body, raising fears of a new paternalism. In 2007, without warning, this government intervened in the Northern Territory, ostensibly to protect children against abuse. Strict paternalistic controls were imposed, for example, over Aboriginal people's welfare benefits. The intervention continues to divide opinion, both among Aboriginal people and the population at large. When the federal Labor Party won government in the 2008 election, it did little to alter the intervention, probably because opinions about its impacts continued to be so divided. Labor's major policy goal in Indigenous affairs is to close the socioeconomic gap, which, despite some encouraging improvement, persists. Life expectancy, to take just one example, is 12 years less for Indigenous men, and 10 years for women.

Ethnic Identity Today
About 400,000 Australians today identify themselves as Aboriginal, and there are doubtless many more people possessing some Aboriginal ancestry who have melded into the population at large. Rates of intermarriage between Aboriginal and non-Aboriginal people are increasing. As in the population at large, about 80% of Aboriginal people live in urban areas. Just over half of them live in just two states: New South Wales and Queensland, but are small minorities in both, whereas in the Northern Territory they constitute a significant (if still minority) proportion of the population. Two criteria are germane to Aboriginal identity: self-identification and the recognition of this claim by an unspecified "Aboriginal community". A notable highlight of the Indigenous year is NAIDOC (National Aboriginal and Islanders Day Observance Committee) Day, which is observed via ceremonies, celebrations, and balls nationwide.

The spectrum of Aboriginal people's social situation in Australia today is vast, covering a small minority of well educated bureaucrats and professionals occupying senior positions, and at the other extreme are a larger minority in remote regions who speak English as a second language and in a few cases have experienced first contact with Whites in their lifetimes. Between these ends of the spectrum are most of the population, who can be located in varying social categories. As a group, Aboriginal citizens are situated overwhelmingly below the Australian average on all social indicators. Generalizing from such diversity is a risky but not impossible endeavor, because the Aboriginal population is notably united by pride in their identity and the continuing struggle for equality. Notionally, under Australian law, all citizens, including Indigenous Australians, are subject to the same rights and obligations. Yet the Aboriginal people are acutely aware of the extent of inequality and the racism, both structural and personal, to which they are subject.

Over most of the continent, alienation from land and traditional resources has been extensive and the impacts of the European invasion have been hardest and longest felt in the southern and eastern regions, and the southwest. Aboriginal people there are predominantly of mixed descent and hugely outnumbered, and their main focus has been on cultural revival. Where colonial impacts have been greatest, Aborigines' sense of unity has been substantially derived from a shared history of oppression and experiences of racism, which may carry greater moral weight among non-Aborigines than would appeals to shared traditions. In their consciousness-raising endeavors, Indigenous leaders have generated a political ideology that has focused on this shameful history, probably because it resonates strongly with a majority of Aboriginal people. To a considerable extent, "Aboriginality" tends to be reduced to that essence, or inner something, or distinctive "spirituality" possessed by everyone who is Aboriginal. In remote Australia, identity is not an issue, whereas for those of mixed descent who are light skinned and look more "European" than Aboriginal it is a major concern, because they face "hints of inauthenticity" from the non-Indigenous majority. Many wear black, red, and yellow emblems (the colors of the national Aboriginal flag). Conscious of their motivations and objectives, they tend to objectify their Aboriginality and associated traditions, and have been active in cultural borrowing from other areas when necessary. The notion "cultural revival is survival" (a once popular slogan) is linked to issues of identity, pride, land rights, local solidarity, and belonging. Many Indigenous people are knowledgeable about the Australian political system and aware of the potential held by tradition either to legitimate their claims to a greater share of resources or to impede the efforts of state agencies or other parties to impose change to which they object. Legislation, particularly that relating to Aboriginal heritage protection, is one of the few tools available to them for the effective exercise of some measure of power against the hegemony of the "whitefella".

Language

In 2008, 19% of Indigenous people aged 15 years and over and 13% of Indigenous children (aged 3–14 years) spoke an Aboriginal or Torres Strait Islander language. Creoles are spoken in several areas, particularly in northern regions. Many language centers operate in rural and remote Australia, and there is considerable investment in language research and recording, and in supporting language education. There are bilingual schools, particularly in central Australia and the Northern Territory, but in recent years bilingual education has become controversial, with opponents claiming that it retards the effective acquisition of English and mainstream education. About 70% of Indigenous children (aged 3–14 years) and 63% of Indigenous people aged 15 years or over are involved in cultural events, ceremonies, or organizations. Today, about two thirds of Indigenous Australians today identify with a clan, tribal, or language group. In Southern Australia, many languages have been revived, and many people believe they are crucial to cultural health, as a keystone to identity, Law, and land claims.

Art Production

Petroglyphs and rock paintings have been part of Aboriginal culture for at least 40,000 years, and everywhere ochres were used for body decoration in connection with rituals. In the desert interior, ground drawings were common, as were sand paintings. The introduction of paints and other materials that are both portable and enduring has resulted in new media and forms of expression in the visual arts. Since the 1970s there has been a dramatic rise in the output of Aboriginal art, on canvas and bark, and there are national awards and major exhibitions in every state. Many prominent artists show very successfully in Europe and North America and command prices in five or six figures. Basketry, pottery, sculpture, and glasswork are all part of the prodigious Aboriginal art production. The art market now provides a significant source of income for a large number of artists.

Festivals

Besides the many cultural and eco-tourist centers and businesses that promote Aboriginal culture and artifacts to tourists, music and cultural festivals are held in most states. A notable example is Garma, in the Northern Territory, attracting visitors from all over the country to camp, sing, and dance with the Yolngu people. There are popular Aboriginal dance companies in several states, and opera and pop singers with big followings. The theme of survival is celebrated annually on Australia Day, January 26th, a public holiday on which Australia marks the establishment of the first British colony, in Sydney. Indigenous people label it "Invasion Day", or more popularly, "Survival Day", on which concerts and other events are staged around the country. The last two decades have seen a large increase in Aboriginal representation in the performing arts.

Sport

The most widely recognized Aboriginal people in Australia's media today are sportsmen, who are significantly overrepresented in both Australian rules football (10%) and rugby (11%), but many women have also achieved sporting fame, notably tennis star Evonne Goolagong and Olympics gold medal winner (400 metres), Cathy Freeman. There are also many Aboriginal female and male participants in a variety of amateur sports such as netball and basketball.

Sovereignty Issues and Relations with National and Local Governments

Xenophobia directed at "the yellow peril" (especially Chinese) in the 19th Century led to the White Australia policy, which restricted immigration by non-Whites. Although the Aborigines ceased to be a threat long ago, prejudice against them appears to have deep roots in the Australian psyche; and in the case of those of mixed descent, the notion that these generally light-skinned people are somehow inauthentic lingers. The promulgation of a pan-Aboriginal ideology, which began in earnest in the 1970s, was accelerated when the Federal Government established an elected Aboriginal advisory body, the National Aboriginal Consultative Committee. The NACC provided a major impetus for an increased national Aboriginal presence, but its most prominent leaders and spokespersons were Aboriginal people of mixed descent, whose ethnic identity became a target of attacks both from White Australians and some Aboriginal people in remote areas. A penchant for associating cultural characteristics with skin color, shared by many Aboriginal and well as non-Aboriginal Australians, has at times operated to challenge the authenticity of some urbanized Aborigines of mixed descent.

Other challenges for Aboriginal nation-builders have been to overcome the problems of distance and diversity of lifestyle and outlook, and to present a unified front and a positive self-image. Any claim to represent Aboriginal people is potentially in conflict with strongly maintained traditional values surrounding local autonomy, which limit the ability of individuals to "speak for" others. Recognition of Aboriginal sovereignty has waxed and waned as a goal articulated by Aboriginal leaders; it is currently not a major theme in public discourse. Rather, in recent times there has been a focus on amending the Constitution to include recognition of the Indigenous Peoples as having had prior sovereignty, or being the "First Australians". The current government, with the support of the Opposition, established an expert panel that included some prominent Indigenous leaders, to investigate and make recommendations on the way in which such constitutional recognition might best be achieved.

Relations with governments at all levels have generally been fraught. Following colonization, and especially after federation in 1901, Aboriginal people were not included as citizens with the full array of rights entailed in this status. Until the 1967 Referendum, only the states could make laws specifically dealing with the Indigenous people. At both state and federal levels, there are departments or agencies for Indigenous affairs. Local governments deal with some issues, and some predominantly Indigenous communities are municipalities in their own right. Political action (as opposed to violence or passive resistance) began to develop in the 1930s and by the 1970s focused on land rights. Over many decades prior to the 1980s, there had been a largely hidden policy of removing children by government fiat from their natural parents, with devastating consequences. In the 1990s, a well-publicized national enquiry into "the stolen generations" was conducted. A 1994 Australian Bureau of Statistics survey revealed that more than 10% of Indigenous Australians over the age of 25 reported being separated and raised in isolation from their natural families. Many non-Aboriginal Australians were deeply moved to learn how severe, widespread – and recent – were these government-inflicted traumas and gross violations of human rights.

Several organizations have since been working towards the goal of reconciliation and there are Reconciliation Action Plans nationwide. These bodies have had great success in reuniting members of the stolen generation with their kin. In 2008 in the federal parliament, along with the Prime Minister offered an apology to members of the stolen generations, the symbolic importance of which was tremendous. Broadcast nationwide, it triggered an emotional reaction in the society at large.

On matters of social justice, the Australian Human Rights Commission has an Aboriginal and Torres Strait Islander Social Justice Commissioner, whose Annual Report, on the enjoyment and exercise of Indigenous human rights and recommendations to government for addressing issues in these areas, has become a major reference work for all those interested in Indigenous Australia.[5]

Land Rights
For the last 50 years, land rights have loomed large in Indigenous political struggle. Notable breakthroughs include both federal and state legislation specifically recognizing Indigenous Australians' claims of ownership (e.g., the Aboriginal Land Rights [Northern Territory] 1976 and the the Anangu Pitjantjajara Yankunytjajara Land Rights Act 1981). The most momentous legislation, to date, however is the Native Title Act 1993. In 1992, in *Eddie Mabo and others v the State of Queensland*, the High Court of Australia handed down an historic judgment that signalled an important legal as well as symbolic change in relations between the nation's two Indigenous Peoples and Australian society at large. The Court accepted that, under common law, the Native title of Australia's Indigenous inhabitants could be recognized. This invalidated a 200-year-old legal fiction which held that the continent was *terra nullius*, "a land without owners". The Court nevertheless found that Native title did not carry with it any basis for challenge to the sovereignty of the colonizers. The Court also found that grants of freehold and some leasehold titles by the Crown extinguish Native title, thus rendering most of southern and eastern Australia unavailable for Native title claims. In fact, since most of Australia's Aboriginal people live in urban areas and large country towns, only 10-30% of their number could potentially gain some security of tenure. The fight for Indigenous land rights continues to exert a powerful symbolic force on Aboriginal people despite the small proportion of eligible claimants. Despite successful Federal Government moves to weaken the Native Title Act and protracted legal chal-

---

5.   The Annual Report is published electronically at www.humanrights.gov.au/social-justice/sj_report/sjreport12/].

lenges to the claimants, the pace of successful resolutions has picked up.

An important aspect of Mabo is that it provided a nexus between the "political" and the "cultural" dimensions of Aboriginality. Native title, though itself an artifact of Western legal reasoning and therefore alien, established the legal basis for constructive Aboriginal political action. Yet this is not the only reason why the notion of Native title was so rapidly embraced by Aboriginal people. Native title specifies, and therefore legitimizes, Aboriginal "culture", in the form of "laws and customs" as the key determinant of title. The synthesis of these two powerful elements made the Mabo decision a momentous step towards Australian *and* Aboriginal nation-building. An unfortunate consequence of the Mabo decision, while impelling Aboriginal people towards rapprochement with other Australians, has been the pressure placed on Aboriginal unity because of competing land claims. Nevertheless, the decision stood to improve the bargaining powers of Indigenous Australians in their political negotiations with agents of the dominant society. Initially, there was vehement opposition to the decision by state governments, pastoralists, miners and many Australians who see compensatory and ameliorative measures as discrimination against them. Others believed that the decision improved the chances of achieving a lasting reconciliation with Indigenous Australians. Back in 1901, when the colonies federated, the new nation's Constitution specifically excluded the Aborigines.

Another major point of focus by Indigenous leadership and organizations, governments, and NGOs has been the glaring disadvantage of Aborigines and Torres Strait Islanders on every measure of well-being, especially health, education, and employment. For example, median incomes for Aboriginal people are 35% of those of non-Indigenous Australians. The goal of "closing the gap" is a 21st Century theme in Indigenous affairs, particularly in regard to health status. Raising educational attainment and reducing welfare dependency are also often-stated goals, and there is continuous debate about how best to achieve them.

Outlook for the Future

Generalizing about Aboriginal Australia today is extremely difficult because of its enormous regional and social diversity. Certainly, there will be an increasing melding of the two "nations" in Australia, though the two contrasting population pyramids (showing a much younger, but shorter-lived, Indigenous population that is increasing more rapidly than the national rate) will not soon blend into one. The rhetoric of a "dying race" has long since disappeared, the Aboriginal population having reached its lowest point 70 years ago. Recognizing Aboriginal antiquity adds some 60,000 years to the comparatively fleeting 200-year tenure of the Europeans in Australia. Regrettably, many non-Aboriginal Australians continue to blame the victims rather than acknowledging the enduring impact of the long history of dislocation, marginalization, oppression, and racism underlying Aboriginal disadvantage.

A small but significant number of influential Indigenous people are now working in the professions, academia, media, politics, and business. University graduation rates are increasing and leadership programs have successfully launched hundreds of young Aboriginal women and men into well-paid positions. An Indigenous national television network now exists. According to the Australian Bureau of Statistics, educational attainment for Aboriginal and Torres Strait Islander Australians has increased appreciably since the mid-1990s. In 2008, 37% of Aboriginal and Torres Strait Islander people aged 18 years and over (adults) had attained a minimum of Year 12 or a skilled vocational qualification, more than double the rate in 1994 (16%). Over the same time period, those completing a minimum of Year 10 or basic vocational qualifications increased from 48% to 71%. While relatively few Aboriginal and Torres Strait Islander adults continued on to complete a Bachelor degree or above, the rate increased to 5% in 2008.

The political reality is that people identifying as Aboriginal are a tiny minority of Australia's population, and until relatively recently have been excluded from control over any significant resources. There are notable changes occurring, particularly in Western Australia and Queensland, the two big mining states that currently account for much of Australia's very solid economic situation via mineral exports. After decades during which local Indigenous people were almost entirely excluded, the industry now provides training programs and employment in mining and associated service industries. Also, with the recognition of land rights and Native title, payments of mining royalties to affected Indigenous communities and land councils are occurring in many remote region; this presents major organizational challenges, like how to achieve an equitable redistribution among the Aboriginal land owners, and the extent to which the revenues available will be used for the long-term benefit of the affected populations. Material improvements in employment opportunities and income should have positive effects on housing and health levels.

Closing the glaring socio-economic gap will undoubtedly continue to be a major element of government policies towards Indigenous Australians. Despite improvements in their material conditions, health problems remain severe, and Western lifestyle diseases, notably diabetes, cardiovascular diseases, and renal failure now claim a disproportionately high number of victims. Another huge challenge is how best to combat alcohol abuse and associated violence and death, which are widespread among Aboriginal people nationally. A 2008 survey found that 17% of Indigenous people aged 15 years and over drink alcohol at risky to highly dangerous levels. Indigenous people are also twice as likely as non-Indigenous people to be daily smokers, and to suffer higher levels of psychological distress and have shorter lifespans than the population at large. In many areas, Aboriginal community life is severely marred by massive and chronic unemployment, and domestic and other forms of violence. The failure of 40 years of policies promising self-management (yet never permitting Aborigines to formulate new strategies and learn from their missteps) has led to strong calls by prominent Aboriginal leaders for a complete rethink of the relevant government policies. They want properly empowered communities devising their own strategies to escape from "welfare dependency" and engaging productively with the mainstream economy, while tackling head-on the social ills that plague most communities.

Indigenous Australians are now an increasingly visible physical and cultural presence in most major cities, and a significant demographic component of local populations in the sparsely populated northern and central regions. (A large surge in people identifying as Aboriginal occurred in the 1990s and could be related to this more amenable social milieu.) Notable Aboriginal cultural achievements in art, music, literature, sport, film, and dance have received much media attention; there are nationally televised Award nights, such as the Deadlies in music, and awareness of positive images of Indigenous people appear to be seeping into the national consciousness in a decidedly positive way. The frequency with which Indigenous Australians appear in the media, and in increasingly, in a mostly positive guise, would probably amaze North America's First Nation Peoples. A small but significant number of influential Indigenous people are now working in the professions, academia, media, politics, and business. Leadership programs have successfully launched hundreds of young Aboriginal women and men into well-paid positions.

Aboriginality as expressed mainly via a political rhetoric of resistance, based on shared oppression, has not disappeared, but is today matched by a more culture-centered emphasis on Aboriginal commonalities, continuity and pride in survival, and aspiration to mainstream participation, to which members of the dominant society tend to react more positively. Through mass media reporting, as well as media aimed specifically at them, Indigenous Australians are able to see more and more of their number succeeding in a wide range of endeavors: sport, the arts, professions, and employment in government and non-government agencies. This growth in role models may well help expand young Indigenous people's conceptions of what is possible out in the society at large.

Native Hawaiians of the USA

'Umi Perkins

University of Hawai'i at Manoa

*O*n January 17th, 1993, between 20,000 and 30,000 people, mainly Native Hawaiians, marched to 'Iolani Palace in Honolulu to observe the one hundredth anniversary of the overthrow of the Hawaiian Kingdom. The palace, often described as "the only royal palace on American soil," was the symbolic site of a radical revision of history, which eventually threw open questions including whether or not Hawai'i was American soil at all. At the rally, the representatives of the United Church of Christ (UCC) read a formal apology for the Church's role in the 1893 overthrow. The UCC apology became the template for another apology later that year – Public Law 103-150, the Apology Resolution signed by President Clinton on November 23rd 1993, which "urges the President of the United States to also acknowledge the ramifications of the overthrow of the Kingdom of Hawai'i and to support reconciliation efforts between the United States and the Native Hawaiian people."

But while Hawaiians (and Hawai'i) focused on reestablishing sovereignty and governance, an underlying, and perhaps underappreciated project consisted of a radical reframing of Hawai'i's history. Through a settler's historiography this history was suppressed in various ways, at times through outright distortion and propaganda, and at other times through omission. A reframing of Hawaiian history reveals a sovereignty in suspension, or rather, competing sovereignty claims stemming from the initial intervention in what some consider Hawai'i's last "legitimate" government, the Hawaiian monarchy. At stake in these historiographies is not only the outcome of the issue of Hawaiian sovereignty, but of Hawaiian subjectivity itself. In this chapter, I use the terms Hawaiian, Native Hawaiian, and Kānaka Maoli interchangably to describe the Indigenous people of the Hawaiian Islands. I discuss the distinctions between the terms, review the history of the Hawaiian people, and examine issues of identity and sovereignty. All these issues stem from understandings of the history on which they are based. This history is formed through the often contested practices of historiography.

Historiographies

Hawaiians had a rich oral history tradition, with orators able mnemonically to recite thousands of lines of genealogical histories. The 2000-line Kumulipo creation chant was an example of such oral history (Beckwith, 1972). With the arrival of missionaries in 1820, a rapid drive toward literacy occurred, followed by the transcribing of oral traditions by a generation of Western-trained Hawaiian scholars. Hawai'i produced over one hundred Hawaiian-language newspapers between 1834 and 1948 (Nogelmeier, 2010). David Malo and Samuel Kamakau epitomized this generation of historians trained at the Lahainaluna Seminary on Maui. Malo came to be seen as a prophetic figure when in 1837 he wrote "if a big wave comes in, large and unfamiliar fishes will come from the dark ocean, and when they see the small fishes of the shallows they will eat them up" (Daws, 1968, p. 106).

Because of the imperialism to which Malo was referring, at the turn of the twentieth century this oral tradition committed to paper was erased from popular and even scholarly consciousness by the bans on Hawaiian language in the 1890s (Shutz, 1985). The Hawaiian language came close to extinction in the mid-twentieth century, but in the 1980s and 1990s a revival of the language reopened this archive of Hawaiian language sources. Only approximately two percent of this archive has been translated to English today, and contemporary scholars have read only a relatively small portion of it. For the bulk of the twentieth century, the ruling "oligarchy" had as its historian Ralph Kuykendall, who came to Hawai'i in 1922 "at the invitation of the Historical Commission of the Territory of Hawaii" (Kuykendall, 1938) and produced the multi-volume *The Hawaiian Kingdom*, which failed to use any Hawaiian language sources, but was the standard history of the Kingdom era for a half century. Gavan Daws's 1968 *Shoal of Time* became (and still is) the standard history text, but it took a blandly liberal stance that did not particularly acknowledge the unique position of Hawaiians as the islands' Indigenous people.

In the 1990s and 2000s, while the nineteenth century historians were being rediscovered, a new generation of Hawaiian historians produced a new historiography with revised histories of key periods. Lilikalā Kameʻeleihiwa's *Native Land and Foreign Desires: Pehea Lā e Pono Ai?* (1992), Jonathan K. Osorio's *Dismembering Lāhui: A History of the Hawaiian Kingdom to 1887* (2002), and Noenoe K. Silva's *Aloha Betrayed: Hawaiian Resistance to American Colonialism* (2004) epitomize this "revisionist" historical school. The section below is organized by "Monarch" or ruling chief. While Hawaiians, in short, have begun to (re)tell their own history, it is still an elite, rather than a people's history. Below is a summary of the state of the revised and rediscovered, yet incomplete, "new" history. Because of the contingencies of historiography, there are, more accurately, a multiplicity of histories.

Histories

For several decades, archaeological and ethnohistorical evidence pointed to settlement of Hawai'i circa 300-400 AD from Southern Polynesia, mainly the Marquesas and Tahiti (Cordy, 2000). One scholar has recently suggested a later date, circa 900 AD (Kirch, 2012). After several centuries of settlement and expansion, the Hawaiian Islands congealed politically into four Kingdoms, or complex chiefdoms, until the late eighteenth century. After the arrival of Captain James Cook in 1778, Western weapons became a factor in Native Hawaiian warfare, most of which aimed at unifying the disparate chiefdoms. By 1795, wars of conquest had consolidated three of these Kingdoms under Kamehameha, a chief from the island of Hawai'i. Kaua'i, the "separate kingdom" that had never been conquered militarily, capitulated in 1810, uniting the entire archipelago for the first time (Joesting, 1984). Kamehameha I became the progenitor of a line of kings who brought Hawai'i into the modern era. American Protestant Missionaries arrived in 1820, bringing both literacy and capitalism, aiding Hawaiians in the formation of a nation-state and setting the stage for the loss of Native control of land. In 1848, Hawaiians voluntarily privatized land, in what Banner (2007, p. 128) has called "preparing to be colonized." At the same time, however, the Hawaiian Kingdom was preparing to prevent such a colonization by gaining international recognition of its status as a sovereign state (Sai, 2008).

The nineteenth century brought rapid modernization economically, with the rise of sugar and related industries such as pineapple, shipping, and banking, and politically under a succession of monarchs, Kamehameha I through V, William Lunalilo, Kalākaua, and Liliʻuokalani. By the late nineteenth century, Hawaiʻi was a fully recognized nation-state with numerous international treaties including treaties of friendship and reciprocity with the US (Daws, 1968, p. 119). Many debate which event constituted the crucial turning point in the loss of Hawaiian sovereignty. Some claim it was the 1893 overthrow, others the 1848 privatization of land or the abandonment of Hawaiian religion in 1819. Still others claim Western contact itself had the most impact, beginning with the arrival of Captain James Cook in 1778.

Cook: "Contact"

What some have called the "Lono myth" – the idea of the deification of the first foreigner to arrive in Hawaiʻi – initiated an international debate in anthropology between Marshall Sahlins and Gananath Obeyesekere. The Sahlins-Obeyesekere debate, over whether Hawaiians did or did not perceive Cook as the god Lono, is an example of the complexities of the practice of historiography generally and ethnohistory in particular. It began with Sahlins's (1995, p. 105) assertion, uncontroversial at the time, that "in January 1779 … Captain Cook was put through the customary rites of welcome to Lono." Obeyesekere (1992, p. 8) notes, in explaining his initial interest in Cook's apotheosis:

> I was completely taken aback at [Sahlins'] assertion that when Cook arrived in Hawaiʻi the natives believed that he was their god Lono … Why so? Naturally my mind went back to my Sri Lankan and South Asian experience. I could not think of any parallel example in the long history of contact between foreigners and Sri Lankans or … Indians.

Obeyesekere (1992, p. 3) rebuked Sahlins's assertion that Cook was perceived by Hawaiians as the god Lono, with a post-colonial intervention:

> I question this 'fact,' [of Cook's perceived deity] which I show was created in the European imagination of the eighteenth century and after and was based on antecedent 'myth models' pertaining to the redoubtable explorer cum civilizer who is a god to the 'natives.' To put it bluntly, I doubt that the native created their European god; the Europeans created him for them. This 'European god' is a myth of conquest, imperialism, and civilization—a triad that cannot be easily separated.

Sahlins (1995) retorted that as a Native Sri Lankan, Obeyesekere was not privy to "how Native [Hawaiians] think." Sahlins (1995, p. ix) held that "in speaking for 'native' others ... depriving them of their own voice" and "spinning [Hawaiians'] history out of our [bourgeois] morality" Obeyesekere was "doing no one a favor."

One problematic source for Obeyesekere is Kamakau, who nominally appears to concur with Sahlins. To discredit Kamakau, Obeyesekere (1992, p. 164) wrote:

> Kamakau has excellent accounts of native cosmology and historical genealogies, but his evangelical prejudice forces him to translate Hawaiian cosmology into a kind of pantheism with a supreme being at the top. Furthermore, Kamakau has serious problems of identity. His strong evangelical conviction has the passion that one associates with recent converts.

Kamakau's Christianity, then, is reframed as the simplistic, over-zealous faith of the recently converted. According to Kamakau (1992), Hawaiians' idea of Cook as the god Lono was short-lived. Hawaiians thought at first that he was Lono, but not later because he failed a test: "Here is the test of a god: if we tempt them and they do not open their gourd container, which holds their ancestral gods ('aumakua) then they are themselves gods, but if they open the sacred gourds (*ipu kapu*) [if they yield to the temptation of low-ranking women], then they are not gods – they are foreigners (*haole*)" (p. 96). A Hawaiian perspective emphasizes the importance of genealogy, the highest of which is that of gods (who are ancient ancestors), who would not demean their rank by mating with maka'āinana (commoners).

While some noted anthropologists came down on the side of Sahlins (Salmond, 1997), Robert Borofsky (2000, p. 440) distilled the substance of the Sahlins-Obeyesekere debate with the question "what should be the role of ethnographic history (and ethnographic historians) in this new "borderland" politics –now that indigenous scholars, from Hawai'i to Haiti, challenge the right of Western scholars to speak about "others" in other times?" Anthropologists such as Ty Kāwika Tengan and others have attempted to describe what a Native anthropology would look like (White & Tengan, 2001).

Another issue in Hawai'i's historiography of this period is the population at the time of contact. It is the subject of fairly intense debate, and only estimates exist. At the low end, in 1972 Robert Schmitt estimated 200,000 – 250,000, but this was a downward revision of the original estimate by James King, an officer in Captain Cook's entourage, of 400,000. David E. Stannard (1989) revised this estimate to 800,000 to 1 million, based on three methods. The debate remains unresolved, and disparate estimates are used today, albeit within the range mentioned above. The population debate has bearings on the extent of the impact of contact with *haole* – foreigners.

Messengers from Kaua'i related to the people of O'ahu that Cook was a *haole* from the land of other Western sailors previously known (probably Spanish). They said that *haole* would "possess the land." Trade began, as Beaglehole (1992: 639) relates: "nails, bits of iron, even iron tools, the only things that could be used for trade, were exchanged ... for roots and small pigs." Cook was killed in 1779 in an altercation while trying to take Kalaniopu'u, King of Hawai'i Island, hostage to regain a stolen longboat. Several accounts exist of Cook's death. James King, an officer in Cook's crew, described it tactically:

> Capt Cook now gave up all thought of taking Terreoboo [Kalaniopu'u] onboard with the following observation to me, 'We can never think of compelling him to go onboard without killing a number of these People' ... a fellow armed with a long Iron Spike and a Stone ... made a flourish with his Pah hou ah [pahoa – dagger] and threatened to throw his stone upon which Cook discharged a small shot at him ...[did not penetrate] ... The Capt then fir'd a ball and killd a Man. They now made a general attack and the Capt gave orders to the Marine to fire and afterwards called out 'Take to the Boats' ... after being knocked down I saw no more of Capt Cook.

Watts (p. 536), another member of Cook's crew, relates that Cook

> received a stab from the Chief behind him somewhere near the shoulder blade upon which he staggered a few paces & fell into the Waster when two or three Natives Jumped on him and beat him about the head with stones until he expired notwithstanding some brave personal struggles even in the Agonies of Death.

Kamakau (1992, p. 103) writing from oral history and with not a little Christian zeal, is somewhat more judgmental:

> Captain Cook struck Ka-lani-mano-o-ka-ho'owaha with his sword, slashing one side of his face from temple to cheek. The chief with a powerful blow of his club knocked Captain Cook down against a heap of lava rock. Captain Cook groaned with pain. Then the chief knew that he was a man and not a god, and that mistake ended, he struck him dead together with four other white men.

The British burned houses and killed in retaliation, but a truce was reached, and the two ships left Hawai'i. "Contact," which Greg Dening (1980) asserts is "too pretty a word for what occurred," inexorably altered Hawaiian society by initiating a period of continual foreign arrivals. Between 1779 and 1794, 45 vessels arrived in Hawai'i, bringing, among other things, weapons that became a factor in Kamehameha's effort to unify Hawai'i.

Kamehameha's Unification of the Hawaiian Islands

Kamehameha ended serious internal political conflicts (the end of war), created a unified Hawaiian identity as I show below, and established a singular Hawaiian nation-state. Kamehameha's birth was rife with intrigue, as his parentage was later found to be in dispute, and his life was under threat from its inception. Prophecies foretold that the chief who was born under a comet would grow to kill the King. Because of the fear that the king of Hawai'i Island, Alapa'inui, would kill the young chief to preempt his own demise, on the night of his birth Kamehameha's mother was in flight. He was born aboard a canoe and landed at Kokoiki, Kohala, Hawai'i Island (Desha, 2000, p. 25). His mother Keku'iapoiwa was captured by Alapa'i's soldiers but allowed to sleep the night under guard.

A chief of Kohala, Nae'ole, rescued Kamehameha by pulling him out through a hole in the wall of the house and escaping through the Kohala Mountains. Nae'ole was *Iwikuamo'o* of Keku'iapoiwa and *kahu* of the infant Kamehameha. Nae'ole hid Kamehameha and took him on a long journey through Kohala, where the Kohala people protected him. Kamehameha was thus raised in secrecy in the Kohala Mountains.

Kamehameha was eventually caught at approximately the age of nine. Alapa'i, who was old by then and felt little threat from the young chief, changed his mind and invited Kamehameha to his court. There Kamehameha gained a reputation for intelligence and as an excellent warrior (Desha, 2000, p. 28). After the death of King Kalaniopu'u, Hawai'i Island was divided between three major groups of chiefs, including Kamehameha.

Over ten years Kamehameha's rivals were worn down, culminating in the dramatic sacrifice of his cousin Keouaku'ahu'ula, chief of the Ka'u district at Pu'ukohola *heiau* (temple) in Kohala (Desha, 2000). By 1791 Hawai'i Island was completely under the control of Kamehameha. Kamehameha next prepared to attack O'ahu. At this point Kamehameha instituted a law that became foundational even in the State of Hawai'i: *Kanawai Malalahoe*, the Law of the Splintered Paddle. The law instructed the chiefs to "Let the old men go and lie by the roadside, let the old women go and lie by the roadside, let the children go and lie by the roadside and no one shall harm them" (Desha, 2000, p. 213). This law balanced security and freedom so effectively that the State of Hawai'i incorporated it into its Constitution in 1978. Article 9, section 10 of the 1978 Constitution of the State of Hawai'i (on Public Safety) provides:

> The law of the splintered paddle, mamala-hoe kanawai, decreed by Kamehameha I – Let every elderly person, woman and child lie by the roadside in safety – shall be a unique and living symbol of the State's concern for public safety (http://hawaii.gov/lrb/con/).

Continuing his pursuit of unification, in 1795, Kamehameha launched the campaign that culminated in the Battle of Nu'uanu, which put him in control of all the islands except Kaua'i and Ni'ihau. Kamehameha launched an attack on Kaua'i, but encountered a storm and returned to O'ahu. Despite two failed attacks on Kaua'i, by 1810 Kaua'i king Kaumuali'i felt he could not evade the impending takeover of his kingdom, and agreed to meet Kamehameha at Honolulu Harbor on O'ahu. According to Kamakau (1992, p. 196), Kaumuali'i said to Kamehameha "here I am; is it face up or face down?" inquiring whether he would live. Kamehameha dismissed the suggestion but said that the lands of Kaua'i were his gift to Kaumuali'i. This act subsumed Kaumuali'i and Kaua'i under Kamehameha's rule, and completed the 30-year process of unification.

The legacy of Kamehameha was the end of wars, political unification of the islands under one nation, and socio-cultural unification of the people under one shared identity. Not all Hawaiians feel that Kamehameha was *pono* – a "righteous" conqueror, but the war and bloodshed of Kamehameha's wars had a purpose in that it allowed Hawai'i to deal with the emerging threat from foreign powers. Kamehameha gave the new nation the name of his home island, and thus his political act also embedded issues of identity, which I discuss below. Kamehameha died on May 8, 1819 (Kamakau, 1992, p. 210). His last words expressed the Hawaiian idea of *pono* – righteous balance: "E 'oni wale no 'oukou i ku'u pono 'a'ole i pau" [Endless is the good that I have given you to enjoy] (Kamakau, 1992, p. 210). His heir Liholiho, eldest of his high-ranking sons, would attempt to guide Hawai'i through one of its most tumultuous periods.

Liholiho – Kamehameha II

The three most powerful *ali'i* at the time of Kamehameha's death were Liholiho, Ka'ahumanu, favorite wife of the King, and Kekuaokalani, son of Kamehameha's brother, who had been named *kahu* or guardian of the war god *Kū* (Kame'eleihiwa, 1992, p. 83). These *ali'i* had to contend with Western-influenced disease and depopulation, mercantilism, and the objectionable behaviors of Westerners, who did not feel that Hawai'i *kapu*, sacred law that ordered Hawaiian society, applied to them.

In 1820, American Calvinist and Congregationalist missionaries arrived in Hawai'i. In opposition to Hawaiian norms of behavior, Calvinists in particular were austere, egalitarian (with respect to their congregation), and ethnocentric (Kame'eleihiwa, 1992). The protestant work ethic, for example, in many ways opposed Hawaiian views on collectivity and *kuleana* (responsibility). Sent by the American Board on Foreign Missions (ABCFM), the missionaries were involved in the "Great Awakening," the religious renewal in the US, which became a compelling "push factor," impelling American missionaries to travel to places like Hawai'i. A Hawaiian man, 'Ōpūkaha'ia or "Henry Obookiah," travelled to the East Coast of the US in 1809, converted to Christianity and began lecturing to theology students that they should travel to Hawai'i and convert Hawaiians to Christianity (Dwight, 1830). He died in 1818 in Cornwall, Connecticut, but a company of missionaries and their families sailed for Hawai'i, including four young Hawaiians who had briefly settled in New England.

The self-appointed leader of the "Pioneer company" of missionaries, Hiram Bingham, expressed the view of some of the missionaries upon the first contact with Hawaiians: "the appearance of destitution and barbarism among the chattering and almost naked savages … was appauling…can these be human beings! [sic]"(Bingham, 1848, p. 81). This view would partially inform later interactions, but those behind mission efforts had varying views on the duty of "civilizing" the Native. The evangelical president of Brown University, Francis Wayland, whose text was used to teach political economy to the chiefs, wrote "the son of God has left us no directions for civilizing the heathen, and then Christianizing them. We are not commanded to teach schools in order to undermine paganism … If this is our duty, the command must be found in another gospel; it is not found in the gospel of Jesus Christ" (Hutchison, 1987, p. 84).

Meanwhile, a power struggle developed between Lilholiho and Ka'ahumanu. The main supporters of the missionaries were Ka'ahumanu, Keopuolani, and Kapi'olani (Kame'eleihiwa, 1992, p. 111). These ali'i women were seeking a new *akua* (god) since the abolishment of the *aikapu* – the law separating men and women in some roles. The missionaries were initially used as pawns in the power struggle between Ka'ahumanu and Liholiho. Liholiho was skeptical of missionary intentions, and initially only gave them a one-year probationary period to stay in Hawai'i. For Hawaiians the most positive legacy of early impacts was the development of a Hawaiian orthography. Ironically, the value of the written language was that it would allow for the preservation of Hawaiian culture, traditions, and history at a time when they were at risk. Another concern at the time was the loss of sovereignty, a concern that would preoccupy the Monarchs for the following seventy years. To address this concern, Liholiho took a trip to England to request that Great Britain establish a protectorate over Hawai'i. Liholiho and his wife and half-sister Kamāmalu died of measles in London (Kame'eleihiwa, 1992, p. 110). England pledged friendship, but did not promise to take on another world power on Hawai'i's behalf.

Kauikeaouli– Kamehameha III

Kamehameha III was Kauikeaouli the younger brother of Liholiho. Kauikeaouli's name meant "placed on a dark cloud," which seemed to signal the dark cloud the cloud of Western imperialism during his reign. Kauikeaouli responded to the threat with a strategy of Westernizing the Kingdom. Thus, his goal was Westernization as a means to preserve Hawaiian sovereignty. Hawaiian *ali'i* believed the country's sovereignty was threatened. Imperialism and colonialism was occurring in Australia, New Zealand, and the Society Islands (Kame'eleihiwa, 1992, p. 176).

Hawai'i was affected by gunboat diplomacy by the U.S. in 1826, France in 1839, and Britain in 1843 (Kamakau, 1992, p. 359-364). *Ali'i* attempted to address concerns by seeking advice from foreigners Hiram Bingham in matters of religion, missionary doctor Gerrit Judd and William Richards in matters of politics. The former missionary Richards advocated "three paths to foreign *mana*" (power): Christianity, Western government and laws, and capitalism (Kameʻeleihiwa, 1992, p. 174). Hawaiians could see that the economic and military superiority of foreigners were connected to writing and the institutions of government and trade, and incorporated these principles in the first constitution. The Constitution of 1840 was part of this general effort toward Westernizing Hawaiʻi.

The 1840 Constitution stated: "No law shall be enacted which is at variance with the word of the Lord Jehovah." It established three branches of government, and defined the powers of the king. It also confirmed that land was held by the king – as heir to Kamehameha I, "to him belonged all the land … though it was not his private property" (Hawaiian Laws, 1840-1841). Whaling grounds were discovered by 1830 and whaling became the new pillar of Hawaiʻiʻs economy. Whalers became involved in the newly established sugar industry, owned by Ladd and Co. The first plantation was opened at Kōloa, Kauaʻi in 1835. The sugar industry dominated Hawaiʻiʻs economy, controlled by the "Big Five" companies, which held monopolistic control of jobs and over laborers for a century and a half.

To elude the continued threat of imperialism, Kauikeaouli sent three envoys, Richards, Sir George Simpson and Timoteo Haʻalilio, to Europe and the US to secure recognition of Hawaiʻiʻs independence (Kamakau, 1992, p. 367). While the envoys were away, the British Naval Captain George Paulet responded to complaints of unfair treatment from a British resident, forcing Kauikeaouli to conditionally cede sovereignty to Britain on February 25th, 1843 (Kamakau, 1992, p. 359-364). This takeover was later determined to be illegal, or at least against British policy, and Admiral Richard Thomas restored Hawaiian sovereignty on July 31, 1843. Even this happy event was subject to historical dispute. Herman Melville (1964, p. 284), who was in Hawaiʻi at the time of the Paulet affair, wrote of his horror at Hawaiians' ostensible suspension of the laws in an appendix to *Typee*:

> …his Majesty [Kamehameha III] announced to his loving subjects the reestablishment of his throne, and called upon them to celebrate it by breaking through all moral, legal and religious restraint for ten consecutive days, during which time all the laws of the land were solemnly declared to be suspended … Who that happened to be at Honolulu during those ten memorable days will ever forget them! The spectacle of broad-day debauchery, which was then exhibited, beggars description … It was a sort of Polynesian saturnalia.

Later that year, in London on November 28, 1843, the British and French Governments jointly recognized Hawaiian independence in writing in the Anglo-Franco proclamation (Sai, 2008). The Hawaiian Kingdom's independence was recognized by the vast majority of independent states by the end of the nineteenth century, including many with diplomatic representatives in the Hawaiian Kingdom in 1893: the United States, Britain, France, Portugal, Japan, Italy and others (Sai, 2008).

The intervention by Paulet led William Richards to advise Kauikeaouli that a system of proprietary rights to land was a necessity. Not only would this system discourage would-be imperialists by showing Hawai'i to be a "civilized state," it would provide for fee-simple title to land for Aboriginal Hawaiians "separate and distinct from each other" (Alexander, 1891, p. 109). In case of an overthrow, *maka'āinana* (commoners) would have ownership of land under a land tenure system that the invading country would likely respect.

The 1848 Māhele was a division of all the lands of Hawai'i between the King and 252 individuals, mainly chiefs (Kame'eleihiwa, 1992). The Kuleana Act provided for *maka'āinana* claiming the lands they cultivated from the lands divided in the Māhele. According to Alexander (1891) "convinced that the ancient system was incompatible with their further progress in civilization, the King and chiefs resolved to separate and define the undivided shares which each individual held in the lands of the Kingdom."

The land tenure system of the kingdom consisted of a three-tiered system of interest in land: the King, all classes of *ali'i* (chiefs) in their capacity as *konohiki* (land supervisors), and the *maka'āinana* (commoners) each held a one-third undivided interest in all the land in the Kingdom. The system of proprietary interests, consisting of fee-simple title, leaseholds and life estates existed on top of this dominion of vested rights in land.

The results of the Māhele and Kuleana Act were as follows: *ali'i* and some foreigners received 40% of the land, the king 23%, the government 37%, and the *maka'āinana* less than one percent (Kame'eleihiwa, 1992). These figures have led the Māhele to be regarded as one of the most detrimental events for Hawaiians, but new research is challenging this view. Some have found that *maka'āinana* received the majority of land *value* (i.e., the most valuable lands) and that they held on to this land for a generation. Further, Robert Stauffer (2004) found that Aboriginal Hawaiians lost land after 1874 due to a non-judicial foreclosure law – a law that allowed foreclosures on mortgages without judicial oversight, a fact that explains the lack of written records. Research has shown that *maka'āinana* received approximately 150,000 acres (5% of all land in Hawai'i) in government land sales through the minister of interior. This brings the total closer to five percent of the land in the Kingdom, and when combined with Stauffer's finding on value suggests that Hawaiians received the vast majority of land value in the Kingdom.

Alexander Liholiho – Kamehameha IV
Despite adherence with the "paths to foreign mana," concerns about maintaining Hawai'i's independence in an era of worldwide imperialism remained. Resident sugar growers were pushing for annexation to the US or a reciprocity

treaty with the US that would eliminate tariffs on exported Hawai'i sugar. The resulting goals of the brothers Alexander Liholiho and Lot Kapuāiwa were to strengthen sovereignty and the monarchy, and the establishment of a reciprocity treaty with the US. The stipulations of the reciprocity treaty included mutual free trade between the US and Hawai'i. But reciprocity treaty negotiations failed because some in the US felt the US would lose important tax revenue needed for the post Civil War reconstruction. The reciprocity treaty would also increase competition for Louisiana sugar growers. This reinforced a desire of sugar growers to achieve annexation to the US.

The means used by the monarchs to strengthen monarchy and national independence was to achieve closer ties with Great Britain. This was because Britain was a constitutional monarchy (as was Hawai'i) and would thus support the same government in Hawai'i. Increased ties with Britain would diminish the possibility of annexation to the US. The Royal couple's supported the Anglican Church as a means of strengthening these ties with Britain. Tragedy struck the Royal family, however, with the death of four year old Prince Edward Albert Leiopapa a Kamehameha, and the early death of Alexander Liholiho at age twenty-nine (Osorio, 2002).

Lot Kapuāiwa – Kamehameha V

Kamehameha V, Lot Kapuāiwa, was known as the "last of the old style *ali'i*." Staunchly pro-Hawaiian, he brought back public hula performances. Lot Kamehameha, as he called himself, significantly changed the Constitution in 1864, requiring literacy and property ownership as voting qualifications. He also removed the position of *kuhina nui*, on the grounds that the appointed position had too much unchecked power as a mere appointee of the king. For the method he used in changing the Constitution, Kapuaiwa is often remembered as a despot. A. Grove Day (1984, p. 69), an associate and co-author of Kuykendall, notes that he "favored a stronger monarchy that verged on despotism." But by eliminating a powerful appointed position, Kapuaiwa in fact reduced his own power (Sai. 2008). Kamehameha V was thus maligned in given settler histories. The brothers increased ties with Britain, increased the strength of the monarch's position, and improved the security of Hawaiian sovereignty. Lot Kapuaiwa, however, had no designated heir at the end of his reign. The Constitution provided for an election in such a case. This led to the first election of a monarch in Hawaiian history. William Lunalilo won this election handily over David Kalākaua, but only reigned for slightly over a year. Kalākaua won the next election in 1874.

Kalākaua – Bayonet Constitution

Kalākaua's opponent during the election of 1874 was dowager Queen Emma. US businessmen supported Kalākaua, and he won by a vote of the legislature of 39 to 6. Following the election a riot broke out, led by the supporters of Queen Emma, and two US and one British ship were required to quell the riot.

Kalākaua's goals were to modernize Hawai'i in order to solidify political independence and renew Hawaiian practices to strengthen the *lāhui* (nation) (Osorio, 2002). Seeing that the population was continuing to decrease, Kalākaua's motto for the Hawaiian Kingdom was "*Ho 'oulu Lāhui*" – increase the nation/race. Kalākaua planned to modernize Hawai'i's economic development via increased government income by means of a reciprocity treaty.

As Merry (2000) notes, rapid Westernization of the Hawaiian legal system and bureaucratic infrastructure was meant to replicate Western governmental structures, thereby preserving Hawaiian sovereignty. But one price of Westernization was that the new legal system criminalized many aspects of Hawaiian culture, and diseases decimated the population (Merry, 2000). The sugar industry and other related industries were controlled by a small group of Hawai'i-born and foreign-born *haole* who became a self-proclaimed oligarchy. The most powerful of these men were a tiny group of the sons of the first American missionaries, the so-called "mission boys" (Daws, 1968, p. 292). This small, wealthy group conspired to strip Kalākaua of political power with the "Bayonet Constitution" in 1887 (Lili'uokalani, 1964, p. 177). Kuykendall called the 1887 Constitution the Hawaiian Magna Carta despite the fact that there had already been three previous Constitutions. The 1887 Constitution made a near-majority of the small Euro-American population, disenfranchising most Hawaiians, and gave a full veto to the king's cabinet (Osorio, 2002). The cabinet, allied with sugar interests, renewed the reciprocity treaty with the stipulation that the US would control Pearl Harbor – this was done against the king's will.

Lili'uokalani – Overthrow

After a gradual erosion of the power of the monarch over an 80-year period, the Haole oligarchy staged a *coup d'etat* in 1893. As Queen Lili'uokalani was about to promulgate a new constitution (to replace the "Bayonet Constitution"), non-Hawaiian business leaders, most connected with the sugar industry, overthrew the Queen with the aid of US Marines (Coffman, 1998). The Marines acted at the request of John Stevens, US Minister to the Kingdom of Hawai'i, but without the knowledge or authorization of Congress or the President. The oligarchy proclaimed itself a provisional government, elected Sanford B. Dole President, and proceeded to lobby the US Congress to annex Hawaii. Their aim was to become a territory, thereby avoiding foreign tariffs on sugar (Coffman, 1998, p. 126).

President Grover Cleveland opposed the annexation of Hawai'i and the overthrow. Cleveland sent Senator James Blount to investigate and, in denouncing the overthrow, Blount produced one of the most scathing critiques of US foreign policy in American history. On the basis of the Blount Report (1893), Cleveland pushed for reinstatement of Queen Lili'uokalani. A majority of Congress was pro-annexation, however, and this led to a standoff between Congress and President Cleveland until William McKinley was elected in 1896 (Silva, 2004). Because of the Blount Report, the provisional government declared itself the Republic of Hawai'i On July 4th, 1894, in response to Cleveland's demand to reinstate Queen Lili'uokalani, and denounced the US interference in its internal affairs (Russ, 1961).

Kuykendall (1967, p. 650), in a fashion typical of a historian in service of power, worded his description of the period this way: "Thus the ripe fruit was to be left dangling, but the United States had posted trespass notices and presumably would patrol the orchard." Kuykendall's *The Hawaiian Kingdom* does not discuss the annexation, but rather ends in 1894, restricting itself literally to "the Hawaiian Kingdom" period and missing the entire aim of the overthrow – annexation to the US – an aim that Cleveland's successor William McKinley would attempt to achieve.

McKinley was in favor of annexation, but while a majority of Congress was also in favor of annexation, there was not a *two-thirds* majority necessary for a treaty of annexation. A joint resolution, the Newlands resolution, was resorted to as a means of annexing Hawai'i, with the admittance of Texas as a state (not as a territory) used as a precedent. This resolution is still a point of contention that many in the Hawaiian sovereignty movement claim nullifies the annexation of Hawai'i, because the resolution was an internal law not even binding on the illegal Republic of Hawai'i, much less the Kingdom (Sai, 2008). "Annexation" occurred in 1898 despite a petition signed by 38,000 Hawaiians – most of the 40,000 living at the time (Silva, 2004).

When Noenoe K. Silva discovered the anti-annexation petitions a decade later, and one hundred years after the fact in 1998, it became clear not only that Hawaiians had opposed annexation, but that nearly every living Hawaiian man, woman and child had registered their resistance, and had done so nonviolently (Silva, 2004). Along with Wilcox's insurgencies, which consisted of several hundred armed Royalists, Hawaiian resistance to American control was firmly established as historical fact. This historiography shows the extent to which the present-day movement was bound up alternately in historical contingency and rootedness. It was contingent on historical events, but rooted in Hawaiians' ancestors' actions, and present-days Hawaiians' ability to (re)discover and interpret those actions. Silva's discovery of the petitions, for example, was only possible because of her fluency in Hawaiian language, itself contingent on the renewal of language programs.

The Territory of Hawai'i

In 1907, the name of Honolulu High School was changed to McKinley High School (Wist, 1940). At the ceremony unveiling the statue of William McKinley, champion of the annexationist's hopes, Sanford Dole and Lorrin Thurston were present. In McKinley's hand is a document, which says "Treaty of Annexation." The same year, the US State Department published a *History of the Department of State*, which states that Hawai'i was annexed by treaty (Sai, 2008). Both sides thus engaged in a cover-up of the fact that no annexation treaty existed, accentuating the need for a treaty.

The history of the Hawaiian people during the first half (even two-thirds) of the twentieth century has yet to be written. Hawaiians seemed to fade into obscurity as the plantation elite solidified their hold on political and economic power. What discernable Hawaiian social organization existed was first in the Territorial legislature, which Hawaiians controlled until the 1920s, in civic organizations, such as the Hawaiian Civic Clubs and Royal Orders, such as the Royal Order of Kamehameha and Hale o nā Aliʻi. Another discernable area of Native Hawaiian activity was in labor unions. One of the most important figures in the Hawaiʻi labor movement was a Hawaiian – Harry Kamoku. Kamoku was involved in one of the most contentious labor battles in Hawaiʻi history, the Hilo Massacre, in which union members boycotting a ship were fired upon with buckshot (Puette, 1988). The unions caused a gradual change in Hawaiian party affiliation from Republican to Democrat, which reflected the general trend.

The Territory of Hawaiʻi came into existence after the Spanish-American war in 1900 with the proclamation of the Organic Act. The Territorial government was Republican and business dominated, and the power of the sugar-based oligarchy had reached its zenith. An alliance between haole plantation elites – Republicans – and Hawaiians led to a political arrangement in which the Hawaiian Prince Jonah Kūhiō Kalanianaʻole went to Congress, where he pushed for sugar interests, and finally for a homesteading program for Hawaiians through the Hawaiian Homes Commission Act in 1921. The Hawaiian Homes program allowed for leases of government lands for one dollar per year to Native Hawaiians who could prove 50% blood quantum. The program was fraught with corruption and was largely ineffective.

Of the plantation owners, more is known. They held economic power through the "Big Five," five companies that held the bulk of economic power in Hawaiʻi. Noel Kent (1983, p. 70-71) described the close-knit group that exercised this power:

> The Big Five companies (Castle and Cooke, C. Brewer, American Factors, Theo. Davies, Alexander and Baldwin) continued to be controlled by the long-entrenched *haole* families, still very much in charge of the businesses inherited from their missionary and merchant forefathers … Decisions were the prerogative of such men, sitting in leisurely ease in their plush offices or in the elegance of the Pacific Club.

Lawrence Fuchs (1961, p. 43) describes this ruling set in his social history of the period:

> … the haoles – approximately 5 per cent of the populations of the islands – constituted an elite group of Caucasians, nearly all of them of American or British stock. A small group of missionary descendants …

comprised the inner core; their dominant purpose was the control of Hawaii. They governed the islands in a leisurely but conscientious fashion, primarily from the offices of the major sugar agencies. They lived in stately mansions surrounded by royal palms in the hills of Honolulu, or in large sprawling houses set on manicured lawns in rural areas.

For decades, however, the immigrant population grew and the oligarchy lived on borrowed time. In 1954, a "Democratic revolution" transpired in which Americans of Japanese Ancestry (AJAs) were swept into political office *en masse* based on their forty-five percent plurality in the Hawai'i population (Daws, 1968, p. 380). The sugar industry, still powerful, achieved a victory in the movement for statehood, when the Jones-Costigan Act threatened to treat territories as foreign producers of sugar in terms of tariffs (Daws, 1968, p. 332). The Statehood Act passed in August of 1959. Hawaiians were swept up in the fervor of the drive for Statehood, with many prominent Hawaiians supporting it, but a subaltern resistance to Statehood and memory of the Kingdom, documented by Dean Saranillio (2009), has recently come to light.

Statehood and Hawaiian Renaissance
Statehood initiated a development boom that began the paving over of Hawaiian sites and led Hawaiians to question the cultural costs of development (Cooper & Daws, 1985). Throughout this period, the condition of the Native Hawaiian population was generally abysmal. From the time of Western contact in 1778 until 1893 there was a ninety to ninety-five percent decrease in the Native Hawaiian population from between 400,000 and 800,000 to 40,000 (Stannard, 1989). By the mid-1970s the Hawaiian language was nearly extinct. Today Native Hawaiians, like Indigenous Peoples throughout the world, experience the lowest levels of education, income, and life expectancy and the highest levels of incarceration, drug use, homelessness, infant mortality, and obesity in the state (Trask, 1999, p. 17).

In 1978, Hawaiians played a prominent role in the State Constitutional Convention, making Hawaiian language one of the official state languages and creating the Office of Hawaiian Affairs (OHA) (Coffman, 2009). One significant area of cultural revitalization was language. The bans on the use of Hawaiian language in schools and government were not overturned until the 1980s. At that time, Hawaiians followed the Māori system of "language nests" (*Kohanga Reo*) and instituted a system of Hawaiian language immersion schools – *Punana Leo* was the name of the preschool system. Today, there are 32 schools in which Hawaiian is the medium of instruction for all subjects (11 preschools and 21 primary and secondary schools) (http://ahapunanaleo.org). This was an outcome of the second cultural renaissance beginning in the 1970s, and corresponding with ethnic movements globally, which had a profound effect on Hawaiian identity.

Identities

In 1964, the renowned Hawaiian writer John Dominis Holt asked in his essay *On Being Hawaiian*, "what is a Hawaiian?" Holt (1964, p. 11) noted that he had "been compelled to ask [himself] these questions for many years. Is a Hawaiian a Hawaiian by blood, or genes? Yes, of course!" While vague, this definition – that "Hawaiian" meant to have ancestry dating back to Hawai'i's original inhabitants – came to be accepted even in recent Federal legislation. But it diverged from the received definition of the time, established by the 1921 Hawaiian Homes Commission Act, which required a blood quantum of 50 percent, and came to be the standard upon which all subsequent Federal Native Hawaiian programs were based.

The name "Hawai'i" itself has a genealogy as recent as Kamehameha's conquest (ca. 1800), when he supplanted Cook's moniker, the "Sandwich Islands," and applied the name of his home island, Hawai'i, to the entire archipelago. The term "Hawaiian" derives from this relatively late date. An American, Captain William Finch (Sai, 2011, p. 34) made the first note of the use of the term:

> The Government and Natives generally have dropped or do not admit the designation of Sandwich Islands as applied to their possessions; but adopt and use that of Hawaiian; in allusion to the fact of the whole Groupe having been subjugated by the first Tamehameha [Kamehameha], who was the Chief of the principal Island of Owhyhee, or more modernly Hawaii.

Like the Māori of New Zealand and the Maohi of Tahiti, Hawaiians could only view themselves as the "true" or authentic people – Kānaka Maoli, until the Western-influenced unification in 1810.

Outside of Hawai'i, the term "Hawaiian" is used as "Californian" would be, connoting a mere resident. But in Hawai'i, it is well understood that "Hawaiian" means Native Hawaiian, of which only 289,000 of Hawai'i's 1.3 million residents declared themselves to be in the 2010 census (http://www.census.gov). Another 238,000 Native Hawaiians live on the US mainland, for a total of 527,000 Native Hawaiians in the US (http://www.census.gov). The Hawaiian renaissance, described below, made being Hawaiian "desirable," as did benefits from the Federal and State governments and admission to Kamehameha Schools, a private preparatory school founded by Princess Bernice Pauahi Bishop in 1887 with an endowment now approaching $10 billion. Many non-Hawaiians began to practice Hawaiian culture (hula, music, canoe paddling, lei making), and claim to be "Hawaiian at heart," which shows the impact of the renaissance – previously, many "part-Hawaiians" would emphasize their other ethnicity/ies, particularly Caucasian. Many of the prominent families of the early- to mid-twentieth century were Hawaiian-Caucasian, including those who claim to (and seem actually to) have ties to the royal family/ies. For example, Abigail Kawananakoa, a direct descendent of Prince David

Kawananakoa, was recently granted the right to be buried at Mauna'ala, the Royal Mauseleum, where the Kamehameha dynasty monarchs are buried.

The prestige of the hapa-haole also changed at some point in the twentieth century between 1930 and 1970, when it became in vogue not to be Caucasian. Incidentally, the term "hapa" recently has been taken on by many of mixed-Asian ancestry. Some claim that the 1931 Massie affair, an "honor killing" of a Native Hawaiian for the alleged rape of a military dependent, incited and brought pre-existing anti-"haole" sentiments to the surface (Rosa, 2000). No evidence of rape was ever found, and the epithet "honor killing" was used by David Stannard in his book of that title. The Massie case is often compared to mainland cases such as Rosewood, and generally seems to show the same pattern. It is sometimes noted that the Massie case was the origin of the term "local." The Hawaiian renaissance and the effects of ethnic movements nationally and globally may have contributed to this shift in the relative status of ethnic groups in Hawai'i. In 2010 Samoan-German Gubernatorial candidate Mufi Hanneman tried to gain "local" support by stating publically that "I look like you," i.e., non-Caucasian (DePledge, 2010).

John Rosa (2010, p. 53) notes the subtle distinctions between how people are categorized and how they may self-identify in Hawai'i:

> People here [in Hawai'i] more commonly identify as "Hawaiian," "Chinese," "Filipino," "Samoan," or even "haole," for example, rather than as one of the race designations found in census 2000: White; Black or African American; American Indian and Alaska Native; Asian; and Native Hawaiian and Other Pacific Islander.

Jonathan Okamura (2008) suggests a binary racial hierarchy in Hawai'i today that has *haole*/Caucasians, Japanese, and Chinese as an upper class, and Filipinos, Hawaiians and Samoans as an underclass. Hawaiian identity is embedded in, and complicated by this local identity – to be Hawaiian is usually to be local, but not always, and not vice versa. J. Kehaulani Kauanui writes of the "de-racination" implicated in a non-local Hawaiian identity. As the Hawaiian renaissance gained momentum in the late 1980s, Hawaiian identity began to give way to a notion of Hawaiian nationality.

Sovereignties

In 1988, at age 16, I attended a very early sovereignty rally with my mother, a professor of Hawaiian literature. The rally was organized by Kekuni Blaisdell, a physician who is now considered the father of the sovereignty movement. Neither I nor my mother had considered the prospect of Hawaiian sovereignty, as Hawai'i was still at the tail end of a process of Americanization, with "local" people trying constantly to prove they were "American enough." Yet here was a Hawaiian, very successful in the newly-Westernized Hawai'i, advocating the idea of not being American at all. It was a difficult idea to grasp, but within five years the notion that some model of sovereignty would be implemented was considered inevitable.

The Hawaiian Sovereignty movement evolved as the political manifestation of a larger Hawaiian movement – the Hawaiian Renaissance. Aspects of Hawaiian culture such as hula and Hawaiian language, formerly banned and on the brink of extinction, emerged into the public eye. At the same time, land struggles such as Kahoʻolawe, where in 1976 young Hawaiians occupied an island used for military target practice, politicized a culturally based movement.

The land struggles of the 1970s were immediately followed by two movements that catalyzed the Hawaiian renaissance. In 1976, the traditionally designed voyaging canoe Hokuleʻa sailed to Tahiti using ancient, and nearly lost, techniques of navigation. Hokuleʻa captured the imaginations of many Hawaiians and instilled a sense of pride in, and fascination with, their own culture, which had formerly been marginalized. A movement to reclaim the island of Kahoʻolawe, which was used since World War II for naval bombing exercises brought attention to the issue of Hawaiian land and created a political consciousness among Native Hawaiians and a generation of Hawaiian activists. George Helm and Kimo Mitchell, young leaders of the Kahoʻolawe movement, lost their lives in the Kahoʻolawe struggle and became symbols of Hawaiian resistance to the American military presence. Kahoʻolawe and Hokuleʻa were followed by a tremendous upsurge in participation in Hawaiian cultural practices, and in the 1990s, the sovereignty movement.

Models of Hawaiian sovereignty were, from the outset, plural. Kekuni Blaisdell advocated a kind of decolonization of the mind, emphasizing that the word "Hawaiian" was not actually Hawaiian, and that "Kānaka Maoli" (the true people) was the appropriate term. This new way of thought corresponded, for him, with a nationality based on Kanaka Maoli ancestry in an independent Hawaiʻi. Another independence advocate, Pokā Laenui, a.k.a. Hayden Burgess, argued that because citizenship in the Hawaiian Kingdom was not based on ethnicity, neither should it be in a restored Hawaiian nation. (The Hawaiian Kingdom had several thousand non-native citizens, mainly Portuguese and Chinese).

Ka Lāhui Hawaiʻi (the nation of Hawaiʻi), which came to be the largest sovereignty group with a membership of 22,000, argued that independence was not realistic and that Hawaiians should follow the tribal model of Native Americans. Led by Mililani Trask (its Kiaʻāina, or Governor), the group turned out in large numbers at the 1993 march on ʻIolani Palace and was active in legislative politics. Trask was a member of the United Nations Working Group on Indigenous Affairs, and helped draft the UN Declaration on Indigenous Rights, passed in 2009. Her sister Haunani-Kay Trask gained international recognition for her book *From a Native Daughter: Colonialism and Sovereignty in Hawaiʻi* (1991), and both gained some notoriety at home for their controversial public comments. The Trasks reflected an outward-looking approach that emphasized solidarity with, and learning from, other Indigenous Peoples.

Ka Lāhui's "nation-within-a-nation" approach led to a decade-long effort to pass the Akaka Bill, which I discuss below, and which continues in modified form. In the 1990s and 2000s many sovereignty groups emerged, including Henry Noa's Reinstated Hawaiian Kingdom, which became the Hawaiian Kingdom Government.

In the mid- to late-1990s, Keanu Sai began to make the argument that what Hawaiians should aim for was not sovereignty, but restoration of governance. Sai's argument was based on the lack of a treaty of annexation, the legal and logical conclusion of which was that Hawai'i *remained* a sovereign, independent nation-state under military occupation. This approach also reinforced an emphasis on international *public*, rather than *Indigenous*, law. After using this argument to throw into question the validity of land titles, Sai was convicted of "attempted theft of land," but not sentenced to any prison time. The Hawai'i State Supreme Court upheld this decision, despite the fact that larceny (theft) is defined as "taking, with the intent to steal, *personal* property," [emphasis mine] i.e., not real property or real estate. Sai took his argument to the International Court of Arbitration at The Hague, Netherlands, in 1999. The case was accepted by the court, a *de facto* recognition of the continuity of Hawaiian sovereignty, but the substance of the case hinged on whether US involvement was necessary – the US refused to participate.

To further test the veracity of his ideas he completed a Ph.D. in Political Science at the University of Hawai'i, Mānoa. His dissertation was entitled *The American Occupation of the Hawaiian Kingdom: Beginning the Transition from Occupied to Restored State* (2008), and the Deans of the University of Hawai'i's William S. Richardson School of Law and the School of Law at the University of London's School of Oriental and African Studies (SOAS) were on his dissertation committee.

Later, Sai began to argue that the agreement made between Queen Lili'uokalani and President Grover Cleveland to restore the Queen to the throne constituted a treaty, which, according to case law, is still in effect. Sai sued the US, specifically Secretary of State Hillary Clinton for failure to comply with the Cleveland-Lili'uokalani agreement. The suspended nature of Hawai'i's sovereignty is seen in the response of US Attorney General Eric Holder, which suggested that this issue would not be address during the Obama administration.

The fact that the view of Hawai'i's status as "occupation" was spreading is seen in veteran journalist Tom Coffman's second edition of his acclaimed book *Nation Within*. The first edition carried the subtitle "The Story of America's Annexation of the Nation of Hawai'i" (Coffman, 1998). In the second edition this was revised to "The History of the American Occupation of Hawai'i" (Coffman, 2009). Coffman (2009) wrote in a note on the second edition:

in making this change, I have embraced the logical conclusion of my research [and] am prompted to take this step by a growing body of historical work by a new generation of Native Hawaiian scholars ... [i]n the history of Hawai'i, the might of the United States does not make it right.

But as Sai's line of reasoning began to take hold, so did a drive for Federal recognition, initially through the "Akaka Bill."

Akaka Bill

From 1999 to 2012, continual efforts were made by the Hawai'i Congressional delegation and Office of Hawaiian Affairs to pass the Akaka Bill, or Native Hawaiian Government Reorganization Act. For "mainstream" Hawaiians – who were either entrenched in the US system (many work for the US military), patriotic toward the US, poorly informed about Hawaiian history, or simply unmoved by arguments for Hawaiian independence – the notion of creating a Hawaiian nation without seriously altering the Federal and State apparatuses was appealing. Former OHA Chairwoman Haunani Apoliona said "what is good for the Indigenous population, Native Hawaiians, is good for all [of] Hawai'i" (Pang, 2007).

The backdrop was that legal challenges to Hawaiian entitlements programs were materializing as a sort of backlash to the sovereignty movement. One challenge was successful: in *Rice v. Cayetano* (1999), the US Supreme Court (SCOTUS) upheld a challenge to Hawaiian-only voting for the trustees of the Office of Hawaiian Affairs (Kauanui, 2002). Today, non-Hawaiians vote for OHA trustees. Challengers to Hawaiian entitlements were buoyed by this victory and went after the Hawaiian preference policy in admissions to Kamehameha Schools (Watson, 2006). The Schools settled out of court to prevent one challenge from reaching the US Supreme Court. Other challenges took on the Department of Hawaiian Home Lands policy of granting leases of land to Hawaiians of 50% blood quantum.

Hawaiian leaders began to view the Akaka Bill as a means to circumvent future challenges to Hawaiian entitlements. The strategy was that by redefining "Hawaiians" as a political group – a citizenry of a nation – rather than an ethnic minority, challenges based on racial discrimination (or "reverse" racism) would fall away. OHA spent millions of dollars lobbying for the bill, with no success. But while a majority of Hawai'i, both Hawaiians and non-Hawaiians including Republican Governor Linda Lingle (2002-2010), supported the Akaka Bill, opposition to the bill immediately began to take shape. But there was a false dichotomy in the perception of this opposition. Most viewed the issue simply in terms of "for and against." In fact, there were *four* positions that emerged.

Most who supported the bill did so for similar reasons – to protect entitlement programs and achieve general self-determination and governance, albeit under US auspices. But the opposition congealed into three camps, each of which held a competing notion of Hawaiian subjectivity. The first camp opposed the bill because, they felt, it gave too many "special rights" to Native Hawaiians, who they viewed as simply an ethnic minority. This camp took organizational form in the Grassroot Institute, and tended to be comprised of non-Hawaiians, but in 2013, Dr. Keli'i Akina, a Native Hawaiian who had run for OHA trustee, was selected as executive director of Grassroot Institute. There were also a small number of other Hawaiians who opposed the Akaka Bill, and Hawaiian sovereignty for the same reasons as Grassroot Institute. A second camp opposed the bill because it would constitute the first time Hawaiians would willingly concede American jurisdiction. This camp tended to consist of Hawaiian independence advocates, some of whom united in the anti-Akaka Bill coalition Hui Pū. A third camp, mainly consisting of the adherents of Keanu Sai's view, argued that the bill, as a piece of legislation in an occupying, but *foreign* country, had no effect whatsoever on Hawaiians.

Senator Daniel Akaka, the bill's sponsor, retired from the Senate in 2012 and Daniel Inouye, ranking member of the Senate, died the same year. With the Akaka Bill an impossibility, OHA pursued a new strategy of gaining Federal recognition through executive order. While some Native American tribes have gained recognition through this method, a moratorium seems to have been placed on this route to recognition. Part of this process, were it to occur, is to once again rewrite Hawaiian history – this time in terms of Federal legal precedents. In the process, Hawaiian subjectivity will also be "rewritten," or at least one version reinforced: that of Hawaiians as subjugated Americans. But because this process must simultaneously condemn and accept the known historical and legal injustices in Hawai'i, to do so is to undermine and ignore as inconvenient the very legitimate claims of independence advocates. Doing so accepts power over law, perhaps even expediency over "truth."

Conclusions

The historiographies underlying the truth-claims of the contestants over the Hawaiian sovereignty question show the significance of both contingency and rootedness. Hawaiian nationalities and identities (as potential "tribal" member, "citizen-subject" of a Kingdom, mere State resident, or "local"), and subjectivities (as narrators of their own histories or passive receptors of others' imposed interpretations) connect the past (history) with the present (social action). Edward Said noted that while struggles over land appear to occur in the realm of politics, they are actually engaged in the realm of *discourse*. As Said (Silva, 2004, p. 15) noted:

> The main battle in imperialism is over land, of course; but when it came to who owned the land, who had the right to settle and work on it, who kept it going, who won it back, and who now plans its future – these issues were reflected, contested, and even for a time, decided in narrative.

Similarly, while the contests over Hawaiian land, sovereignty and governance appear to occur in the realm of politics, they actually take place in the process of the formation of historical narratives.

Because many historical questions are unsettled and contested, Hawaiian sovereignty remains in a kind of suspension. The 1993 Apology Resolution acknowledged the illegality of the overthrow, but did not acknowledge the quite logical conclusion that annexation was therefore illegal. If annexation is a legal process (as opposed to conquest), and this process occurred illegally, it follows that annexation did not occur. But logic and politics can inhabit different realms, leaving a suspended state, the resolution of which is not readily apparent. It seems that an international court, rather than the SCOTUS, which cannot be expected to rule against itself, will need to adjudicate on the Hawaiian claim. Efforts to enter this arena are underway. In 2013, for example, the Acting Hawaiian Kingdom filed for redress with the International Criminal Court. As of this writing, there appears to be a "race" between adherents of Federal recognition and independence, with progress on both fronts. It remains to be seen which route, if any, will bring Hawai'i's "sovereignty" out of suspension. In the larger context, as Niklaus Schweizer (1999, p. 381) asserts, the Native Hawaiian movement is an evolutionary, rather than a revolutionary process, with Hawaiians building the institutions of "sovereignty" – whether through federal recognition or independence – within the existing structures.

References

Aha Punana Leo
http://www.ahapunanaleo.org

Alexander, William DeWitt.
1891. *A Brief History of Land Titles in Hawaii*. Hawaiian Annual. Honolulu: Hawaiian Gazette Co.

Banner, Stuart.
2007. *Possessing the Pacific: Land, Settlers, and Indigenous People from Australia to Alaska*. Cambridge: Harvard University Press.

Beaglehole, J.C.
1992. *The Life of Captain James Cook*. Palo Alto: Standford University Press.

Beckwith, Martha W. (ed.).
1972. *The Kumulipo: A Hawaiian Creation Chant*. Honolulu: University of Hawai'i Press.

Bingham, Hiram.
1848. *A Residence of Twenty-one Years in the Sandwich Islands*. Hartford: Hezekiah Huntington.

Coffman, Tom.
1998. *Nation Within: The Story of America's Annexation of the Nation of Hawai'i*. Kane'ohe: Epicenter.

Coffman, Tom.
2003. *Island Edge of America: A Political History of Hawai'i*. Honolulu: University of Hawai'i Press.

Coffman, Tom.
2009. *Nation Within: The History of the American Occupation of Hawai'i*. Kihei: Koa Books.

Cordy, Ross.
2000. *Exalted Sits the Chief*. Honolulu: Mutual Publishing.

Day, A. Grove.
1984. *History Makers of Hawaii*. Honolulu: Mutual Publishing.

Dening, Greg.
1980. *Islands and Beaches: Discourse on a Silent Land : Marquesas, 1774-1880.* Belmont: Dorsey Press.

DePledge, Derrick.
2010. Hannemann Spins Facts to Run Down Abercrombie. *Honolulu Star-Advertiser*, Aug. 17, B1.

Fuchs, Lawrence.
1961. *Hawaii Pono: "Hawaii the Excellent" An Ethnic and Political History.* Honolulu: Bess Press.

Hawai'i
Hawaiian Laws 1840-1841. Honolulu: Hawaiian Government Press.

Holt, John Dominis.
1964. *On Being Hawaiian.* Honolulu: Topgallant Publishing.

Joesting, E.
1984. *Kauai: The Separate Kingdom.* Honolulu: University of Hawai'i Press and Kauai Museum Association, Limited.

Kamakau, Samuel.
1992. *Ruling Chiefs of Hawai'i.* Honolulu: Kamehameha Schools Press.

Kame'eleihiwa, Lilikala.
1992. *Native Land and Foreign Desires: Pehea La e Pono Ai?* Honolulu: Bishop Museum Press.

Kauanui, J. Kehaulani.
2002. The Politics of Blood and Sovereignty in Rice v. Cayetano. *PoLAR: Political and Legal Anthropology Review* 25(1): 110-128.

Kent, Noel J.
1983. *Hawaii: Islands Under the Influence.* New York: Monthly Review Press.

Kirch, Patrick Vinton.
2010. *How Chiefs Became Kings: Divine Kingship and the Rise of Archaic States.* Berkeley, CA: University of California Press.

Kirch, Patrick Vinton.
2012. *A Shark Going Inland Is My Chief: The Island Civilization of Ancient Hawai'i.* Berkeley: University of California Press.

Kuykendall, Ralph S.
1938. *The Hawaiian Kingdom Volume I: 1778 – 1854*. Honolulu: University of Hawai'i Press.

Kuykendall, Ralph S.
1953. *The Hawaiian Kingdom Volume II: 1854 – 1873, Twenty Critical Years*. Honolulu: University of Hawai'i Press.

Kuykendall, Ralph S.
1967. *The Hawaiian Kingdom Volume III: 1874 – 1893, the Kalakaua Dynasty*. Honolulu: University of Hawai'i Press.

Lili'uokalani.
1964. *Hawaii's Story by Hawaii's Queen*. Rutland: Charles E. Tuttle Co.

MacGregor, Davianna Pomaika'i, dir.
1992. *Kaho'olawe Aloha 'Āina* (videorecording). Honolulu: Nā Maka o ka 'Āina and Protect Kaho'olawe 'Ohana.

Melville, Herman.
1964. *Typee*. New York: Signet.

Newcomb, Steven T.
2000. Justice Memo Shows US Never Legally Annexed Hawaii. *Honolulu Advertiser*, March 12: B3.

Nogelmeier, M. Puakea.
2010. *Mai Pa'a i ka Leo: Historical Voice in Hawaiian Primary Materials. Looking Forward and Listening Back*. Honolulu: Bishop Museum Press.

Okamura, Jonathan.
2008. *Ethnicity and Inequality in Hawai'i*. Philadelphia: Temple University Press.

Osorio, Jonathan K.
2002. *Dismembering Lāhui: A History of the Hawaiian Kingdom to 1887*. Honolulu: University of Hawai'i Press.

Puette, William J.
1988. *The Hilo Massacre: Hawaii's Bloody Monday August 1st, 1938*.

Rosa, John P.
2000. Local Story: The Massie Case Narrative and the Cultural Production of Local Identity in Hawai`i. *Amerasia* (26)2.

Rosa, John P.
2010. Race/Ethnicity. In *The Value of Hawai'i: Knowing the Past, Shaping the Future*. Craig Howes and Jonathan Kay Kamakawiwo'ole Osorio, eds. Pp. 53-60. Honolulu: University of Hawai'i Press.

Russ, William Adam.
1961. *The Hawaiian Republic, 1894-98: And Its Struggle to Win Annexation*. Selinsgrove: Susquehana University Press.

Sahlins, Marshall.
1995. *How "Natives" Think: About Captain Cook, for example*.

Sai, David Keanu.
2008. *The American Occupation of the Hawaiian Kingdom: Beginning the Transition from Occupied to Restored State*. Ph.D. dissertation, Department of Political Science, University of Hawai'i, Mānoa.

Sai, David Keanu.
2011. *Ua Mau ke Ea: Sovereignty Endures*. Honolulu: Pū'ā Foundation.

Saranillio, Dean.
2009. *Seeing Conquest: Colliding Histories and the Cultural Politics of Hawai'i Statehood*. Ph.D. dissertation, Department of American Culture, University of Michigan, Ann Arbor.

Schutz, Albert J.
1994. *The Voices of Eden: A History of Hawaiian Language Studies*. Honolulu: University of Hawai'i Press.

Schweizer, Niklaus R.
1999. *Turning Tide: The Ebb and Flow of Hawaiian Nationality*. Berne: Peter Lang.

Silva, Noenoe K.
2004. *Aloha Betrayed: Hawaiian Resistance to American Colonialism*. Durham: Duke University Press.

State of Hawai'i.
1978. *The Constitution of the State of Hawaii*. http://hawaii.gov/lrb/con/.

Stauffer, Robert.
2004. *Kahana: How the Land was Lost*. Honolulu: University of Hawai'i Press.

Supreme Court of the United States.
1999. *Rice v. Cayetano.*

Trask, Haunani-Kay.
1999. *From a Native Daughter: Sovereignty and Colonialism in Hawai'i.*
Honolulu: University of Hawai'i Press.

United States.
1893. Report of U.S. Special Commissioner James H. Blount to U.S. Secretary
of State Walter Q. Gresham Concerning the Hawaiian Kingdom
Investigation.

United States Congress.
Public Law 103-150; to Acknowledge the 100th Anniversary of the January
17, 1893 Overthrow of the Kingdom of Hawai'i, and to Offer an Apology to
Native Hawaiians on Behalf of the United States for the Overthrow of the
Kingdom of Hawai'i.

United States Department of Commerce.
2012. United States Census Bureau. 2010 Census Shows More than Half of
Native Hawaiians and Other Pacific Islanders Report Multiple Races.
http://www.census.gov/newsroom/releases/archives/native_hawaiian/cb12-
83.html.

Watson, Trisha Kehau.
2006. Civil Rights and Wrongs: Understanding Doe v. Kamehameha Schools.
Hulili: Multidisciplinary Research in Hawaiian Well-Being. Honolulu:
Kamehameha Publishing.

White, Geoffrey M. and Ty Kāwika Tengan.
2001. Disappearing Worlds: Anthropology and Cultural Studies in Hawai'i
and the Pacific. *The Contemporary Pacific.* (13) 2.

Wist, Benamin.
1940. *A Century of Public Public Education in Hawaii.* Honolulu: Hawaii
Educational Review.

Māori of New Zealand

Margaret Mutu

University of Auckland

The Indigenous Peoples of Aotearoa[1] New Zealand are made up of more than one hundred and twenty *iwi* or nations whose size ranges from between several hundred members for the very small ones to over one hundred thousand for the largest. We identify ourselves according to our one or, more usually, several iwi affiliations and also according to our *whānau* (extended family) and our *hapū* (grouping of *whānau*). Hapū are the economic units in our society. Iwi are groupings of hapū who come together mainly for political purposes and their membership is usually determined by descent from a common ancestor. My main iwi affiliations are: Ngāti Kahu, Te Rarawa, and Ngāti Whātua of the northern regions of the country. Like all Māori, I have many other affiliations which I can call on as a result of genealogical connections ranging back over many centuries.

The territories of the hapū and iwi range over the entire country with almost all located in the northern island. Each hapū has a territory over which they hold mana whenua or ultimate and paramount power and authority in respect of the land, derived originally from the gods and handed down to us by our ancestors. The notion of *mana whenua* subsumes many aspects of the English cultural notion of sovereignty but is far broader and deeper. Spiritual dimensions of the world are an essential element of mana whenua and all pervasive in our thinking. Mana whenua of each hapū invariably overlaps with that of neighboring and closely related hapū.

The name Māori as an overall descriptor for the Indigenous people of Aotearoa New Zealand is one that only came into use when the need arose to distinguish iwi from foreigners. The word māori translates as normal, uncontaminated or ordinary as opposed to tauiwi which means foreigner. We also describe ourselves is Tangata Whenua, the people of the land. This term carries the inherent meaning of having responsiblity for and power and authority in respect of the well-being of the land in the specific area that one's hapū holds mana whenua. The name Māori is pervasive and is used almost exclusively throughout the literature.

In this chapter I will consider the present situation of Māori providing a brief history of how we came to be in a state of marginalization, poverty, and landlessness in our own land and why we are constantly battling and protesting against the White colonizers we call Pākehā.[2] I will provide an overview of the damage colonization has done to us, the struggle we have undertaken to maintain our identity, our language and our culture and the steps we have tak-

---

1.   Aotearoa, according to our traditions, was the name first given to the country when our ancestors arrived here more than fifty generations ago. New Zealand is the name Dutch visitors gave the country many generations ago and which Europeans in general use. For Māori Aotearoa is our country in all its myriad Māori aspects while New Zealand is those aspects that European immigrants occupy and use alongside us.

2.   The word Pākehā means a person of European origin. While many Pākehā in New

en in the fight to restore what was stolen from us. Despite Pākehā assertions to the contrary, we never ceded sovereignty to them. I outline some of the strategies we have adopted to have our sovereignty and right to self-determination recognized and upheld in the face of a fraudulent legal system that has been used to manipulate, suppress, oppress, punish, and kill us. The final part of the chapter provides a brief consideration of our outlook for the future.

Background

Despite our current situation the numerous hapū and iwi of Aotearoa still hark back to our oral traditions to confirm who we are and what our role is in our ancestral lands. Each hapū and iwi has its own specific traditions and they all recall lengthy genealogies, including the deeds of the ancestors, and the territories over which the hapū hold mana. For more than 85 per cent of the time humans have lived in New Zealand, the only people here were Māori. Oral traditions record Aotearoa (the North Island) and Te Waipounamu (the South Island) being the home of our Polynesian ancestors for at least fifty generations. Seven generations ago, foreigners from Europe started arriving. Some who chose to stay assimilated into our communities and made worthy contributions. International trade relations between Māori and the British were very strong for at least two decades (Petrie 2006). And the descendants of those traders and other early visitors who married into our hapū are still considered to this day to be members of our hapū.

From the outset other European visitors were lawless, barbaric, and uncivilized, and they greatly exercised the patience and wisdom of our *rangatira* (leaders) and elders. Their behaviour was driven by delusions of ethnic and cultural superiority which were an anathema to our rangatira. Yet the British authorities recognized that the sovereignty of New Zealand resided with each of the hapū, and they acknowledged a written declaration to that effect, He Whakaputanga o te Rangatiratanga o Nu Tireni (A Declaration of the Sovereignty of New Zealand)[3] in 1835. Five years later a treaty of peace and friendship called Te Tiriti o Waitangi or in English, The Treaty of Waitangi, was entered into by a large number (but not all) hapū and the British (Mutu, 2010, p. 35). The main purpose of the treaty was to formalize the delegation of responsibility for the two thousand lawless British immigrants residing amongst the hapū to the head of the British who, in 1840, was the Queen of England. At the time, hapū hugely outnumbered the British by at least fifty to one with estimates of a total Māori population ranging between one hundred

---

a significant number strongly object to being called this name and variously adopt the names White, European, European New Zealander or, for those who deny their European origins, New Zealander.

3.   The English translation sent to London was entitled "Declaration of Independence".

and several hundred thousand. The treaty reaffirmed British recognition of Māori sovereignty. It was written in *te reo Māori*, the Indigenous language,[4] taken to many parts of the north island of the country and signed by more than five hundred rangatira.

To this day hapū continue to rely on this treaty in all their dealings with the British Crown. The Crown for its part, however, has never ensured that either it or its subjects living in New Zealand adhered to it. Furthermore Pākehā subsequently produced a document written in English which claimed that Māori had ceded sovereignty to the British Crown and they used this to fraudulently claim New Zealand as their own. When Tangata Whenua would not relinquish control, armed conflict resulted.

The first wars against the British took place in the north in the 1840s, in the region where the treaty was first signed. In a series of battles, Ngāpuhi chiefs roundly defeated the British and eventually sued for peace on condition that the British stopped their lawless behaviour. However the British proceeded to try to lay claim to the lands of hapū throughout the north, signing land deeds written in te reo Māori, which simply assigned temporary use rights. They did the same over almost the entire South Island. Yet the British, again fraudulently, claimed that each of these transactions was an English custom land alienation. Almost one hundred and forty years were to pass before a government appointed commission of inquiry, the Waitangi Tribunal, issued findings that none of these lands had been sold and underlying Native title remained unextinguished (Waitangi Tribunal, 1997, p. 7).

As hapū further south saw what was happening in the north, they started refusing to make land available for British immigrants. And so, in the 1860s, the British, with many more resources than they had twenty years earlier, waged war in the Waikato, Mātaatua and Taranaki regions, confiscating huge tracts of land as they went, driving hapū out of their territories and killing or imprisoning those who refused to allow the British to steal their lands. This combined with British diseases, from which hapū had no immunity, decimated the hapū. By the beginning of the twentieth century, the Māori population had been reduced to 42,000 and many British immigrants were celebrating the demise of the entire Māori population (Kukutai, 2011, p. 14; Mikaere, 2011, p. 72). Less than seven million acres of their original sixty-six million acres of land was still in hapū control. Today only approximately 3.7 million acres remains in hapū control with only small areas clawed back through the Treaty

---

4. Although there are a number of dialects of te reo Māori, they are all mutually intelligible. As such there is only one Indigenous language in Aotearoa New Zealand.
5. The New Zealand government has never ratified the genuine treaty – but then neither has it accepted the fraudulent document as part of New Zealand law. Instead it has included "the principles of the Treaty of Waitangi" – see endnote 7.

of Waitangi claims extinguishment process implemented in 1992. The Māori population however is now possibly larger than it has ever been at 712,300 (Statistics New Zealand, 2016). This is 16 per cent of the total population of the country.

Despite the increase in population, most of the 20th century saw Māori struggling to survive as the British Crown continued to pursue the confiscation of all hapū land and the complete marginalization of the Indigenous people of the country. In the 1950s the need for cheap labor in city based industries saw governments enticing and then actively moving impoverished whānau from their rural homelands into the cities. Major social problems ensued as government assimilation policies broke up traditional societal structures of whānau, hapū and iwi. The colonists proudly pursued a White New Zealand policy, actively encouraging the stigmatization of being Māori. The combination of all the negative effects of colonization has led to inevitable poor socio-economic outcomes. The 2013 Census, Statistics New Zealand publications and other government reports have shown that:

- 84.4 per cent of Māori live in urban areas (in 1936 it was about 13 per cent, in 1951, 23 per cent, in 1981, 80 per cent (Groot et al., 2011, p. 235));
- 9.1 per cent of Māori hold a Bachelor's degree or above compared with 18.6 per cent of the European population;
- Māori unemployment is 14.8 per cent, nearly three times the non-Māori rate of 5.5 per cent;
- The average age of Māori is 17 years less than non-Māori;
- Life expectancy for Māori males is 7.4 years less than non-Māori males, and 7.2 years less for females and although socioeconomic status impacts on health, "high-income Māori still have a 40 per cent higher death rate than low income Europeans" (Cram, 2011, p. 151);
- Māori are 2.29 times more likely to die of cardiovascular diseases than non-Māori, 1.77 times more likely to die of cancer, 5.2 times for diabetes, 2.59 times for respiratory diseases, 1.94 times for accidents, 1.5 times for suicide, 3.5 times for homicide (Robson & Purdie, 2007);
- A significant majority of gang members in New Zealand are Māori (Taonui and Newbold, 2011, p. 212);
- Māori children are much more likely to be assessed as abused or neglected than non-Māori children and die of child maltreatment at more than twice the rate of non-Māori children (Cooper & Wharewera-Mika, 2011, p. 172);
- Māori are 15 per cent of the population but 51 per cent of the prison population while New Zealand Europeans/Whites make up 68 per cent of the population but only 37 per cent of the prison population. The situation for Māori women is even more dire: 61 per cent of women in prison are Māori compared with 33 per cent Whites. Apprehension,

prosecution and convictions rates for Māori men help explain these statistics: they are four to five times higher than those of non-Māori men, and Māori men are seven times more likely to be given a custodial sentence than White men. Māori women are ten times more likely than White women to be given custodial sentences (Webb, 2011, p. 250-1). For a large number of whānau being imprisoned has become a normalized part of their lives and for many it no longer carries any stigma (McIntosh, 2011, p. 276-7). Māori are one of the most incarcerated people in the world;

- It is no wonder then that more than 128,000 Māori have taken leave from their ancestral homeland to live and work in Australia (Hamer, 2007; Kukutai & Pawar, 2013).

Fighting Back

Those who managed to stay at home and survive on their ancestral lands were able to preserve our culture, traditions, and customs but struggled to do so with little land and few people to keep the communities viable. The imposition of legislation and policies designed to wipe out the Māori language had a devastating effect on the preservation of the culture and resulted in at least two generations being denied access to much of their ancestral heritage. But rather than fostering loyal, obedient, and subservient English-speaking British subjects, it bred deep and growing anger and resentment. The specific causes of the anger and resentment for each hapū throughout the country were openly discussed on the traditional communal gathering places, the marae. These narratives, recounted time and again on marae throughout the country, became part of the oral traditions of each hapū and were passed down the generations. Survival of the institution of the marae has been key to the survival of Māori as a people, even though most who have been dislocated to urban environments have either lost contact with their own ancestral marae or are only able to return to them occasionally.

By the 1970s the anger and resentment were no longer confined to discussions on the marae. As the city populations of Māori grew, the younger generations became impatient and started adopting the civil rights and anti-apartheid movements' methods of open protest. Protest was not new to Māori, but large scale protest which drew us together from different hapū and iwi was. Even so, many Māori, fearing Pākehā retaliation, opposed protest and kept advocating diplomatic solutions. However in 1975 the first major national protest march took place demanding an end to the confiscation of Māori land. The petition which accompanied the march drew 60,000 signatures (Harris, 2004, p. 74).

The Waitangi Tribunal

The result of the 1975 Māori Land March was the establishment in the same year of the Waitangi Tribunal, a permanent commission of inquiry set up to inquire into Crown breaches of the principles of the Treaty of Waitangi[6] and to make recommendations to the Crown for removal of the prejudice caused. The government's primary intention was not to address the numerous breaches of the Treaty but rather to remove the increasingly embarrassing protest from the streets and away from public and international view (Oliver, 1991, p. 9-10). Māori, on the other hand, took claims to the Tribunal seeking:

- Return of stolen lands, waters, seas, fisheries, airways, minerals, and other resources;
- Protection of the natural environment from desecration and unsustainable development;
- Restoration and recognition of our language and culture;
- Equitable access to commercial opportunities and to government resources and services including education, health, housing, and social welfare;
- Recognition and upholding of our mana and sovereignty.

More than two thousand five hundred claims have been lodged to date with the Tribunal.

Despite the legislative and administrative constraints the Tribunal operates under, including being severely underfunded for most of its existence, it has issued more than one hundred and twenty reports upholding several hundreds of the claims against the Crown. Among its many recommendations addressing each of the issues brought before it has been the return of lands and other resources stolen from whānau and hapū. It has also recommended that the Crown not steal further lands – in particular, in 2004, the country's foreshores and seabed (Waitangi Tribunal, 2004).[7] Its recommendations aim to reverse the damage done by colonization. Most of its reports rewrite the country's history to record the gross deception and unlawful conduct of the Crown in its relationship with Māori. This includes the landmark 2014 report which found that contrary to White and Crown assertion, Ngāpuhi, the country's largest iwi

---

6. The "principles" of the Treaty of Waitangi are yet another Crown attempt to by-pass the original treaty. The 1975 Treaty of Waitangi Act which established the Waitangi Tribunal gives the Tribunal the impossible task of reconciling 'the Treaty in the Māori language' (the valid Treaty) and 'the Treaty in the English language' (the fraudulent document) and coming up with a set of 'principles' against which to make recommendations. As a Crown body the Tribunal (wrongly) assumed – without inquiring - that the Crown claim to sovereignty was legitimate. The 'principles' it arrived at were based on this with the result that all its recommendations fall well short of upholding hapū and iwi sovereignty. That false assumption was only formally challenged in 2010 by the iwi who originally negotiated the treaty, Ngāpuhi, when they took a claim for the government to recognise the fact that they had never ceded sovereignty. In 2014 the Tribunal upheld their claim. See also Mutu, 2010; Mikaere, 2011.

7. The government's refusal to consider the Tribunal's recommendations in this case led to

who were the first signatories to Te Tiriti o Waitangi, did not cede sovereignty to the British Crown when they signed the treaty in 1840 (Waitangi Tribunal, 2014). While this report sent shock waves through the White population and *The Telegraph* in London referred to it as "the historical bombshell" (Mutu, 2016), Māori throughout the country drew on its findings to demonstrate that they still hold ultimate and paramount power and authority throughout their territories, not the White government. The Tribunal reports also record the multiplicity of on-going atrocities committed by the Crown against Māori. They are often very strongly worded in their criticism of the Crown. For example, in the 1996 Taranaki Report, the confiscation of lands and marginalization and denigration of Māori that persisted without ending to the present day in Taranaki was described as the "holocaust of Taranaki history" (Waitangi Tribunal, 1996, p. 312).

A number of the Tribunal's reports have also recorded and explained the very special bond we have with our ancestral lands which we know as Papatūānuku, our Earth Mother. The Tribunal has carefully articulated the values we hold in respect of the natural environment which forbid the desecration, pollution, and destruction of Papatūānuku that Whites, and particularly their local governments, so often visited upon her at the behest of White developers with an insatiable greed for monetary gain. On a number of occasions hapū and iwi have turned to the Tribunal for relief when they have been unable to have legislation that was enacted to protect the environment, properly implemented by local government in their territories (Wheen & Ruru, 2004, p. 97-112; Waitangi Tribunal, 2011).

While some Pākehā have supported the Tribunal, it has raised the ire of many others, including a number of White historians. They attacked the Tribunal, calling for it to be abolished. Large sections of the White population have strongly amnesic tendencies about the atrocities committed as they illegally seized control of huge tracts of Māori land (Mutu, 2011, p. 42). From their position of privilege, dominance, and control of the country, they often articulate feelings of unbearable pain at having to come to terms with the true history of the country. They react angrily and often viciously (Hamer, 2004, p. 7; Abel & Mutu, 2011) to being reminded of their deeply entrenched racism and to being told that their claims to ownership and control of the country's lands and resources are not legitimate (Mutu, 2011, p. 4). As a result, successive governments have shown distain and disrespect for the Tribunal's reports and recommendations, ignoring most of them, despite the fact that the Tribunal

---

the largest protest march ever seen in the country as 50,000 Māori and our supporters descended on parliament in May 2004. The government still proceeded with the confiscation although iwi have issued public statements that they will not allow the legislation to be implemented in their territories.

is a Crown-appointed judicial body (Mutu, 2011, p. 108). Instead they threatened the Tribunal that they would downgrade its powers or abolish it if it ever used its legal powers to make recommendations that are binding on the Crown (Hamer, 2004, p. 7), a very serious breach of the rule of law.

Governments have also sought to extinguish claims by bullying claimants into "settling" their claims for an average of less than 0.1 per cent of what was lost (Mutu, 2005, p. 202-204). However the small amounts of money that are made available are then almost all recovered by the Crown because if Māori claimants want any of their stolen lands back, the Crown forces them to pay market value for them. Many hundreds of claims taken to the Tribunal are extinguished in this process without the permission of the claimants, and none of the claims are adequately addressed. Many of those who have settled have had to litigate to either have their settlements implemented (Chen, 2012) or to try to stop the government violating them.[8] Governments have ignored repeated recommendations of international human rights bodies to reach agreement with Māori on how their claims are to be settled (Stavenhagen, 2006; Anaya, 2011; United Nations Human Rights Council, 2014). Claimants have warned governments that their behaviour means it is inevitable that the "settlements" will be revisited by future generations despite government assertions that they are full and final. However, while "settlements" do not remove the prejudice, they have resulted in at least a small number of iwi being able to start recovering an economic base.

Recovering Our Language

One claim that the Crown did not completely ignore was that taken against its actions in trying to exterminate our language. It was one of the early claims lodged in the early 1980s and resulted in the Māori language, te reo Māori, being recognized as an official language and a Māori Language Commission being established. In the lead up to the Tribunal's inquiries, protest had played a key role in gaining recognition for te reo Māori and rescuing it from its endangered state. British colonisers waged war on the language for over one hundred years as part of their drive to dismantle and destroy our society and culture.[9] Compulsory attendance in schools saw generations of Māori children beaten and punished for speaking their own language, inculcating a fear of speaking it within the hearing of any White person. For decades the language was stigmatized. Yet it was the children of these traumatized children who

---

8. For example, Tainui and Ngāti Whātua o Ōrākei in respect of rights of first refusal over Crown held lands included in their settlements and Te Ohu Kaimoana in respect of the 1992 national fisheries settlement (Mutu, 2017).
9. The Education Act of 1867 directed that instruction in the schools be carried out in English, as far as practicable. The Native Schools Amendment Act of 1871 provided for establishment of village schools and instruction in English only (Biggs, 1968, p. 74).

were at the forefront of the fight against the stigmatization. Their parents did not pass te reo Māori on to them, and they began to suffer identity crises when they could not understand the proceedings of crucial events and ceremonies conducted on their ancestral marae, one of the few places where te reo Māori remained the only appropriate language. In the early 1970s a group of young Māori initiated a nationwide petition calling for the inclusion of te reo Māori in schools. It gathered 30,000 signatures. Despite the ridicule and personal harrassment suffered by these young activists, particularly from White media, the government introduced te reo Māori as an optional extra for schools and teacher training for Native speakers (Harris, 2004, p. 48). Yet progress within the White school system was unacceptably slow so in the late 1970s Māori started establishing our own te reo Māori-centred schooling system starting with our babies and pre-school children.

Kohanga Reo, language nests for pre-schoolers, were started in peoples' homes, in garages and on marae, resourced and run by volunteers. Government recognition and support was only forthcoming when it became clear that Māori were serious about Kohanga Reo and would continue to run them with or without government assistance. Once minimal assistance was made available Kohanga Reo sprang up around the country. They were followed by *Kura Kaupapa Māori* (te reo Māori immersion primary schools), *Whare Kura* (te reo Māori immersion secondary schools) and eventually, *Wānanga* (tertiary, Māori-focussed institutions). Although many students who started in Kohanga Reo did not remain in this system through to tertiary level, mainly because of the lack of resources available to these schools and Wānanga, the graduates they produced were proud and confident in their own ancestral world and language and much more successful academically than their White school and university counterparts.

Māori success, however, is perceived by many Pākehā as a threat to White hegemony, and so government bureacrats moved to undermine the Kohanga Reo and Wānanga in particular. They imposed restrictions and obstacles aimed at assimilating Māori education initiatives into the White education system. They succeeded in removing the head of the largest wānanga and significantly reducing its enrolments (Fox, 2006, p. 68). In the Kohanga Reo, enrollments plummeted and many closed (Waitangi Tribunal, 2011, ch. 5). The Waitangi Tribunal reported that the reduction of numbers of speakers of te reo Māori meant that the language is approaching a crisis point, identifying the failure of Crown to carry out its responsibilities to te reo Māori as the main cause (Waitangi Tribunal, 2011, ch. 5).

Broadcasting

Although education is seen as the most powerful form of language and culture preservation and enhancement, broadcasting was also identified early on by rangatira as another powerful medium. The battle here was just as gruelling as Whites fought shamelessly to have either total control over any Māori participation or to exclude us, and in particular, to prevent us having our own television service. Despite minimal government funding there is a network of twenty-three iwi radio stations operating around the country. The first one started broadcasting in the early 1980s (Mane, 2000). Their licenses require them to broadcast a minimum of eight hours a day in te reo Māori, they are run by Māori for Māori and offer news, sports, current affairs, talkback, music, and entertainment programmes which are of relevance to their listeners. These include indepth interviews with iwi and hapū elders on history, customs and oral traditions from throughout the country, advertising and coverage of hapū, iwi, regional, and national events from a Māori perspective and the promotion of the work of Māori musicians (which is rarely given air time on White stations).

The battle to be allowed to launch the Māori Television Service was protracted and bitter. It started with attempts to correct the pronunciation of White announcers on national television, demanding more Māori people on television and greater recognition of te reo Māori (Harris, 2004, p. 48). However, like education, that changed to establishing our own television service. Legal battles ensued as successive governments, at the behest of White television and media interests, ignored court rulings and fought to keep Māori out of the industry. The service was finally launched in 2004 admidst threats from the National opposition party to disestablish it when they came to power. However its success in delivering Māori and Indigenous peoples' focused television has unexpectedly attracted many non-Māori viewers. The service promotes itself as a world class Indigenous broadcaster and eschews the White television preponderence for English and United States of America programs in favor of those that are produced locally. It also broadcasts international Indigenous and non-Western programs which are not available on the White television networks. Like iwi radio it broadcasts news, sports, current affairs, music, and entertainment programs of relevance to their target audience including programs on hapū and iwi traditions, local and national kapa haka (traditional dances and songs) competitions and iwi sports and culture festivals. A number of our leaders and experts who are regularly subjected to racist attacks and demonized by White media are given safe air time on a daily basis on both Māori television and iwi radio. However although the services are careful to adhere to legal broadcasting standards, they are both dependent on government funding and tread a delicate path between maintaining the confidence and support of their target audiences and not upsetting their White funders.

The Battle for Sovereignty and Self-Determination

The longest on-going battle Māori have fought against our White colonizers is for recognition of our mana, that is, our version of sovereignty, and our right to self-determination. British authorities formally recognized and acknowledged our sovereignty in the 1830s. During that period and for some time after the entire country was still firmly in the control and under the authority of the myriad hapū that made up its population. It was the hapū, under the leadership of their rangatira, who controlled the lands, seas, resources, and people within the territories over which they held absolute and paramount authority.

Initially many rangatira were prepared to believe the assurances provided by missionaries and British bureaucrats about the good intentions of the British Crown and Queen Victoria's undertaking to control her lawless subjects. Others distrusted them from the outset. In the 1840s it was of little import given the numerical superiority of the hapū. On the ground, rangatira continued to exercise their power and authority. They never accepted British assertions of White Supremacy, including their proudly declared White New Zealand policy of the later part of the nineteenth century and for most of the twentieth century. They never accepted the bullying behavior of Whites or their denial of Māori sovereignty. Neither did they accept their disregard for the sanctity of Papatūānuku, Mother Nature, as they raped and pillaged her for material and monetary gain. However, the damage wrought by these attitudes and behaviors was both destructive and devastating and rangatira often gathered to discuss ways to address it.

Te Whakaminenga o Ngā Hapū o Nu Tireni

The first recorded gathering to deal with Pākehā lawlessness was known as Te Whakaminenga o ngā Hapū o Nu Tireni (The Gathering of the Hapū of New Zealand). It was a gathering of mainly northern rangatira who had been meeting to discuss a range of issues, including the problematic foreigners, since the early 1800s. This was the gathering that authorized and signed the 1835 document He Whakaputanga o te Rangatiratanga o Nu Tireni (The Declaration of Sovereignty of New Zealand). It was these same rangatira who signed Te Tiriti o Waitangi in the north in 1840 (Healy et al., 2012; Waitangi Tribunal, 2014). Between these hapū they controlled all the territories of the north, and further south in Waikato and in the east at Māhia. Te Whakaminenga has continued with its mainly northern focus to this day, although the gathering became marginalized and severely weakened for long periods as Whites attacked and undermined the authority of rangatira.

The Kīngitanga—The King Movement

Immediately to the south of the northern iwi are the Tainui confederation of iwi of the Waikato region. During the 1850s as the hapū and iwi of the central North Island resisted the theft of their lands, a number of iwi of the central North Island, including Tainui, came together and formed the Kīngitanga or King Movement in 1858. The movement based its structure on the British monarchy, selecting a king as their overall leader. It was a response to the extremely hostile actions of the British government as it attempted to take control of the fertile Waikato river lands. In exercising their mana and sovereign rights and forbidding Whites to enter their territories, Tainui's actions were interpreted as a direct challenge to and denial of White assertions of power and sovereignty. In 1863 British troops invaded the Waikato lands, intent on taking control. They provoked a war and then confiscated 1.2 million acres of land disingenuously claiming that Waikato iwi were rebels in a flimsy attempt to justify their actions. The King and his people were rendered virtually landless and forced to retreat into neighboring iwi lands. They remained in exile for twenty years before returning to a new legal and political order. Despite the social, economic, and cultural damage sustained by Waikato-Tainui during this period, the Kīngitanga remained in tact with Te Kauhanganui/ Te Whakakitenga o Waikato,[10] its parliament, being established in 1889 and still operating today (Waikato-Tainui website; Cox, 1993, p. 55-60).

For the next 120 years Waikato-Tainui sought justice and redress and finally and reluctantly signed its first Deed of Settlement in 1995 (Waikato-Tainui website). It returned control of 47,048 acres or three per cent of the lands stolen. A monetary payment of $70 million was made with the Deed acknowledging that this fell well short of the $12 billion owed to Waikato-Tainui (Mutu, 2011, p. 26). Six monarchs had led Waikato-Tainui to this point where they could finally start recovering their economic base. The Kīngitanga remains an influential force in the Māori world to this day.

Te Kotahitanga—The Māori Parliament[11]

While Waikato-Tainui concentrated on the Kīngitanga, other iwi were also coming together to try to address the damage being wrought by White colonists. Initial exclusion from the White Parliament and then token representation of four seats in 1867 (rather than the twenty Māori were entitled to) resulted in Māori eventually setting up their own parliament in 1892. Between the 1860s and the 1880s a number of iwi confederation movements developed around the country. The major concern for all of them was on-going theft of land by Whites and in particular, the operations of the Native Land Court. After several gatherings in their own territories, the confederations started meeting together in venues around the country. Over a period of several years they debated and then developed the structure and operational rules for a parliament made up of representatives of all iwi except Waikato-Tainui, who already had their own Kīngitanga movement and chose not to participate.

By the late 1890s the parliament's founding document carried 38,000 signatures, and that at a time when the total Māori population was 42,000. Te Kotahitanga mirrored the structure of the White Westminster parliament but operated on the basis of He Whakaputanga o te Rangatiratanga o Nu Tireni of 1835, Te Tiriti o Waitangi of 1840 and section 71 of the Constitution Act 1852

---

10. In 2015 Te Kauhanganui was restructured and renamed Te Whakakitenga o Waikato.
11. Information in this section is drawn mainly from Cox, 1993, p. 61-70; Walker, 2001, p. 88-99; Keane, 2010; Bargh, 2010.

of the White parliament. Section 71 provided for iwi autonomy within defined districts.[12] The full name of the Māori parliament was Te Rūnanga o te Kotahitanga mō te Tiriti o Waitangi (The Council of Rangatira and Elders for National Unity under Te Tiriti o Waitangi) and it was established to unite Māori, draw up legislation that returned power over hapū lands to those hapū and to reject White courts and institutions. It had 96 members from iwi throughout the country and operated in accordance with Māori law. It allowed the four Māori members of the Pākehā parliament to participate in order to be able to inform that body of their decisions so that they would be incorporated into legislation developed there. It is often referred to as Te Pāremata Māori (the Māori Parliament).

Te Kotahitanga first met in the Hawke's Bay region on 14 June 1892. Over the eleven years that it was in existence, it met many times and debated many issues, particularly those relating to the relationship of the British Crown and iwi. It drew up and passed legislation but when the four Māori members took it to the White parliament, White members refused to discuss it and walked out of the House. They would not tolerate any talk of a Māori parliament or Māori determining anything to do with their own welfare. In the end it was one of these Māori members of the White Parliament who worked within Te Kotahitanga to eventually convince it to close down after having effectively undermined its work. This strategy of using our own against us is a weapon that Whites have always wielded very successfully and continue to use to this day. We call our own who do this kūpapa (traitors) and despite the shame that label carries, there are many who infiltrate our organizations to this day in an attempt to have Whites, and particularly the government, control us, or, if they cannot achieve that, to destroy our organizations.

National Māori Congress[13]

Although Te Kotahitanga was closed down, its principles and the wish to revitalize it have always been with us. The next body that was based on the principle of national unity was the National Māori Congress. It was established in 1990 and was made up of rangatira and other iwi representatives from almost all iwi round the country. Its main purpose was to bring iwi together to form a united front for the practical recognition of our mana and sovereignty. It met on many occasions throughout the country and operated for almost eight years. It discussed and made decisions on a range of issues impacting on iwi and was severely critical of several of the Crown's deeply racist policies and legislation, particularly the Crown's unilaterally determined policy for the ex-

---

12. In practice local Pākehā administrators refused to implement section 71 and it was never given effect. (Cox, 1993, p. 36-7).
13. Information for this section is from Cox (1993, ch. 7) and my own knowledge and experience as a member of National Māori Congress representing Ngāti Kahu.

tinguishment of claims taken to the Waitangi Tribunal, a policy dubbed "the fiscal envelope" (Mutu, 2011, p. 17-27). National gatherings were convened, and the need for constitutional change in the country was identified as being crucially important for the future well-being of Māori as a people. Despite the very deeply respected membership of Congress, the Crown would not tolerate its own asserted authority being questioned and potentially undermined. Infiltration followed by a divide and rule strategy ensured the demise of Congress.

National Iwi Chairs' Forum[14]
From the late 1990s, the possibility of re-establishing the economic bases of hapū and iwi started to emerge with the so-called "settlements" of some of the Tiriti o Waitangi claims against the Crown. The first settlement related to fisheries and although it drew Māori into legal battles for eleven years, Māori are now a significant and powerful player in the New Zealand fishing industry (Mutu, 2012, p. 120). Two relatively large settlements for claims that were valued in excess of $12 billion followed for Tainui in 1995 and Ngāi Tahu in 1997. The settlements of these claims were each valued by the Government at $170 million and returned small amounts of land, and cash to purchase other lands. Since then sixty nine much smaller settlements have been legislated and a further thirty or so are at various stages approaching legislation. The government has claimed that all the settlements have a total monetary value of just over one billion dollars. Most of that is made up of money retained by the government as they force Māori to pay market value for their own lands that were stolen from them. Although most who have settled have been able to grow their settlements substantially, they have never been enough to address the appalling socio-economic statistics listed earlier.

In 2005, Ngāi Tahu called the elected chairpersons of each of the iwi throughout the country together to see how we could support each other to be able to properly exercise our mana and sovereignty and better maximize the benefits of settlements. We agreed to set up the National Iwi Chairs' Forum and to avoid having the Crown, which today is effectively the government of the day, involved in any way other than at our behest and on our terms.

The Forum has undertaken several projects, one of which is to draw up models for a constitution for the country based on tikanga (our own laws), He Whakaputanga of 1835 and Te Tiriti o Waitangi of 1840. The project is being undertaken because while many Māori believe that He Whakaputanga and Te Tiriti are the country's constitution, Whites assert that the country has no written constitution. And they refuse to contemplate anything that could possibly challenge their very privileged lifestyle and so avoid debate on a written

---

14. This section derives from my knowledge and experience as a member of National Iwi Chairs' Forum representing Ngāti Kahu.

constitution (Mutu, 2011, p. 96-7). Those Pākehā who have given the matter some thought are also aware of the inevitability of having to include He Whakaputanga and Te Tiriti in any written constitution. As the Indigenous people who have ultimate responsibility for our country, we have taken this initiative based on the advice provided by Māori experts and communities throughout the country.[15] The group responsible for this work, Matike Mai Aotearoa – the Independent Working Group on Constitutional Transformation, published their report in 2016 (Jackson & Mutu, 2016). The governance models it recommends are being discussed with both Māori and non-Māori around the country. It's recommendations include that a constitutional convention for Māori be convened in 2021 and then one for the whole country to be organised with the aim of achieving constitutional transformation by 2040, that is, 200 years after the signing of Te Tiriti o Waitangi.

The Forum has also taken on several other specific projects aimed at insuring that Māori sovereignty is upheld in practical terms. These include Māori ownership of water, of minerals (including petroleum), and of the foreshore and seabed; the need for Māori control over and, if necessary, prevention of mining and oil drilling; Māori control over our own education, health and housing and over the New Zealand contribution to climate change. All of these projects have required discussions with the government. This has made adhering to the requirement of no Crown involvement less straight forward. Furthermore some iwi leaders still believe that Crown support and validation is required and government Ministers, bureaucrats and kūpapa are shameless in their attempts to infiltrate and influence the work and decisions of the Forum. While we could all learn well from the lessons of Te Whakaminenga, Te Kotahitanga and National Māori Congress, it remains to be seen whether we will do so.

Recourse to International Instruments

From the outset of relationships with Whites, our rangatira have sought international support in our disputes and battles with them. Initially they approached the British monarchs but by the early 1900s their lack of honor and integrity had became clear. And so our rangatira tried the League of Nations,[16] but the White government successfully blocked our access there. However, since the 1960s increasing support has been forthcoming from the United Nations. The International Convention on the Elimination of All Forms of Racial Discrimination of 1965 required the New Zealand government to give

---

15. Consultation was conducted over four years in 252 *hui* (gatherings) and in seventy *rangatahi* (youth) meetings.
16. In 1924 Tahupōtiki Wiremu Rātana, a political and religous leader, sent a delegation to the League of Nations in Geneva calling for intervention to return confiscated land and the implementation of Te Tiriti o Waitangi. They were denied access.

up its White New Zealand policy. It could not ratify the Convention until it had passed the 1971 Race Relations Act outlawing racism. The Act has been steadily weakened since then and now affords little or no protection for Māori from racist attacks. And although the White New Zealand policy may have been formally abandoned and removed from legislation, it remains *de facto*.

Three United Nations Special Rapporteurs have visited New Zealand and reported on the situation of Māori: Erica-Irene Daes in 1988, Rodolfo Stavenhagen in 2006, and James Anaya in 2011. Each report has been severely critical of the New Zealand government's treatment of Māori, and each time the government has ignored the report. The United Nations Committee for the Elimination of Racial Discrimination issued a decision against the government in 2005 for its discrimination against Māori in respect of the 2004 Foreshore and Seabed Act. In 2014 the United Nations Human Rights Council was critical of the on-going racism and discrimination against Māori and made a number of specific recommendations to remedy this.

During this period from the 1980s until 2007, Māori were active participants in drafting the United Nations Declaration on the Rights of Indigenous Peoples. When the General Assembly adopted the Declaration in 2007,[17] the New Zealand government could no longer maintain its façade of good race relations it had maintained in the United Nations for many years. It joined the other English speaking colonial governments of Australia, Canada, and the United States to be one of the four states who voted against the Declaration. In 2010, as a result of international pressure and pressure from their Māori Party coalition partner, they very begrudgingly supported it. When the Māori Party announced New Zealand's support in the United Nations, the Prime Minister desperately tried to play down the significance of the Declaration. However Māori knew the significance and were jubilant as the news of the support filtered through from New York. But as yet the government has refused to allow reference to it in any government policy or legislation.

The articles of the Declaration the New Zealand government is most vehemently opposed to are those declaring Indigenous peoples' right to self-determination, autonomy, and self-government. In the United Nations General Assembly they specified that they opposed the articles relating to our right to our lands, territories, and resources, our right to have our lands and resources that were stolen from us returned or fully compensated for, and the right to decide matters that directly impact on us (United Nations General Assembly, 2012). Consideration of each of the 46 articles shows that the New Zealand

---

17. The adopted version of the Declaration is a much weaker statement than that agreed by Indigenous Peoples and fails to fulfil the aspirations of those who pursued a full articulation of the human rights of Indigenous Peoples (see for example Churchill, 2011; Newcomb, 2011).

government is non-compliant with almost all of the articles of the Declaration.

Outlook for the Future

Māori determination to survive as a people and to preserve our language, culture, mana, and sovereignty has been under concerted attack for more than one hundred and seventy years by Whites whom we welcomed as our guests. What has become clear is that no amount of bullying is going to force us all to assimilate into a foreign culture or to accept a subordinate position on our own ancestral lands. Our current situation is dire and whānau, hapū, and iwi have been struggling on many fronts to free ourselves from the landlessness, poverty, deprivation, and marginalization that Whites have forced on us. Yet after being threatened with near extinction at the beginning of the twentieth century, we are now in a position to start making real gains in taking back power and control over our own lives.

The key to our survival has been the resilience of our marae as the institution that has preserved our culture. There are over one thousand throughout the country, each upholding the mana of its own whānau and hapū, although even there, encroachment of White culture can happen if whānau are not vigilent. Building, restoring, and maintaining our marae involves major communal efforts and must be supported into the future.

Our language can be heard on our marae and on a daily basis on Māori radio and television, even though it still remains threatened. It is the only language used in kapa haka, our traditional songs and dances, and local, regional, and national festivals and competitions attract huge followings of young Māori and their whānau. We have our immersion schools, kohanga reo, kura kaupapa Māori, and whare kura, and our tertiary wānanga preserving our language and producing a small but steady flow of graduates well grounded in our own knowledge bases, histories, and worldviews. Out of the universities we now producing another small but steady stream of professionals in the Pākehā world, some of whom use their training to help our people. This is particularly so in law, where we now have a small number who have been appointed to the judiciary, in medicine, in education, and in the arts. The number of Māori academics is steadily increasing and with it an emerging literature grounded in our peoples' struggles to retain our mana and our identity. Yet our culture will not be secure until a much greater number of us live our lives according to the underpinning values of our culture. For that to happen, curriculum in White schools, where most of our children are, must change to include the true history of our country, to make Māori language compulsory and to normalize being Māori.

On the economic front landlessness remains a huge problem, although a few hapū and iwi have been able start recovering parts of their territories. The fight to recover our lands will probably take several generations, and each generation will find new ways to achieve that goal. While greater influence in parliament would help, we remain handicapped with only seven Māori seats in a parliament of one hundred and twenty one seats. Seventeen other members of parliament acknowledge their Māori ancestry, but unless Māori adhere to the dominant White agenda in parliament they are effectively marginalized. Despite this, iwi will nevertheless become significant players in the agriculture and forestry industries once the Crown has fully relinquished its claims to exotic forest lands and large state farming operations. However, insuring that control of the lands is returned to those who are mana whenua rather those who managed to get to the Crown officials first is proving to be a stumbling block that must be cleared. We are well on the way to taking back control of our fisheries, but we are still battling for control of our waterways, our minerals, including our petroleum, and our foreshore and seabed. Some extensive Māori business networks have been formed across a number of industries as Māori entrpreneurship starts to regain strength.

The most important task ahead of us is securing the constitutional transformation necessary to provide us with legal security for our human rights. The lack of a written constitution in New Zealand has greatly privileged Whites and severely disadvantaged Māori, leaving us subject to the political whim of Whites. New Zealand's support for the Declaration on the Rights of Indigenous Peoples in 2010 nevertheless signals a turning point in this area although it will be up to Māori to lead the change. Respected Māori High Court judge and Chairman of the Waitangi Tribunal from 1983 to 1999, Sir Edward Taihākurei Durie, in a message to the Māori Party after the announcement in the United Nations said,

> ...I would still rank the day that New Zealand gave support to the Declaration as the most significant day in advancing Māori rights since 6th February 1840 [when Te Tiriti o Waitangi was signed].

> I do not overlook that the Declaration has only moral force. The same is said of the Treaty. Important statements of principle established through international negotiation and acclamation filter into law in time through both governments and the courts, which look constantly for universal statements of principle in developing policy or deciding cases.

> Most significant for the present is the statement that recurs throughout the Declaration that Indigenous people should be dealt with through their own institutions (Harawira, 2010).

References

Abel, Sue, and Margaret Mutu.
2011. There's Racism and Then There's Racism – Margaret Mutu and the Racism Debate. *The New Zealand Journal of Media Studies* 12(2).

Anaya, James.
2011. *The Situation of Māori People in New Zealand.* Geneva: United Nations Human Rights Council. Available at http://unsr.jamesanaya.org/country-reports/the-situation-of-maori-people-in-new-zealand-2011, accessed July 7, 2012.

Bargh, Maria.
2010. Lessons from the Māori Parliament. In: *Māori and Parliament: Diverse Strategies and Compromises.* Maria Bargh, ed. Pp. 17-27. Wellington, Huia Publishers.

Bargh, Maria. (ed.)
2010. *Māori and Parliament: Diverse Strategies and Compromises.* Wellington: Huia Publishers.

Biggs, Bruce.
1968. The Maori Language Past and Present. In: *The Maori People in the Nineteen Sixties.* Eric Schwimmer, ed, pp. 65-84. Auckland: Blackwood and Janet Paul.

Chen, Mai.
2012. Post-Settlement Implications for Māori–Crown Relations. In: *Treaty of Waitangi Settlements.* Nicola Wheen and Janine Haywood, eds, pp. 182-200. Wellington, Bridget Williams Books.

Churchill, Ward.
2011. A Travesty of a Mockery of a Sham: Colonialism as 'Self-Determination' in the UN Declaration on the Rights of Indigenous Peoples. *Griffith Law Review* 20(3), 526-556.

Cooper, Erana, and Julie Wharewera-Mika.
2011. Healing: Towards an Understanding of Māori Child Maltreatement. In *Māori and Social Issues.* Tracey McIntosh and Malcolm Mulholland, eds. pp. 263-282. Wellington: Huia Publishers.

Cox, Lindsay.
1993. *Kotahitanga: The Search for Māori Political Unity.* Auckland: Auckland University Press.

Cram, Fiona.
2011. Poverty. In *Māori and Social Issues*. Tracey McIntosh and Malcolm Mulholland, eds, pp. 147-168. Wellington: Huia Publishers.

Daes, Erica-Irene A.
1988. Confidential Report by Professor Erica-Irene A Daes, Chairman-Rapporteur of the United Nations Working Group on Indigenous Populations, on visit to New Zealand, 2-7 January, 1988. Athens: E A Daes.

Fox, Derek.
2006. Education: Te Wananga o Aotearoa: Who's at the Helm Now? In *Mana Magazine* no. 69, April–May 2006. P.67.

Groot, Shiloh, Darrin Hodgetts, Linda Waimarie Nikora, and Mohi Rua.
2011. Māori and Homelessness. In *Māori and Social Issues*. Tracey McIntosh and Malcolm Mulholland, eds, pp. 235-248. Wellington: Huia Publishers.

Hamer, Paul.
2004. A Quarter-century of the Waitangi Tribunal. In *The Waitangi Tribunal: Te Roopu Whakamana i Te Tiriti o Waitangi*. Janine Haywood and Nicola R Wheen, eds, pp. 3-14. Wellington: Bridget Williams Books.

Hamer, Paul.
2007. *Māori in Australia Ngā Māori i te Ao Moemoeā*. Wellington: Te Puni Kōkiri. Available on http://www.tpk.govt.nz/en/in-print/our-publications/publications/maori-in-australia/download/tpk-maorinaustralia2007-en.pdf, accessed July 7, 2012.

Harawira, Hone.
2010. *The Declaration of Rights of Indigenous Peoples*. Speech delivered in Parliament Wednesday 21 April 2010; 3.10pm.

Harris, Aroha.
2004. *Hīkoi: Forty Years of Māori Protest*. Wellington: Huia Publishers.

Haywood, Janine, and Nicola R. Wheen. (eds).
2004. *The Waitangi Tribunal: Te Roopu Whakamana i te Tiriti o Waitangi*. Wellington: Bridget Williams Books.

Haywood, Janine, and Nicola R. Wheen. (eds).
2012. *Treaty of Waitangi Settlements*. Wellington: Bridget Williams Books.

Healy, Susan, and Ingrid Huygens, Takawai Murphy, and Hori Parata.
2012. *Ngāpuhi Speaks*. Whāngārei, New Zealand: Te Kawariki & Network Waitangi Whāngārei.

Jackson, Moana, and Margaret Mutu.
2016. He Whakaaro Here Whakaumu Mō Aotearoa : The Report of Matike Mai Aotearoa – *The Independent Working Group on Constitutional Transformation*. Auckland, the University of Auckland and National Iwi Chairs Forum. Available at http://www.converge.org.nz/pma/Matike-MaiAotearoaReport.pdf, accessed October 4, 2016.

Keane, Basil.
2010. Kotahitanga. In *Māori and Parliament: Diverse Strategies and Compromises*. Maria Bargh, ed, pp. 9-15. Wellington, Huia Publishers.

Kukutai, Tahu.
2011. Contemporary Issues in Māori Demography. In *Māori and Social Issues*. Tracey McIntosh and Malcolm Mulholland, eds, pp.11-48. Wellington: Huia Publishers.

Kukutai, Tahu, and Shefali Pawar.
2013. *A Socio-demographic Profile of Māori living in Australia*. Hamilton: National Institute of Demographic and Economic Analysis, University of Waikato. Available on http://www.waikato.ac.nz/__data/assets/pdf_file/0006/156831/2013-WP3-A-Demographic-Profile-of-Maori-living-in-Australia.pdf, accessed 2 October 2016.

McIntosh, Tracey.
2011. Marginalisation. In *Māori and Social Issues*. Tracey McIntosh and Malcolm Mulholland, eds, pp. 263-282. Wellington: Huia Publishers.

McIntosh, Tracey, and Malcolm Mulholland. (eds).
2012. *Māori and Social Issues*. Wellington, Huia Publishers.

Mane, Jo.
2000. *A History of Iwi Radio – Te Reo Tautoko: Māori Language Radio Broadcasting*. Unpublished MA dissertation. University of Auckland.

Mikaere, Ani .
2011. *Colonising Myths, Māori Realities, He Rukuruku Whakaaro*. Wellington: Huia Publishers.

Mulholland, Malcolm. (ed.).
2006. *The State of the Māori Nation*. Auckland: Reed.

Mulholland, Malcolm, and Veronica Tāwhai. (eds).
2010. *Weeping Waters: The Treaty of Waitangi and Constitutional Change.*
Wellington: Huia Publishers.

Mutu, Margaret.
2005. Recovering Fagin's Ill-gotten Gains: Settling Ngāti Kahu's Treaty of
Waitangi Claims Against the Crown. In *Waitangi Revisited: Perspectives on
the Treaty of Waitangi.* Michael Belgrave, Merata Kawharu and David
Williams, eds, pp. 187-209. Melbourne, Oxford University Press.

Mutu, Margaret.
2010. Constitutional Intentions: The Treaty Texts. In *Weeping Waters: The
Treaty of Waitangi and Constitutional Change.* Malcolm Mulholland and
Veronica Tāwahi, eds, pp. 13-40. Wellington, Huia Publishers.

Mutu, Margaret.
2011. *The State of Māori Rights.* Wellington: Huia Publishers.

Mutu, Margaret.
2012. Fisheries Settlement: "The Sea I Never Gave". In *Treaty of Waitangi
Settlements.* Janine Haywood and Nicola Wheen, eds, pp. 114-123.
Wellington: Bridget Williams Books.

Mutu, Margaret.
2016. Māori Issues. *The Contemporary Pacific: A Journal of Island Affairs,*
Vol.28, No.1, pp 227-237.

Mutu, Margare
2017. Māori Issues. *The Contemporary Pacific: A Journal of Island Affairs,*
Vol.29, No.1.

Newcombe, Steven T.
2011. The UN Declaration on the Rights of Indigenous Peoples and the
Paradigm of Domination. *Griffith Law Review* 20(3), 576-607.

Oliver, W.H.
1991. *Claims to the Waitangi Tribunal.* Wellington: Department of Justice.

Petrie, Hazel.
2006. *Chiefs of Industry: Early Tribal Enterprise in Early Colonial New
Zealand.* Auckland: Auckland University Press.

Reid, Papaarangi, and Bridget Robson.
2006. The State of Māori Health. In *The State of the Māori Nation*. Malcolm Mulholland, ed, pp. 17-31. Auckland: Reed.

Robson, Bridget, and Ricci Harris. (eds).
2007. *Hauora: Māori Standards of Health IV: A study of the years 2000-2005.* Wellington: Te Rōpū Rangahau Hauora a Eru Pōmare. Available at http://www.hauora.maori.nz/downloads/hauora_complete_web.pdf, accessed July 7, 2012.

Robson, Bridget, and Gordon Purdie.
2007 Mortality. In *Hauora: Māori Standards of Health IV: A study of the years 2000-2005*. Wellington: Te Rōpū Rangahau Hauora a Eru Pōmare. Bridget Robson and Ricci Harris, eds. Available at http://www.hauora.maori.nz/downloads/hauora_complete_web.pdf, accessed July 7, 2012.

Statistics New Zealand.
2016. *Māori Population Estimates – Mean Year ended 31 December 2015 - tables*. Wellington: Statistics New Zealand. http://www.stats.govt.nz/browse_for_stats/population/estimates_and_projections/MaoriPopulationEstimates_HOTPMYeDec15.aspx, accessed October 2, 2016.

Stavenhagen, Rodolfo.
2006. *Report of the Special Rapporteur on the Situation of Human Rights and Fundamental Freedoms of Indigenous People*. Mission to New Zealand. E/CN.4/2006/78/Add.3. 13 March 2006, Geneva, United Nations Human Rights Commission available at http://www.converge.org.nz/pma/srnz-march06.pdf, accessed July 7, 2012.

Taonui, Rawiri, and Greg Newbold.
2011. Māori Gangs. In *Māori and Social Issues*. Tracey McIntosh and Malcolm Mulholland, eds, pp. 209-234. Wellington: Huia Publishers.

United Nations Committee on the Elimination of Racial Discrimination.
2005. Report on the New Zealand Foreshore and Seabed Act 2004, Decision 1(66), 66th Session, 11th March 2005. UN Doc CERD/C/66/NZL/Dec.1. Geneva: United Nations.

United Nations General Assembly.
2007. *United Nations Declaration of the Rights of Indigenous People*. New York: United Nations. Available at http://www.un.org/esa/socdev/unpfii/documents/DRIPS_en.pdf, accessed July 7, 2012.

United Nations General Assembly.
2012. GA/10612 available at http://www.un.org/News/Press/docs/2007/
ga10612.doc.htm, accessed 19 April 2012.

United Nations General Assembly.
2014. *Report of the Working Group on the Universal Periodic Review: New Zealand.* https://documents-dds-ny.un.org/doc/UNDOC/GEN/G14/131/43/
PDF/G1413143.pdf?OpenElement, accessed 29 Sep 2016.

Waikato-Tainui website http://www.waikatotainui.com/, accessed 5 October 2016. Waitangi Tribunal

All reports are available at http://www.waitangi-tribunal.govt.nz/reports/, accessed July 7, 2012.

Waitangi Tribunal.
1989. *Report of the Waitangi Tribunal on the te reo Maori claim (Wai 11).*
Wellington: The Waitangi Tribunal.

Waitangi Tribunal.
1996. *Taranaki Report: Kaupapa Tuatahi: Te Muru me te Raupatu (Wai 143).*
Wellington: GP Publications.

Waitangi Tribunal.
1997. *Muriwhenua Land Report (Wai 45).* Wellington: GP Publications.

Waitangi Tribunal.
2004. *Report on the Crown's Foreshore and Seabed Policy (Wai 1071).* Wellington: Legislation Direct.

Waitangi Tribunal.
2011. *Ko Aotearoa Tēnei (Wai 262).* Wellington: Legislation Direct.

Waitangi Tribunal.
2014. *He Whakaputanga me Te Tiriti: The Declaration and the Treaty: The Report on Stage 1 of the Paparahi o Te Raki Inquiry (Wai 1040).* Wellington, Legislation Direct.

Walker, Ranginui.
2001. *He Tipua: The Life and Times of Sir Apirana Ngata.* Auckland: Penguin.

Webb, Robert
2011. Incarceration. In *Māori and Social Issues.* Tracey McIntosh and Malcolm Mulholland, eds, pp. 249-262. Wellington: Huia Publishers.

Wheen, Nicola, and Jacinta Ruru.
2004. The Environmental Reports. In *The Waitangi Tribunal: Te Roopu Whakamana i Te Tiriti o Waitangi*. Janine Hayward and Nicola Wheen, eds, pp. 97-112. Wellington: Bridget Williams Books.

Ainu of Japan

Jeffry Gayman

Hokkaido University

This chapter looks at the history, present situation, and outlook for the future of the Ainu people, an Indigenous nation inhabiting the northern islands of Japan, and a group whose fate/identity is now very much intertwined with the surrounding ethnic Japanese population. Much has been written about monoculturalism in Japan, from the angle of *Nihonjinron* (discourses about monoethnic Japan), as well as, in recent years, a slowly expanding alternative response to such an interpretation. In order to understand the current position and future outlook for the Ainu of Japan, it is first necessary to examine their identity by briefly touching upon the relational framework vis-à-vis the wider Japanese social milieu. First, in order are interpretations of group identity in Japan, and how this social/psychosocial phenomenon both negatively and positively affects minority activism within the boundaries of this country. Then, in order is an overview of the characteristics of the physical environment and corresponding lifeways of this Northern people. Beginning in the mid-Tokugawa Era (circa 1700) the Japanese government exerted a constraining influence on the Ainu, an influence that intensified rapidly with the commencement of the Meiji Era (1867-1911), in which Ainu lifeways were curtailed and an aggressive policy of assimilation adopted. The gist of this policy of colonization was to create a social climate of prejudice and discrimination against which the Ainu are still struggling today. A complicated mix of factors included intermarriage, assimilation, and internalized oppression to dampen collective group identity, while welfare colonialism combined with divisive administrative policies to bolster pre-existing factionalisms amongst the Ainu community and thereby hamper the progress of the larger Ainu rights recovery movement. Concerns about ethnic backlash, strongly interrelated to the monocultural Japanese mindset, concretely affected individual Ainu behavior as well as guided the conservative discourse of "gradual implementation" which is currently shaping Ainu policy development. While the Japanese government and *Wajin* (native-born Japanese) academics are—not unexpectedly—proceeding along a conservative tack, the Ainu people are by no means accepting such a lack of positive policy passively. Indeed, Ainu people have been struggling for their collective rights for decades, and pride in this heritage of cultural revitalization/rights recovery activism serves in part to fuel the disparate loci of the current Ainu revitalization movement. Within the final sections of this chapter, the growth in younger generation Ainu who are coming to express a positive embrace of their Ainu identity, thanks in part to the implementation of a 1997 "Cultural Promotion Act", is examined. Also examined is the increased cultural exchange with foreign Indigenous groups and the meaning of these developments for a future Ainu society.

Ainu group identity is torn between conflicting values and loyalties accompanying the above contradictions and tensions, and Ainu policy has stopped short of clear-set policies guaranteeing Ainu self-determination in economic, political, or educational arenas. As regards the future of Ainu "ethnicity" as an identifiable Ainu society demarcated by use of the Ainu language and following Ainu values, one factor for alarm is the advanced age of knowledgeable culture-bearers and the lack of attention that they are receiving in current cultural policy. Whether the strength of the remaining Elders is enough, combined with the enthusiasm of the newly-emerging pro-Ainu youth generation, to weather the factionalism of Ainu society until policy implementation proceeds far enough to stabilize Ainu ethnic identity and cultural transmission, is a question of time, and finally of the support and guidance of the international Indigenous community, who must help the Ainu to cultivate internal solidarity while all the while being considerate of the delicate and contradiction-ridden situation in which the Ainu are placed.

Homogeneous Japan and the Minority Exception
As with other Indigenous groups in liminal situations such as off-reservation Native Americans, or Indigenous Peoples in repressed or discriminated conditions, lack of incentive to "come-out" as Ainu prevents us from knowing the exact population of the Ainu people. Official figures from the Hokkaido government, derived through the cooperation of the Hokkaido Ainu Association, the largest and currently sole representative organization of the Ainu people, put the 2006 population at 23,782 (Hokkaido, 2006), but these numbers are suspect, as they are a derivative figure calculated by multiplying numbers of official members in the Association overall by a flat rate of supposed members per household, and do not take into account Ainu living in the Tokyo metropolitan or other areas of Japan south of Hokkaido. Further, 2006 population figure only represent those Ainu contacted by the Ainu Association who were willing to acknowledge their Ainu heritage. Estimates of numbers of Ainu people hiding their identity, or of those of partial Ainu descent, postulate the actual number to be from three to ten times this amount (70,000 – 300,000).

Ainu identity, as always, remains a nebulous category: the provisional standard implemented by the Ainu Association until several years ago has limited membership to those: 1) born into an "Ainu family", 2) raised by Ainu, or 3) married to a person of Ainu heritage. Definition, however, of who qualifies as "Ainu family", "Ainu", or of "Ainu heritage" has ultimately been determined by the Ainu in each community where there is a branch of the Ainu Association; thus, it is has been until now a subjective criteria. Recently, in an effort to determine target populations for subsequent Ainu policy, the official standard has now been reduced to: 1), those born into an Ainu family, but how this administrative change will ultimately affect the Ainu community at large remains to be seen.

Heavily influencing these figures, and intra-group Ainu dynamics as well, is the phenomenon of passing, possible in many Asian cities in countries which possess minority or Indigenous Peoples within their borders. In Japan this phenomenon is particularly manifest, due to Japanese theories of cultural homogeneity proliferated after World War II, and bolstered even further by a societal value of *Wa*, or, "not making waves". Sanctions against offenders have occurred even amongst the same ethnic community since time immemorial, the most famous being banishment from village affairs, but the people who suffer the most from this custom are Japan's minorities, who are damned if they do and damned if they don't. Japan still has much room left for improvement in its protection of human rights; discrimination in employment and marriage on the basis of ethnic or family background has occurred until the present day, while more extreme cases of physical violence such as knife attacks have occurred against students attending Korean schools. Such discrimination has palpable manifestations for the victims.

In the case of Indigenous Japanese minorities such as the Ainu and Okinawans (Ryukyuans), or the resident Korean and Chinese Japanese—many of whom were brought to Japan as forced labor during Japan's colonial period— these mindsets and cultural values play out on individual and group levels. At the individual level is passing, and on a group level is the bashing against those members of the in-group who would threaten other group member's anonymity by coming-out, or by too stridently "rocking the boat".

Tsuneyoshi et al. (2011) report on how educational programs for "Intercultural Understanding" toward resident Koreans have broken the mold of the "homogeneity discourse", paving the way locally for an open multicultural atmosphere for newcomer immigrant children in Kawasaki City inside the Tokyo urban conundrum. Meanwhile, Peng Er Lam (2005) outlines how various minority groups in Japan have been influenced by the resistance philosophies and tactics of their fellow minorities and/or predecessors.

In the Ainu case, these exceptions to the discourses of the ethnic homogeneity discourse and the culture of *Wa*, while exhibiting limited influence in the cities of Sapporo or the urban conurbations of the Tokyo and Osaka areas, have not had a significant affect on the attitudes of people, neither Ainu nor *Wajin*, in rural Hokkaido. Additionally, the resistance philosophy and tactics of the *Buraku* (outcaste Japanese with origins in the feudal era) liberation movement, while being employed by some hard-core Ainu activists to this day, seem not to have caught on with the "Ainu masses", despite a brief period of active usage during the 1970s and 1980s. On the contrary, these factors still continue to extend the influence that they have in the past. For example, intermarriage between Ainu and *Wajin* seems to have combined with Ainu self-disdain to foster assimilationist attitudes amongst the great majority of Ainu, which produces reticence about one's own identity to the extent that many Ainu do not relate their ethnic identity even to their children.

Ainu Homelands/Ainu Mosir

The Ainu homeland displays a huge amount of diversity in climate, foliage, and fauna, from the mild-wintered grassy coastal regions of southern Hokkaido to the windswept, barren tiny islands of the Kuriles, to the forests of central Hokkaido and Sakhalin, from the marine habitat of the Kuriles to the inland environments of Asahikawa. The region is 1800 kilometers from north to south, and 600 kilometers from east to west, approximating the dimensions of the current Japanese state. Most scholars today support the argument that the Ainu were originally hunter-gatherer inhabitants of the Japanese archipelago who were pushed to the North by rice-cultivating immigrants from the Asian mainland who entered Japan from the southern Honshu region.

Ainu Spirituality and Ainu TEK

As with many Indigenous people, the Ainu are animists, believing in the spirits of animals, plants, and other organic matter, but differing in that the Ainu extend their reverence and respect for the spirits of objects to all man-made materials as well. This deep spirituality culminated in rhythmical songs and graceful dances to the Gods, rich spirit-sending ceremonies and rituals, intricate designs in carving and embroidery, one of the most extensive oral traditions in the world, as well as extensive knowledge for how to live successfully in the harsh northern climate.

Fundamentally a hunter-gatherer society who traded their surplus in far-ranging trade networks to China and Russia, the Ainu generally lived along waterways or in sheltered places along the coast readily accessible for transporting their goods. Ainu traditional ecological knowledge was founded on dictums such as only taking as much fish or game as was necessary, leaving clusters of edible plants and mushrooms for future years, replanting trees upon harvest, and showing respect for all living things. Recent Ainu responses to the increase in bear sightings in the city of Sapporo are telling; the Ainu claim that the bears have been forced to roam into the city in search of food because the *Wajin* have overharvested their natural diet in the nearby mountains that surround the city. Such values were inculcated into children and passed down to the next generation through stories around the fireside at night, told with ingenious creative devices in order to draw the listener into the tale and keep their attention.

As with almost all Indigenous cultures, the Ainu culture is a culture of memory. The longest of the Ainu oral epics is said to take three days and nights to recite. Since the Ainu depend upon the forest for their bounty, young gatherers are admonished to "memorize the location of each plant and tree" so that they will know where to go for it in times of need. One Elder told me that she cannot remember peoples' names but she knows under just which tree on which ridge on which mountain the mushrooms and other edible mountain plants can be found in season; in other words, she possesses a detailed mental map of all of the local forest for miles around. Ainu children were admonished to memorize family Ainu and other patterns by recollecting designs, which their parents had drawn into the ashes in the hearth, then erased. Such training has been referred to as "training for the eyes", the memory of the oral tradition as "training for the ears".

Colonization Delves a Huge Blow to Ainu Society and Culture

Huge changes came about to Ainu society as a result of the expansion of the borders of Japan and Russia, all conducted conveniently under then current international law parlance of "development" of "terra nullius" lands (Harrison, 2008). Ainu were the victims of a number of forced relocations, the most extreme of which being the removal of 841 Ainu in 1875 from southern Sakhalin to Tsuishikari near Sapporo upon Japan's relinquishment to Russia of Sakhalin in the same year. Another example is the forced transfer of 97 Shimushu Ainu from their homeland in the Northern Kuriles to Etorofu near Hokkaido in 1905.[1] Large numbers of both groups died due to the stress of living in an unfamiliar environment.

Beginning with the full-fledged colonization of Hokkaido by the Meiji government in 1869, unilateral prohibitions on Ainu hunting (1872), and fishing (1875) decimated Ainu lifestyles and forced several Ainu communities into near starvation. Ainu lands were appropriated by the Meiji Government, who through a series of land decrees then parceled them out to *Wajin* settlers (1879) and wealthy conglomerates (1892) leaving only the worst and most agriculturally unsuitable land to be reapportioned to the Ainu in an effort to change them into agriculturalists, a policy codified into law with the passage of the paternalistic and blatantly colonial "Hokkaido Former Aborigines Protection Act" (HFAPA) in 1899. The HFAPA essentially forced the Ainu to become agriculturalists and to undergo schooling in the medium of the Japanese language to inculcate into them values of being "loyal citizens of the Emperor". Prohibitions on Ainu tattooing, bear-spirit sending ceremonies, and traditional funerary rites were implemented, thus decimating the Ainu culture. Of the land which managed to stay in Ainu hands, a great deal was cheated out of the illiterate Ainu by conniving *Wajin* merchants who got them to sign it away when they were drunk, as well as during the Agricultural Land Reforms carried out by the American General Head Quarters after World War II to end land monopolies, despite strident protest from Ainu representatives, in what was literally the second "taking away" of their land.

The discriminatory Hokkaido Former Aborigines Protection Act actually remained in effect until 1997, partly because it formed a justification for social welfare measures aimed at the Ainu people. The Ainu Cultural Promotion Act (CPA) replaced HFAPA. The CPA, however, falls far short of official Ainu demands compiled in 1984 for political representation in the form of seats in the national and prefectural Diets, and compensation for historical discrepancies in the form of cultural and educational subsidies and an autonomy fund.[2] Ainu

---

1. Even today descendants of the remaining Kurile Ainu remain in Russia (Kamchatka Times, March, 2012), although no talk of free border crossings between the two countries has been actualized as of the present and none seems forthcoming.

policy, as stands, remains limited to financial support for those cultural and consciousness-raising activities provided for in the legislation of the Cultural Promotion Act: the *manifestations* of Ainu culture, such as dance, song, art, and crafts. Meanwhile, the actual lived culture of the Ainu people, as a manifestation of Ainu society, remains outside of policy, as do all official rights to self-determination as an *ethnic or Indigenous people.* Moreover, the CPA as stands serves to entrench intra-Ainu community feuds through a divisive system of funding, and extends paternalistic mechanisms and structures via the employment of *Wajin* scholars and "specialists" as Foundation advisors and management committee members.

The local and national media, intelligentsia, and above all, scholars working with the support of national academic funding bodies justified Hokkaido colonization policies and paternalistic attitudes toward the Ainu. Theories of eugenics were employed to explain: "inferior" Ainu intelligence, humiliating "medical" tests carried out as late as the 1960s, and unforgivable grave-robbing in the name of scholasticism carried out *en-masse* and occasionally against the direct protest of the local Ainu villagers. Unfortunately, these negative images of the Ainu served to compound the self-denial brought about by experiences of extreme poverty, itself a result of excessive assimilation policies, to produce a devastating spiral of self-dejection. Some postulate that the height of discrimination and Ainu self-loathing occurred during the 1950s and 1960s, during Japan's period of rapid economic growth after World War II and before the worldwide ethnic revival movements. In any event, "internalized oppression" is a readily noticeable phenomenon today, resulting as noted above in Ainu "bashing" of, or allergic reactions to, Ainu activists.

In sum, the current situation of the Ainu in comparison to other Fourth World Peoples is that they are especially disadvantaged: 1) because of lack of a subsistence base upon which to maintain a traditional lifestyle, and 2) because of the ease of passing. Mutually reinforcing synergistic factors found in other Fourth World nations were completely non-existent in the Ainu case until the birth of the Ainu ethnic movement in the late 1960s, after which a small percent of Ainu—mainly activists—came to embrace their Ainu group identity as one element of the struggle for rights. Even today the main factors of ethnicity are essentially not subsistence-related ones except for those of a few Ainu living in the most rural of communities. In other words, the very fact that the only "ethnicity" embraced by the majority of contemporary Ainu is an ethnicity associated merely with "culture" and not with Ainu society, nor with the economic and political rights associated with full citizenship, is a reflection of the Japanese and Hokkaido government's continuing colonialist measures,

---

2.   Nomura Giichi, the former chairperson of the Hokkaido Ainu Association, is said to have personally been negotiating for an amount worth several billion US dollars.

and its refusal to acknowledge The United Nations Declaration on the Rights of Indigenous Peoples (UNDRIP) in any other facet than a cultural one.

Recent Developments in Indigenous Status and the Official Stance on Ainu Policy

Following Japan's endorsement of UNDRIP in September, 2007, pressure prior to the 2008 Toyako G8 Summit, led the Japanese Diet to pass a resolution recognizing the Ainu as an Indigenous people of Japan in June, 2008. Initially hailed as the first implementation of government action based on the UNDRIP, great expectations were held both domestically and internationally toward policy developments, and a Council of Experts on Ainu Policy Countermeasures (hereafter, Council of Experts) and Council on Ainu Policy have since been established, and the former disbanded after completing its mission of submitting an official report on possibilities for implementation of Indigenous policy measures in Japan. However, slowness of progress, lack of transparency, and accusations of partisanship for the Council of Experts have dampened Ainu hopes and led to UN Recommendations for immediate implementation. Here, a brief review of the "official" government stance is in order to get a clearer picture of the current state of Ainu sovereignty. Such a review will also offer explanations of recent Ainu cultural and rights recovery activism, which has arisen in response to the delay in implantation of legislation based on the UNDRIP, and as such, must be viewed as intricately related to the CPA legislation currently in effect and to movements leading up to the actualization of the CPA in 1997.

In a 19 June, 2010, talk to members of WIN-Ainu, an Ainu-lead NPO, Hokkaido University Graduate School of Law Dean and Ainu Council of Experts member Tsunemoto Teruki, distinguished between three types of political self-determination, depending on decreasing level of autonomy: independence, self-government, and political participation (Tsunemoto, 2011). According to this typological gradation by Tsunemoto, *independence* refers to the political action taken, for example after World War II, by various countries in Asia and Africa, namely, separation from the sovereign states to which they had belonged until that time; *autonomy* refers to high-level self-government within a state; and *political participation* refers to the guarantee of voice as a people in the normal political processes of a state.

Tsunemoto goes on to propose four types of interpretations regarding political-economic self-determination of Indigenous Peoples, the first, based on the final provision of the Preamble to the UNDRIP, construing that rights accruing to socioeconomic self-determination can actually demonstrate a breadth of variations according to the particular Indigenous people or to the country in which they find themselves. The second, a construal put forth by some interpreters of the ILO Convention 169, is that this convention, while famous for its definition of Indigenous Peoples, refrains from actually laying forth rights to political self-determination of Indigenous Peoples.

Tsunemoto continues by explaining as the third and fourth construals two unique interpretations proffered by Japan regarding its Indigenous people. Namely 1) The definition accompanying the Nibutani Dam Verdict, which construed Indigenous Peoples as a minority people possessing special rights to culture, pursuant to their Indigeneity, and 2) The Hokkaido Government Council of Experts on Ainu Countermeasures definition, which construed the Ainu as a "people" possessing "Indigeneity" (i.e, having lived in the area "prior" to other peoples) as historical fact, but granted no concordant legal rights. Tsunemoto admits that the latter is "the conception which the Japanese government has adopted [ever since 1997], which has no legal binding effect whatsoever." He goes on to add regarding this fourth interpretation that it is thus possible to have a conception of Indigenous Peoples which recognizes their indigeneity in name but grants no consequent particular legal meaning nor special rights.

Tsunemoto goes on to explain that the Ainu Council of Experts, which he headed, thereby saw it as their task to sort out the significance of the two issues of "definition" and legal effects. The following is an analysis of Tsunemoto's technical explanation.

Tsunemoto puts forth three conceptualizations of the relationship between identity as an Indigenous people and legal rights as such, to explain the Council of Expert's stance regarding this question. First, "appellative conception", represents the stance taken until now by the Japanese government; in other words, that there exists no causal relationship between Indigenous identity and Indigenous rights. This line of thinking, Tsunemoto claims, is indisputably evident in the official government response of the Cabinet Committee which reviewed the legislative bill on the Cultural Promotion Act, to wit, "Ainu indigeneity is not the driving factor behind this legislative bill".

Tsunemoto's second and third conceptualizations, namely, "substantive conceptualization" and "procedural conception", were conceived by the Council in order to overcome the limitations of the "appellative conception" and the CPA on which it is based. "Substantive conceptualization", according to Tsunemoto, stands on the premise, as reflected in the UNDRIP, that Indigenous Peoples possess rights (the preeminent of which would be the right to self-determination) as a natural consequence of being Indigenous. "Procedural conception", being a prescriptive construal, also demands that the government give special consideration to its Indigenous Peoples, but in the form of procedural justice rather than in the form of specific rights, and the means for reparation are to be considered separately.

Tsunemoto proceeds to explain three types of consideration that the Council of Experts employed in adopting the procedural conception: "theoretical", "realistic", and "phased". Firstly, in explaining "theoretical considerations", regarding the issue of the subject of Ainu policy (i.e, who will be allowed to exert Ainu rights) and content (what will be allowed), Tsunemoto points out the dangers of "self-definition"[3] and preemptive policy implementation.

Taking a conservative tack, particularly regarding the content of Indigenous rights, Tsunemoto emphasizes that the concept of Indigenous rights itself is still historically in its formative stages, and admits that the Council concluded that writing a suitable response to the questions of rights, subjects, and group rights, was not feasible in the time period allotted by the Cabinet to the Council.

He proceeds to explain that, consequently, in order to propose a solution to these issues which would persuade the majority of Japanese citizens, the Council adopted "realistic consideration". The Council reasoned first that averting the backlash which was bound to arise from a rights-oriented policy was the safest solution, and assumed that the dual priorities of responding to the immediate issues of cultural revitalization and fulfilling the government's responsibilities through policy would be possible through a procedural approach, and second, that such a phased means of going forward would not necessarily preclude an eventual substantive approach. In other words, once a solid infrastructure had been put into place through a procedural approach, legislators would be able to proceed to the next step of how to actualize a substantive approach.[4]

Herein lies the drawback of Tsunemoto and the Council's conception, but legal protections which ensure Indigenous vitality such as one sees in other countries just, aren't coming into place quickly enough. First, and crucially, the Report of the Council of Experts contains the major drawback, from the point of international Indigenous standards, that it was not compiled with sufficient input from the Ainu community in the first place. Tsunemoto claims that the Council made "concrete" actions to listen to the "actual voice of Ainu living in the present day" by holding hearings during their deliberations in several locations throughout Hokkaido as well as in Tokyo, and he emphasizes that the Council based its deliberations on the actualization of proposals put to the Council by Member Kato Tadashi, Chairperson of the Ainu Association. However, it must be remembered that the Ainu Association is not the sole representative organ of the Ainu people. In this regard, it must be pointed out that the "Hearings" arranged by the Council were not actually public meetings, but sessions closed to all but a few who had obtained the prior consent of the Ainu Association.[5]

---

3. This is regardless of the fact that the Utari social welfare subsidies have been implemented and continue to be implemented de-facto on a "self-definition" basis.

4. In order to actualize the procedural approach, Tsunemoto and the Council members premised Ainu privilege on the right to practice their culture, and in this case interpreted "culture" in the broadest sense of the word; in Tsunemoto's words, "Cultural transmission is dependent in the first place on some kind of economic activity; this is a huge insight that the Council garnered in its study of Indigenous Peoples around the world".

Secondly, no measure has been set in place to codify the report into law. On the contrary, the other part of the "set" that makes up Tsunemoto and the Council's reasoning, namely, understanding on the part of the majority Japanese, is premised, in addition to concerns about aggravated discrimination in the form of backlash, in considerations of the systematic limitations of a democratic government; in other words, that the Law as decided by the Japanese Parliament requires a majority vote within the Diet.

Although Tsunemoto states that the Council has left leeway for an eventual substantive approach, when and where this will be achieved is left in the air. Tsunemoto himself admits that the current Council on Ainu Policy is not charged with re-consideration of the Council's conclusions. If one were to take an extremely pessimistic view of things, perhaps it will take so long for the Japanese government to achieve construction of an infrastructure upon which a substantive approach can be actualized that the original conceivers of this approach will no longer be alive to promote it.

Ainu Ethnicity Today

Ainu ethnicity, as with that of Indigenous and minority groups throughout the world in recent decades, displays ever-increasing diversity. A number of socioeconomic, societal, and individual elements, which play upon and interact with one another in complex and variegated ways, factor into this situation. As explained above, poverty and internalized oppression, consequences of discrimination, remain major influences even today, influences to which the Council on Ainu Policy is supposed to be responding.

Speaking strictly from a demographic standpoint, the number of knowledge bearers raised in the presence of an Elder who spoke the Ainu language, and versed in the etiquette and protocols of Ainu ceremonial and ritual, has dropped to less than several dozen, while numbers of cultural practitioners versed in traditional Ainu song and dance remains slightly more constant, although not numerous. Due to the implementation of assimilation policies from the late 1860s, people who had actually experienced Ainu language or ritual firsthand in this manner were all born before the 1930s. Cultural practitioners in the present largely are comprised from those in the third generation, those who were not themselves raised in the Ainu language and culture, but who learned from someone in the second generation as a child of someone

---

5.   On the other hand, however, it must be noted simultaneously, that at the time of the Council's deliberations, as at present, no official census of Ainu individuals existed /exists to enable the democratic selection of Ainu council representatives through a voting process, thus having forced the Council to rely upon its selection of Ainu individuals through the Hokkaido Ainu Association. Additionally, all third-party petitions submitted through groups and organizations other than the Ainu Association were eventually delivered to the Council, who included them in their deliberations.

raised around a grandmother or grandfather who only spoke the Ainu language and was versed in Ainu ceremonial. Some fourth generation youth, who have personally experienced no onus of discrimination in their personal lives and have gleaned benefits from the results of the implementation of the CPA, are currently active as cultural practitioners, working in Ainu museums or foundations, or employed in Ainu tourism. Most of these youth experienced Ainu language and culture vicariously through time spent with a grandparent who was a second generation Elder. Additionally, some of these youth have proceeded through higher education to obtain Masters Degrees and one is even the possessor of a Doctoral Degree.

Efforts to revive the knowledge of Elders via organized or unorganized and formal or informal apprenticeships has been occurring in fits and starts since the late 1970s, attendant upon a rise in ethnic consciousness accompanying the Ainu rights revival movement, while the organized transmission of traditional song and dance has an older history, reaching as far back as the early 1950s in organizations such as the *Obihiro Kamui to Upopo* Cultural Preservation Society, and even further in the often criticized Ainu tourism centers of Shiraoi, Asahikawa, Akan and Biratori. The Kawamura Kaneto Ainu Museum in Asahikawa, the oldest Ainu-run museum, has been in continuous operation since 1916. Ainu run and operated museums also exist in Biratori and Shiraoi.

The Cultural Revitalization/Rights Recovery Movements
Cultural Revitalization

The Ainu cultural revitalization movement manifests in sites throughout the island of Hokkaido, as well as in the Kanto region, in a variety of sizes, shapes and forms, from cultural preservation societies, 17 out of 20 of which have been designated by the nation as intangible cultural heritages, as well as community Ainu language classrooms in 14 communities,[6] down to family or individually-based organizations. Most are locally based and combine a pre-set yearly agenda of community-centered ceremonies and events with participation in "pan-community" gatherings, retreats, and cultural exchange, although recent years have seen an increase in Prefecture-wide groups such as the Nikaoppu Dance Troupe.

In addition to the "pan-community" gatherings such as the Shakushain Festival in late September, and the Marimo Festival in early October, both of which have been going on for over 50 years, the Ainu Association has gathered youth from throughout the prefecture for annual youth retreats as well as occasional international cultural exchange. Meanwhile, the Foundation for

---

6. According to my 2013 survey (Agency for Cultural Affairs, 2013), all but four of these classrooms had been relegated to virtual inactivity by 2009 cuts in funding from the Hokkaido Government.

the Research and Promotion of Ainu Culture (FRPAC), formed as a result of the CPA, has instigated yearly language retreats as well as the Cultural Bearer's Training Initiative at the Ainu Museum, Shiraoi, which brings together specially selected youth from throughout the prefecture.

These classrooms and societies cater to Ainu of all ages and occupations, and have been expanding their activities to include more children, as well as deepening and broadening the quality of their delivery, during the 16 years since the establishment of the Ainu Cultural Promotion Act.

Local Cultural Preservation Societies provide a "place to be Ainu" which supplements Ainu language classrooms, Ainu workplaces and home environments that are so crucial to children. Often organizations in one community embrace children and adults who are members of multiple groups. Cultural Preservation Societies additionally contribute to awareness-raising regarding the Ainu by performing "guest" classes at local schools with Ainu students.

Museums and cultural centers, in addition to employment of full-time Ainu staff, provide paid vocational training courses in "Ainu Culture" lasting from three months to three years, as well as volunteer opportunities to teach and thus, simultaneously, learn, about the Ainu culture, and, in combination with government agencies, represent project implementing bodies for the Iwor Traditional Territory Restoration project now being piloted in several townships. Eventually the latter project will require the revitalization of varied cultural transmission skills and knowledge, but at present systematization of these educational processes is still in its formative stages.

Finally, the Foundation works closely with the Ainu language classrooms, which are under the jurisdiction of the Hokkaido Ainu Association, to implement an Ainu Language Instructors Training Course and a Family Ainu Learning Initiative, which have succeeded in increasing the numbers of enthusiastic young Ainu language instructors and are producing cadres of primary school and middle school Ainu language speakers with the collaboration of their parents. However, it must be noted that these yearly initiatives are limited in duration.

Rights Recovery

One of the most salient areas in which Ainu ethnicity can be recognized is in the ongoing fight for Ainu rights recovery; the right to maintenance of sacred sites and resources, representation in government, increasing autonomy in the Indigenous tourism and cultural exchange arenas, and repatriation of Ainu remains and burial items. Due to elements of rights-recovery activism within the activities of the wider Ainu Association, it is often difficult to distinguish where rights recovery activities end and purely culturally-motivated actions begin in the cultural conservation societies, which are subsidized by Ainu Association funding and whose membership often overlaps with that of the Ainu Association. Indeed, not surprisingly, nearly all rights recovery events exhibit a strong cultural flavor, with participants gathered together garnered in colorful Ainu regalia. Greetings in the Ainu language and sacred ceremonies can also be witnessed.

These activities found their roots in the heady activism of the late 1960s and early 1970s, had developed into a more sophisticated, intellectually driven phase by the early 1980s, and display a strong regional flavor. For example, the efforts of Kayano Shigeru, first Ainu member of the Japanese Diet, and Kaizawa Tadashi, past vice-chairman of the Ainu Association, in Biratori, resulted in the construction of the Nibutani Ainu Cultural Museum as well as victory in the Nibutani Dam Case, which has led to a number of Ainu-cultural related initiatives sponsored by the government but implemented by local Ainu, in Biratori. The efforts of the Sapporo Branch of the Hokkaido Ainu Association resulted in winning not only the construction of the Sapporo Ainu Cultural Exchange Center, but in its being 95% staffed and managed by Ainu living in Sapporo. Asahikawa, where the Kaneto Museum is located, has been the site of a number of nitty-gritty battles between charismatic and iron-willed local Ainu and the Japanese government and business, and the start of the Ainu carving trade which originated there and spread throughout the island, initially began as a means for Ainu activists to gain funds with which to travel to Tokyo and present their case. Ainu from throughout the Prefecture both donated money and stood in solidarity to create and submit the Proposal for an Ainu New Law to the Hokkaido Government in 1984.

The fight does go on, even after the Japanese government's recognition of the Ainu people as being Indigenous. A number of Ainu-driven organizations are in the process of fighting continuing discrimination and colonial structures, questioning government policy, and demanding increased Ainu self-determination. Fundamentally, the issue of whether Japan's annexation of Hokkaido was a colonial process or not comprises the dividing line between the rights and principles outlined in the UNDRIP and the actual current practice of the Hokkaido and Japanese governments. Failure to admit that the development of Hokkaido by the Meiji government was an act of colonialism is equal to failure to admit that colonial structures are still in place today, and stands in opposition to the spirit of the rights outlined in the UNDRIP, and inactivity in the face of colonial acts is occurring. In the last four years alone, at least six organizations have sprung up to advocate or otherwise fight for Ainu rights, the most ambitious being the Ainu Party, led by Kayano Shiro, Kayano Shigeru's son, on the grounds that the Ainu Association has no provision in its charter which will allow it to engage in political activities. Out of the other five organizations, three have been organized to stem violations of Ainu Indigenous rights: the Mopet Sanctuary Network was formed to support the efforts being spearheaded by Ainu fisherman Hatakeyama Satoshi to realize the revitalization of Ainu traditional whaling, and to curtail the creation of an industrial waste disposal facility upstream of a sacred river to the Ainu people. The Hokkaido University Repatriation Research Society was formed to achieve repatriation of Ainu remains and burial items purportedly held by

Hokkaido University, which were not being returned to the Ainu people. The Citizen's Support Association for the Ainu Side Reader formed to halt one-sided censorship and alteration of historical facts in a side reader distributed to local Hokkaido elementary and junior high schools.

The problem is that the rights of the Ainu as an Indigenous people still have not been codified into law, and thereby not implemented into practice, an issue reflected in the submission of the FRPAC, the publisher of the side reader, to demands from the Hokkaido Board of Education, themselves brought upon by the political clout of a lone Hokkaido Assembly member, and in the responses of Hokkaido government officials to enquiries regarding the contradiction of the waste disposal facility construction to rights in the UNDRIP: they replied that the facility was "in the public good", and therefore overrode Ainu concerns.

Meanwhile, Hokkaido journalists were quick to pick up on the criticisms regarding Ainu misuse of funds, but in the de-contextualized conditions of the present, without any concomitant comment regarding historical responsibility of the Hokkaido government for training Ainu staff in bookkeeping, and without comment on historical misuse by Hokkaido government officials of Ainu funds which were supposed to be held in their trust. Similarly, the fact that the Hokkaido government in 2006 misprinted Ainu rate of response to questions about perception of anxiety due to limited financial income of "29.2%" as "0.2%" was only conveniently lightly passed over by Hokkaido journalists.

Remaining Issues

The causes of discrimination against the Ainu people, and feuding between Ainu people is often mistaken to be Ainu generated, rather than seen as a reflection of what it really is, structures of societal inequality perpetuated by paternalistic mechanisms. For example, one sometimes comes across Ainu women who display a strong aversion to anything "rights-oriented" or having to do with "movements". This, again, comes back to, first, the simple desire to lead an ordinary life uncharacterized by stress or strife, and second, an aversion to the idea of being discriminated against as a consequence of openly displaying one's ethnic identity. Yet the real heart of the problem lies in a xenophobic and monocultural society that refuses to accept calls for diversity.

Similarly, paternalistic attitudes amongst scholars and those responsible for cultural preservation-related policies serves to agitate misplaced anxieties amongst Ainu Elders and cultural practitioners about hierarchies of knowledge between them. Of course even without paternalistic Japanese intervention, debates about authenticity will plague any traditional society purporting to achieve cultural revitalization.

Outlook for the Future

One thing is certain: Ainu infighting, which will never be appeased but rather only further inflated under ongoing colonial structures maintained by the Japanese and Hokkaido governments, is also not likely to be conquered through the good efforts of the Ainu people alone. Conscientious Indigenous comrades who have been through the same process of internal fractionalization and are familiar with its pitfalls, and, vice-versa, well acquainted with the techniques for Native reconciliation and solidarity-building will be indispensable for guiding the Ainu through the labyrinth of division-generating dangers to the joys and strengths of cohesion.

References

Agency for Cultural Affairs.
2013. Kikiteki na Jyokyo ni Aru Gengo/Hogen no Hozon/Keisho ni Kakawaru Torikumi no Jittai ni Kansuru Chousa Kenkyu Jigyo (Ainugo) [Research Survey on Conditions of Initiatives for the Preservation and Transmission of Endangered Languages/Dialects (Ainu)]. Commissioned 2012 Research Survey for the Agency for Cultural Affairs, Japan. Sapporo: Research Faculty of Media and Communication, Hokkaido University.

Harrison, Scott.
2008. *The Indigenous Ainu of Japan and the Northern Territories Dispute: Historical Dislocation and Relocation*. Saarbrucken: Verlag Dr. Muller.

Hokkaido Government Department of Environment and Lifestyle, Administrative Division, Ainu Affairs Department.
2006. *Report on Actual Conditions of the Ainu*. Sapporo: Hokkaido Government.

Lam, Peng Er.
2005. At The Margins of a Liberal-Democratic State and Illiberal Society: Minorities in Japan. In *Multiculturalism in Asia*, Will Kimlicka and Baogang He, eds. Pp. 223-243. Oxford: Oxford University Press.

Tsunemoto, Teruki.
2011. Senjyuminzoku no Kenri to Kougi no Bunka [Indigenous Rights and Culture in the Broad Sense]. *Mauko Pirika News*, 2(3/4), 5-13.

Tsuneyoshi, Ryoko, Kaori Okano and Sarane Spence Boocock. (eds.)
2011. *Minorities and Education in Multicultural Japan*. London and New York: Routledge.

Voice of Russia.
2012. Nihonjin Ga Ken Mo, Ojigi Mo, Harakiri Mo Jibun no Bunka ni Sita [Japanese Adapted Swords, Bows and Suicide from Ainu People]. Electronic document, http://japanese.ruvr.ru/2012/02/06/65448380.html, accessed February 9, 2012.

Taiwanese Aborigines

Yuan-Chao Tung

National University of Taiwan

The Indigenous population of Taiwan is 550,268, or 2.34% of Taiwan's total population as of July 2016 (Council for Indigenous Peoples, 2016a). In archives, the Dutch, Spanish, Japanese, Chinese, and others of various eras and from different perspectives have recorded Indigenous Peoples. The comprehensive classification of Indigenous Peoples attempted by officials, traders, or researchers rarely corresponds to Indigenous perception and experiences. Terms such as "raw, cooked or assimilated barbarians" reflected the concerns and conveniences of those who initially classified Indigenous Peoples. These terms were replaced by neutral ethnic identifications by Japanese researchers in late 1890s (Hu, 1998).

An increase from nine to sixteen officially recognized Indigenous groups since 2001 reflects growing respect for subjective identification of being different. The name rectification from Mountain People to Indigenous People and then Indigenous Peoples, has been crucial to transforming the view of Taiwanese society from a Han-Chinese migrant/settler-dominated society to a multi-cultural society. At the same time, discourses of a Taiwanese consciousness have matured: Taiwan's Indigenous people are a distinctive constitutive component. This socio-political reorientation is further affirmed by constitutional amendments and the passing of Indigenous People Basic Law ("Basic Law") in 2005. The current struggle for autonomy tests to what extent the ideal of a multi-cultural society will be substantiated.

Formation of Settler Society

Taiwanese Indigenous Peoples are Austronesian language speakers with a connection to other Austronesian speakers in Southeast Asia and Pacific Islands. It is proposed by linguists that Taiwan is likely the point of dispersal of the Austronesian language family, based on the diversities of Formosan languages (Blust, 1995; Ross, 1992). Languages vary so greatly that some are not mutually intelligible. Their differences are also reflected in social structure, ranging from egalitarian to hierarchical societies. Before the first contact recorded in European or Chinese languages, these earliest living Indigenous Peoples maintained social order and reproduced themselves culturally, socially, and biologically.

The first external powers coming to rule Indigenous people in Taiwan were Spanish and Dutch, but their impacts were limited geographically and by time. The Dutch ruled Southern Taiwan for 38 years (1624-1662), leaving a census, Christianity, and a Romanized written language of Siraya, the language of a major Southwest plain Indigenous group (Chou, 1998; Tseng & Tung, 1999). Promoted by the Dutch, Chinese migrants grew in number and expanded from seasonal traders or fishermen to rice or sugarcane farmers. At the end of the Dutch era, the estimate was between 35,000 and 50,000 (Chou, 1998, p. 61). In 1662 after defeating Dutch, Koxinga established his regime and brought with him 25,000 Chinese soldiers. Chinese population gradually grew and equaled that of the Indigenous people in size (ibid, p. 66).

Though the Ching regime ruled a territory smaller than that of the Dutch and endured a shorter time period (1662-1683), it signaled the beginning of the Chinese rule of Taiwan and its Indigenous Peoples.

The Ching ruled Taiwan for more than 200 years. During its rule, regardless of fluctuating policies banning migration away from the mainland, Ho-lo speakers of Fujian Province, and Hakka-speakers of mainly Guangdong and Fujian Province to a lesser extent, moved to Southeast Asia as well as Taiwan. Taiwan was administered under Fujian Province before it acquired the status of province in 1885. Whether long or short, Dutch as well Ching rules both intended to impose their imagery of civilization and implement the 'civilizing process' to the colonized Indigenous people (Chiu, 2008).

Pinpu were seriously affected, while those Indigenous Peoples living in mountainous areas experienced external powers differently. Some Pinpu, Plain Aborigines, maintaining intense interaction with the Ching government, assisted in military maneuvers to suppress resistance activities, and later served as soldier-farmers on rewarded land located between Chinese villages and hilly Indigenous settlements beginning in 1788. Gradually, Pinpu land was transferred to Chinese farmers through debts, marriages, and other causes.

Indigenous Peoples living in mountainous areas were least disturbed by being spatially separated from others. Boundary stones or mounds were set up at the foothills, which reflected the limited official rule of Indigenous Peoples. In 1874, the Ching court was challenged by the Japanese-initiated Mudan Incident, and thus reconstituted its administration of mountainous Indigenous Peoples to prevent further international provocation.

The most significant consequent moves to effactually govern Indigenous areas included the opening of three east-west cross-island routes on north, central, and south Taiwan. Road construction commenced a series of aggressive approaches leading to confrontations with Indigenous groups, and the submergence of Kavalan and Sakizaya groups, who reemerged more than a hundred years later.

The Ching's turn to aggressive governing of Indigenous Peoples terminated abruptly in 1895 when Taiwan was ceded to Japan. Japan, going through Meiji Reform in the 1860s, had transformed into a modern state, adopting scientific methods of survey and investigation to govern more effectively. Its capitalist view of development concerning forestry and products such as logs and camphor reduced Indigenous land to resources, ignoring that it was also home to Indigenous people.

Pacification was a step to clear government access to mountainous areas for resources. Japanese colonial government carried out the pacification policy in 1914 to confiscate weaponry and consequently transform hunters into sedentary farmers. After a few battles to defend a lifeway, mountain-dwelling Indigenous Peoples finally lost their autonomous social order and became subjective to Japanese educational system, police, and government. Mountainous Indigenous areas were subject to a police-dominated administrative system different from plain areas populated by the Chinese, Pinpu, and two Indigenous groups (Amis, Puyuma) who lived on the east coastal plain. The seemingly smooth rule was challenged by the Wushe Incident in 1930, thirty-five years—a generation—after Japanese rule. The Kominka Movement, which honored Indigenous young men serving in military fighting bush wars during the WWII (1937-1945), was the last of the assimilationist policies.

After Japan lost the war in 1945, Taiwan was turned over to the Chinese Nationalist government, and the mass migration of more than two million mainlanders to Taiwan in 1949 changed Taiwan's population make-up and power structure entirely. The Nationalist government followed most Japanese policies concerning Indigenous people, especially the nationalization of Indigenous land and the severe control of weaponry. Indigenous Peoples had occupied a marginal position, whether in politics, economy, or cultural life. This status quo was seriously questioned in emerging Indigenous rights movements beginning in the early 1980s. The leading group named itself Alliance of Taiwan Aborigines and consciously reframed itself as Indigenous people in an internationally meaningful perspective, liberated from national politics.

Indigenous Rights Movement
Immediately after the takeover by the Nationalist government in the mid-1940s, Indigenous elites proposed to recover land lost to the Japanese colonial regime but soon realized the power inequality continued regardless of the change of regime. Though China fought a war against Japan for eight years, there were amazing resemblances in Nationalist and Japanese government policies toward Indigenous Peoples. Near the time when martial law was to be lifted in 1987, Indigenous university students campaigned for Indigenous rights through newspapers, journals, and street protests. It started with a small group of students at National Taiwan University, publishing "*gao-shan-zu* (Indigenous Youth or Green Mountains)" under the strict surveillance of martial law in 1983. A year later, Alliance of Taiwan Aborigines (ATA) was set up and initiated a series of protests over name rectification, land, autonomy, and a specific government office on Indigenous affairs (Hsieh, 1987). These issues significant to the survival of Indigenous people have set the tone for Indigenous rights movement ever since.

ATA's first move was to name itself *yuan-zhu-min* (Mandarin for Aborigines) replacing the official term of *shan-di-tong-bao* (mountainous compatriots) or *gao-shan-zu* (mountainous ethnic group). Since not all Indigenous people live in mountainous areas, *shan-di-tong-bao* and *gao-shan-zu* are partial and incorrect. *Tong-bao* also means the same sibling sets and thus refers to compatriots by extension of imagined blood relations.

The naming issue elaborates to incorporate the right to personal names according to one's own tradition and in one's own language, place names reflecting local knowledge of and historical encounter with the environment in one's language, and self-labeling. Naming involves interpretation of the past, kinship and relation to others. "Indigenous people" is a more inclusive term than mountainous compatriot, and it clarifies the nature of Taiwan being a settler society, and its rule by settler colonialism.

The first sentence of the Indigenous Rights Declaration says that "Taiwan Indigenous Peoples are not the descendants of the Yellow Emperor." "We are Austronesian-speakers, different from the Han of Ho-lo, Hakka and Mandarin speakers and assumed descendants of Yellow Emperor" (Icyang, Parod, et al., 2008, p. 192). The claim of Indigenous status alerted the non-Indigenous population of its designated status of latecomers and migrants. It was not until 1994 that Indigenous people was adopted as the official term, replacing mountainous compatriot. Indigenous Peoples became the official term in 1997.

The right to historical interpretation was one of the earliest issues targeted by ATA. The opening of a newly constructed cultural park surrounding the temple dedicated to Wu Fong ignited protests over the fabrication of the martyrdom of Wu Fong and its inclusion in school history textbooks. Tsou who were said to be responsible for Wu Feng's death and suffered stigma which extended to all Indigenous people assumed them to be headhunters. In two years, Wu Feng's myth was dropped from history textbooks, and in another two years, the Tsou home region was renamed from Wu-Feng County to A-Li-Shan County, honoring the highest mountain in the county.

There are now sixteen Indigenous groups with recognized differences. The basis of recognition has transformed from a long established scholarly classification system adopted by the Japanese government in the early 1920s to a more flexible system accommodating self-identification. The name rectification campaign of Sakizayas from the largest Amis group was such an example (Huang & Su, 2008). Sakizayas scattered into Amis villages and were protected by mixing with Amis when they were defeated by Ching soldiers in 1878. Campaign leaders strategically constructed features distinguishing Sakizayas from Amis to comply with government guidelines (Huang & Su, 2008). Contemporary Sakizaya traditional clothing was based on old black and white photos with colors of symbolic meanings in response to their current situation. The invention of a dramatic ritual of fire gods serves to reconnect them with the defeat in 1878 and the death of their leading couple, now commemorated as the fire gods. Fire destroyed some Sakizayas but also lightened the escape for others. Thus, fire serves as a symbol of rebirth. It took Sakizayas years to find a way to conceptually settle their entangled relationships with the Amis who sheltered and saved them, intermarried with them, and constituted Sakizaya families.

The "'Return Our Land' Movement Alliance" was an alliance of six groups, of which ATA and the Presbyterian Church of Taiwan were the two major advocates. ATA with its young membership of college students some majoring in law or political science, was eloquent on theories of Indigenous rights, expressive in oral and spoken Mandarin, and courageous in street protests. ATA, based in Taipei City and its surrounding urban areas, was limited in its influence on geographically dispersed Indigenous populations. Though the Presbyterian Church entered Indigenous areas mainly after World War II, it rapidly attracted a large following. The faith provided a network of churches as platforms for city-based ATA members to communicate and mobilize for the Indigenous rights movement (Icyang, Parod, et al., 2008). Yu-shan Theological College and Seminary, with its Indigenous faculty and students, upheld organizational and fundraising efforts.

There were three waves of the "Return Our Land Movement," in 1988, 1989 and between 1990 and 1994. The driving force behind the initial land movement was the shortage of land for subsistence, which forced Indigenous youth, male and female, to leave home for survival. Some were drawn to fishing boats, construction sites, coal mines and brothels, enduring harsh working conditions with low self-esteem.

In a practical sense, it is clear that land is critical for the survival of Indigenous Peoples as a people. Campaign pamphlets documented a decrease of acreage under Indigenous control since contact with the Dutch in the early 17th century. The current system of Indigenous reserve was a continuation of the Japanese system. Indigenous residents had rights to use (but not to own) Reserve land for construction as well as cultivation. Japanese administration brought in different concepts of land rights and land use with irreversible consequences. According to Yapasuyongu (2012), under the Japanese rule, a 'scientific' calculation of land needs allowed land for living space (0.2 hectares per person), sedentary farming (1.8 hectares per person), common gathering ground for fire woods (0.5 hectares per person), and animal husbandry or other industry use (0.5 hectares per person). With three hectares of land needed per person, the total Indigenous land area sharply dropped from 1,720,000 hectares at the beginning of Japanese rule to 250,000 hectares when the reserve system was implemented. The acreage again decreased from 250,000 hectares at the latter part of Japanese rule to 240,000 hectares at the time of the land movement in the late 1980s. However, Reserve land available for Indigenous use was further reduced by government expropriation of Reserve land for schools, military facilities, forest reserves, and other public needs, worsening the shortage of land for housing and cultivation. As the population recovered from war, a larger population could not be supported by the same size of Reserve land.

In addition to this, during Japanese rule, Amis and Puyuma living on east coastal plain, and other small pockets of Indigenous areas were classified as general administrative districts apart from Indigenous administrative districts. This classification has been in use 'til today. Amis and Puyuma were officially classified as Plain Indigenous People, were not governed under Indigenous Reserve policies, and gradually lost their land in the market and became uprooted.

Indigenous Reserve policies serve to protect and hinder at the same time. Without ownership, the commoditization of Indigenous land was contained.

The land's value has rested on it being source of subsistence. However, Indigenous Peoples were deprived of land as a source of initial capital for small to mid-scale enterprises common with farming families when Taiwan's economy took off in the 1970s.

The long-term land conditions erupted as the government was preparing for new regulations concerning the development of Reserve land. Tourism was anticipated and new regulations cleared the way in Indigenous areas. In the summer of 1988, the "Return Our Land" movement had its first march on the streets of Taipei City with a large turnout. Its requests grew in its second marching a year later. The government responded to the major requests in two ways. One was to start a procedure of land ownership registry. Five years after continuous use of land that was officially registered for cultivation or housing, land ownership would become available for registered Indigenous leaseholders. The other response was to officially recognize non-Reserve public land used by Indigenous people as Reserve land that could later be converted to private ownership in accordance with the first rule.

Later, the government agreed to check and release idle public land in the government's hands that had been traditional Indigenous land for Indigenous use. Government offices, especially the Bureau of Forestry, which controlled a majority of traditional Indigenous land, were urged to release land for Indigenous use in order to comply with the aforementioned policies.

In the process of land release and registry, many technicalities proved to be a burden on Indigenous households. There were also complaints about newly released land as difficult to use in terms of accessibility, land forms, and soil fertility. Proof of continuing use of land before a specific year as required for registry of land ownership invoked discourses on the eligibility of evidence. Government agencies share similar ideas about what constitutes proof of prior existence and have easy access to maps, census data, and survey reports as possible supporting documents.

Indigenous individuals have sustained this process sometimes with frustrations and defeats. The question of eligibility of evidence and lengthy processes contributed to the third wave of the "Return Our Land Movement" in the early 1990s. The theme was "Anti-occupation, Struggle for Survival, Return Our Land." The march was scheduled on December 10, 1993, on International Human Rights Day at the end of UN Indigenous Year.

Hunters turned Criminals: Rights to Traditional Territories and Autonomy

Land has been re-conceptualized as area necessary to maintain traditional lifestyle and identity. Traditional territory includes land, rivers, sea shores, and ocean if applicable. This definition is a drastic shift from early policy of "terre nullius" during the Japanese time and inherited by the Nationalist government. Traditional territory not only encompasses land, shore, and ocean the most important range of activities; they also provide resources for subsistence, rituals, and other cultural protocols. Land, having been the focus of the

"Return Our Land" campaign, has been replaced by the broader and dynamic concept of traditional area.

Resources available within the area and the human activities engaged with these resources have raised attention to a set of new issues. For Indigenous people to practice traditional knowledge and lifestyle, the following Forest Law, Wildlife Conservation Act, and Controlling Guns, Ammunition and Knives Act are major hindrances. The Forest Law regulates the collecting and use of trees and byproducts in nationally owned forests. Indigenous residents of mountainous areas habitually accessing forests for logs and byproducts have been considered illegal under the Forest Law.

In 2005, the same year the Basic Law passed, a court case lasting for ten years set a precedent clarifying and asserting Indigenous rights to forest products in their traditional territories. Three Smangus men picked a fallen beech trunk, as decided by their tribal meeting. They were sued for breaking the Forest Law and found guilty at first. They appealed, testifying that the spot where they found the fallen tree was in Smangus traditional area, and it was ordered by the tribal meeting to fetch the wood for collective benefit. Ten years later, the judge honored the principle of the Basic Law as well the Forest Law and found them not guilty. During the ordeal, local Atayal in their traditional way asserted their consensus of their living space (Lin, 2015). Smangus, with other fellow Mrqwang groups, met and drew a map with marks significant to them, then made a 'Sbalay' (ritual of reconciliation) to seal their understanding.

The Wildlife Conservation Act (passed in 1989) and Forest Law (amended in 1984) both have severely restricted hunting rights of Indigenous people. Hunting has been important not only as a source of food, but a source of sacrifice to constitute a unique way of life. Even with these restrictions, Paiwan people's mortuary taboos require hunted animals to end the mourning period. Awi Mona (2009) considers it a cultural right to hunt. The proposal of United Nation's Declaration on the Rights of Indigenous Peoples in 1993 facilitated the amendment of Article 21 of Wildlife Conservation Act, to allow Indigenous people to hunt for traditional ritual reasons on Reserve land (Awi Mona, 2009, p. 41). It was again amended to allow hunting for traditional cultural concerns and beyond Reserve land in 2004.

Cases of prosecutions of hunters while hunting during rituals provoked protests. Legal professionals gradually learned to respect new concepts of cultural rights behind amendments of conservation-minded laws. However, the case of Talum, a Bunun hunter who hunted a Formosan serow and a muntjac to quench his elderly mother's thirst for wildlife and was sentenced to three and half years on April 2016 flared up the issue of hunting rights, and pushed to legalize hunting for non-profit self-use. Another focus of amendments is to simplify the application procedure for hunting permits. Currently, it is required to apply for permits with a precise hunting plan of who, where, what, and how many in advance. Hunters prefer to report about the hunting trip afterwards.

The Controlling Guns, Ammunition and Knives Act decriminalizes the manufacturing and possession of guns, ammunitions, and knives by Indigenous people if aforementioned items were hand-made (meaning less efficient and negligible in their impact on wildlife conservation or social order). In most cases of accused illegal hunting, hunters are often prosecuted on two grounds. One is the timing and reasons for hunting, and animals hunted beyond the leniency of Conservation of Wildlife Law. The other is the possession of guns made with more advanced technology and considered not traditionally Indigenous by some prosecutors under Controlling Guns, Ammunition and Knives Act. Commercial Hilti rimfire has been adopted to improve the safety and efficiency of guns. It is argued that Indigenous people progressed with time and they adopted scientific knowledge and methods to better their life like the rest of the society. This argument was accepted by judges in 2013 when the situation first arose.

The concept of traditional territory reflecting the rightful claim of a certain way of life is crucial to autonomy. Its success begins with the establishment of traditional territory. Although survey of Indigenous traditional territory began in 2001, only the Smangus's traditional area was recognized officially in 2007 due to conflicting understandings of traditional territories. Immediately after an official announcement, neighboring Mrqwang groups disputed with officially recognized Smangus boundaries to which they traditionally had access. Involved groups negotiated and reached consensus in their Atayal way.

The Smangus case was important as a landmark, being the first Indigenous group with its territory officially surveyed and recognized. However, it also revealed the sensitivity of imposing foreign conceptualization of bounded territories and exclusive rights (Kuan & Lin, 2008). The public recognition of traditional territory is an important step to local development and autonomy.

As tourism grows in importance in Taiwan's economy, the east coast is becoming a target for developers and hoteliers. The well-known Mei-li Wuan Hotel, a BOT project of Taitung County government, is an example of the trend of tourist investment and the tension between development and environment. Article 21 of the Basic Law requires government agencies or private enterprises to acquire prior informed consent of local Indigenous communities on whose traditional area any development project is proposed. Though there are known shortcomings of the survey of traditional territory and later evolved mapping projects, since traditional area is the foundation of many other policies and laws, hope is high for its official proclamation. Traditional means of dispute resolution, like what Smangus and its neighboring Mrqwang groups applied to solve their boundary issues, could substantiate Indigenous autonomy.

After the unexpected enactment of the Basic Law in 2005, the Council of Indigenous Peoples has begun its long endeavor to implement it. Article 22 of the Basic Law deals with co-management mechanisms for government projects established in Indigenous areas. In 2007, Regulations of Co-management of Natural Resources in Indigenous Areas ("Regulations") have been issued to carry out co-management of Indigenous Peoples with government agencies. The Regulations govern procedures for setting up public projects such as national parks, scenic areas, forestry, ecological conservation areas, et cetera. After obtaining consent from more than half of local Indigenous residents at tribal meeting, a co-management committee should be established. Local Indigenous residents should constitute a majority of the committee to engage with the planning and management of national parks or forestry.

Since 2007, Indigenous people have become involved in co-management committees coordinated by the Bureau of Forestry or National Taiwan University, for example. However, Indigenous residents' participation in co-management is marginal, often limited to low-level daily operations, nothing to do with long-term planning as promised by the Regulations. In addition, Indigenous knowledge is not respected or taken into consideration in resource management, whether it relates to water or forestry (Kuan, 2013).

Cultural and Language Continuity in Formal Educational Systems
Since the late Ching dynasty, there have been repeated records about how Indigenous people learned and could recite classical Chinese literature, or Japanese literary works as proof of successful "civilizing" efforts. Under Japanese rule, in general, Japanese, Chinese and Indigenous children went to separate schools with different curricula. The Nationalist government unified curricula and standardized textbooks for different levels of all schools. Single curriculum and standard textbooks, disregarding existing cultural diversities, had actually served as mechanisms for assimilation before the textbook industry was liberated in 2002.

For Indigenous children, the formal schooling experience has been traumatic in that they had to learn exotic logic and experiences through a foreign language. Even now that the school environment has become friendly, Indigenous students' drop-out rates are clearly higher than their cohorts. Syman Romporan (2014), the famous Tao/Yami writer, mentioned a confusing moment in his early school years. Tao/Yami live on Orchid Island off the east coast of Taiwan; they are the only Taiwanese, Indigenous or not, that are intimate with the ocean. There was one question in a school exam asking if the sun rises from behind the mountain. To Syman Romporan, the sun always rises from the sea on the ocean-surrounded tiny island, but this question was marked incorrect according to his Taiwan-trained teacher.

There were policies, including positive discrimination, to promote the integration of Indigenous students into general educational system (Chou, 2010). The resulting weakening of Indigenous language competence and cultural loss caused concerns and remedies including courses on Indigenous languages and local cultures when the Nationalist government finally lifted the Martial Law in 1987. Measurements to improve the quality of education for Indigenous Peoples made by the Ministry of Education were criticized, as lack of Indigenous subjectivity and systemic perspective and rendered these efforts unsatisfactory.

The promulgation of the Education Act for Indigenous Peoples in 1998 was an important step for the shaping of Indigenous education. Article 2 of the Education Act affirms that the development of Indigenous education is "based on the spirit of diversity, equality, autonomy, and respect for Indigenous Peoples. It aims at the safeguarding of dignity, ensuring the continued survival, advancing well-being and promoting a sense of collective pride in their identity" (see: Ministry of Education http://edu.law.moe.gov.tw/EngLawContent.aspx?Type=E&id=163) Soon, in 2000, the College for Indigenous Studies at National Dong-Hwa University, a college devoted to cultivating Indigenous political and community leaders and government officials, was established. Indigenous Community Colleges organized by local governments offer courses on languages, local histories, traditional rites of passage, et cetera, taught by Indigenous experts, regardless of official credentials. Indigenous community colleges contribute to facilitating the revitalization and continuity of languages and cultures as well as equipping Indigenous people with knowledge and techniques necessary in contemporary living. For example, University of Taipei Indigenous Communities is offering four computer courses with one especially for the elderly in its fall 2016 semester. Just over half (33/65) of its courses are on the languages and cultures of certain Indigenous Peoples.

Tribal school is another alternative available to Indigenous people. Community elders get together to set up a curriculum to educate their youth with traditional knowledge during school break. The newest development is experimental schools that adopt the Indigenous language of the school district as a medium of instruction. The first school has been renamed P'uma by school district communities in Atayal and began to operate in fall 2016. These various forms of knowledge and practices of transmission are availed by the liberating force of the Education Act for Indigenous Peoples. However, there still remain major obstacles in enforcing the Education Act.

The Ministry of Education and the Council of Indigenous Peoples (CIP) are both responsible for enforcing the Education Act, but the coordination between these two government agencies and between national and local county levels is very challenging. Also, the living situation of Indigenous people has changed in the past few decades, which requires reconsideration of affirmative actions. Affirmative action in education guarantees a 25% of difference of test scores for Indigenous students to enhance their chances to enter schools at all levels, and another 10% for students with a certificate of language proficiency of any of forty-two languages and dialects.

The growing percentage of the urban Indigenous population poses a question about what is underprivileged: to be Indigenous or to live in rural areas? Criticism comes from Indigenous people against the requirement of language proficiency, which is disadvantageous to urban-dwelling youth; other criticism questions the eligibility of urban dwellers with access to bountiful educational resources available in the cities. Other than the issue of regional differences, class factors are also considered. Children from elite families are in no way underprivileged enough to take advantage of affirmative action and thus deprive truly underprivileged children of educational opportunities. However, with criticism from Indigenous and non-Indigenous alike, it cannot be denied that Indigenous students are underrepresented in tertiary education, public universities in particular.

Language is central to cultural survival; therefore, CIP encourages students to possess a certificate of language proficiency to be eligible for the 10% bonus test score. Language courses have increased exponentially in all educational institutions as well as other institutions frequented by Indigenous people. Churches in urban areas offer language courses and are supported by CIP (editorial, 2013). Immersion methods or language nests, learned from New Zealand Māori experiences, have been promoted by CIP and adopted in kindergartens of selected Indigenous communities. CIP finally established its own research branch called Indigenous Language Research and Development Center in 2013, responsible to research and develop loan words and new vocabularies, language proficiency tests, syntax and morphology, and last but not least, language revitalization policies.

Being Indigenous in a Global Era

The Alliance of Taiwan Aborigines (ATA) was ahead of its time to name themselves Aborigines instead of mountain compatriots. The United Nations (UN) and International Labor Organization (ILO) have been active in promoting Indigenous rights. UN founded the Working Group on Indigenous Populations (WGIP) in 1982, which set a tone to mainstream Indigenous issues at a global scale. ATA members consciously broke the Nationalist government's allotted slot of minorities by connecting with the international Indigenous movement (Hsieh, 1987). The Vice President to the World Council of Indigenous Peoples (WCIP) was invited to observe the first march for "Return Our Land" campaign; an ILO volunteer attorney was invited in 1990. Soon, Indigenous people began to take part in UN Indigenous issues-related groups. Between 2010 and 2016, the chairperson for the youth work group, a sub group under the United Nations Permanent Forum on Indigenous Issues (UNPFII), was Tuhi Martukaw, an Indigenous Taiwanese woman (Yu, 2016). American, Canadian, Australian, and New Zealander Indigenous policies have served as important references for Taiwan's Indigenous rights advocates.

In addition to the framework of reference provided by the international Indigenous movement, the fact of being Austronesian language-speakers proved to be another basis to distinguish Taiwanese Indigenous people from Sino-Tibetan language family speakers. The beginning paragraph of the Indigenous Rights Declaration straightforwardly states that "We are Austronesian-speakers and different from the Han of Ho-lo, Hakka and Mandarin speakers" (Ichang, Parod, et al., 2008, p. 192). This Austronesian-speaking network also provides Taiwanese people a new image for Taiwanese society, and Taiwan government a new niche to build up international contacts. Yohani Isqaqavut, a Bunun pastor and former Director of the Council of Indigenous Peoples, in his assignment to the post of Representative to the Trade Mission of the Republic of China to the Republic of Fiji in 2008 acknowledged the potential of Austronesian connection.

City-Dwelling Generations

According to the 2016 census, Indigenous people living in urban areas grew to an unprecedented percentage of 46.31% (Council for Indigenous Peoples, 2016b), near half of the entire Indigenous population. This trend poses a challenge to the social cultural reproduction of generations born and growing up away from their Indigenous living context. In a way, the high and growing percentage of outmigration to urban areas reflects on the contemporary composition of Indigenous villages that are now mainly elderly and very young. The foundation of Indigenous cultural and social life is being threatened by outmigration.

Indigenous population movement has been part of the general urban rural migration since the establishment of the first Export Processing Zone in the late 1960s. The migration pattern and resultant settlement pattern reflect the crucial importance of job opportunities. They were first drawn to work on fishing boats and settled in port cities like Keelung and Kaohsiung. Gradually, New Taipei City and Taipei City became home to most indigenous families (Liu, 2009). Taoyuan and Taichung are growing in their importance as regional urban centers.

Early researchers noticed high mobility (Chang, et al., 2010). A series of transformations of economic structures and the nature of available jobs have caused instability. Indigenous migrants with different language competencies, cultural capital, and limited educational credentials were insufficiently prepared for Mandarin and Ho-lo language-dominated communication and market-oriented economy. A pastor who himself grew up in the city lamented that the migration continues from one city to another to pursue blue-collar jobs (p.c. Kino). Distant water fishing, coal mining, and construction had been the three major industries with a significant Indigenous participation.

There are a few well-known incidents that caught people's attention to the labor conditions in these industries and the plight of Indigenous urban migrants. In 1984, Amis workers constituted a majority of the 72 killed in the Haishan coal mine accident. The Amis had been a major group living along east coast, and now they made a living underground. The contrast was so strong that a song called "Why?" was devoted to this accident by a respected Indigenous singer Kimbo (n.d.).

The Tang In-Sheng incident is probably the first incident that pushed the majority of the society to face the suppressive situation in which Indigenous people were embedded (Kuan, 1987). It has maintained a lasting impact. Tang at age 18 came to Taipei for a job. He was first deceived by newspaper ad to mistake a job agency for a hiring restaurant then overworked by the owner of a laundromat where he worked to pay the fees owed to the job agency. Nine days later, when he wanted to quit the job, he became frustrated by the laundromat's owner, who withheld his identity card and verbally insulted Tang. At last, Tang killed the owner, his wife, and their toddler daughter. He has now become a symbol for anti-death penalty campaign.

The Haishan coal mine accident motivated Kimbo to found the Alliance of Taiwan Aborigines the same year. They helped to topple the myth of Wu-feng, the martyr said to sacrifice himself to be killed by the Tsao, to which Tang In-sheng belonged. The myth of Wu-feng was taught at schools, and the Tsao were blamed for the killing. ATA and others worked to reveal the historical formation of the martyrdom of Wu-feng, and finally successfully decolonized history textbooks and place names as mentioned earlier.

Urban migration used to be targeted as an adaptation issue. It has class as well as ethnic/cultural dimensions. Only recently has the cultural reproduction of urban-dwelling Indigenous people and their connection with home villages to substantiate home community development caught attention. In discussion of autonomy, how should Indigenous people living outside of traditional territories be classified, and to what rights they are entitled?

Are Pinpu Indigenous?

Who is Indigenous? What are the criteria to qualify a group of people as Indigenous? The Pinpu, Plains Aborigines, populated the plain areas when the Dutch came to South Taiwan in the early 17th century and when Ching ruled Taiwan several decades later. Pinpu had been generally considered to be highly 'Sinicized' and had lost their own identity. They were known to speak Ho-lo, the major language spoken by migrants and their descendants from Fukien province of China, and could hardly be distinguished from other Ho-lo speakers.

This impression was challenged in the 1990s with a surge of Pinpu studies (Liu & Pan, 1998). The Siraya who lived on the southwest plain under intense Dutch influence have left rich materials written by the Dutch. Though the Siraya spoke Ho-lo in 1990, scholars identified a complex of beliefs and ritual practices followed by Siraya descendants (Pan, 1995). They have conducted a dramatic annual ritual 'night worship,' maintained separate places of worship, and masqueraded the objectified forms of their deities as Han deities. In the Japanese household registry, they were marked as 'cooked barbarians'; however, they lost their status as Indigenous people in the 1950s indirectly through an administrative order. Escape from discrimination has probably contributed to the smooth shift of policy.

As some young people started to quest for the public recognition of their Pinpu identity, their elders scolded them: "We are humans now; why do you want to return to be barbarians?" (Pan, 2000). Efforts have been made to revitalize Siraya language in daily life, with the help of the Romanized Sirayan translation of the Gospel of Mathew, from the Dutch (Chou, 1998). Siraya descendants' request for official recognition was stalled by a series of directors of the Council for Indigenous Peoples. Meanwhile, the Kavalan, a Pinpu group living in northeast and east Taiwan succeeded in being recognized as Indigenous people in 2002 after two decades' struggle.

The Siraya are considered too Sinicized to be Indigenous. There is growing sympathy toward Siraya descendants for their cause and increasing support from Indigenous elite. It is understood that today's Indigenous Peoples suffer from the same assimilative pressure and process that the Siraya went through earlier. Shih (2012, p. 117) mentions that the essentialist understanding of culture and ethnicity contradicts the adjustable cultural expression purported by UN Office of the High Commissioner for Human Rights. However, the Siraya (12,478 in 2009, http://www.tainan.gov.tw/nation/page.asp?nsub=H2A2A0), as a much larger group than the Kavalan (1,368 in 2014, http://www.apc.gov.tw/portal/docList.html?CID=C025000D7FB62524%20), would challenge the distribution of resources once recognized and thus contribute to the prolonged positive reply by the CIP.

The Makkataw of Pingtung County have resumed their quest for Indigenous status in 2015 and soon received positive response from county government. A documentary on the Pinpu struggle of name rectification made in 2014 by Bauki Angaw, a Kavalan director and producer, helped to pressure the CIP to be more responsive. In the presidential apology on August 1st, President Tsai promised to develop a clear policy concerning the Pinpu by the end of September 2016.

What is Transitive Justice for Indigenous People?

With the establishment of the Council of Indigenous Peoples in 1996, the struggle for Indigenous rights has been concentrated on the legal field. Law has become the means of counter-colonial struggle; however, Indigenous communities are overloaded with complicated legal and administrative procedures. Though the living conditions of Indigenous Peoples have improved and their cultures are much more appreciated than before, a full recognition of their status as Indigenous Peoples still awaits.

Most non-Indigenous Taiwanese would not perceive Taiwan as a settler society, in which the Indigenous population has been forced into geographical, political, economic, cultural, and rhetorical margins. The recent debate over whether to include Indigenous peoples' concern in a proposal for Act of Transitive Justice reveals distinguishing interests separating Indigenous Peoples and later comers such as Ho-lo and Hakka speakers.

After the Democratic Progressive Party (DPP) won the legislative and presidential elections in January 2016, issues of transitive justice have been on DPP and its allies' agenda. It is crucial for Indigenous Peoples to resume their status and rights as the autochthonous before the arrival of ancestors of contemporary compatriots during the Ching dynasty. Most descendants of these early Han Chinese migrants, voting nationalist KMT out in last two elections, have developed an identity distinctive from the Mainlanders that arrived Taiwan in 1949. They consider themselves native to Taiwan, compared to Mainlanders and their descendants, regardless of the prior long history of the existence of Indigenous Peoples. Indigenous people's position in the current reinterpretation effort of Taiwanese history goes astray from the political mainstream.

The marginal position of Indigenous Peoples was cruelly revealed after the Democratic Progressive Party won the presidency and became the majority in the legislature in May 2016. Transitive justice has been highly expected of the new government; however, the proposed act of transitive justice by the executive branch was limited to the time period under the Nationalist government between 1945 and 1990. Indigenous legislators of different parties strove for a more time-inclusive act because many laws and regulations that severely impacted Indigenous societies were installed by the Japanese colonial government and inherited by the Nationalist government. The act must trace back to the Japanese era to identify the injustice done to Indigenous Peoples.

For instance, the current Indigenous Reserve system began in the Japanese era. Indigenous Peoples were incorporated into the Japanese administrative system and became minorities increasingly subjective to state power after the pacification campaign in 1914. Guns and ammunitions were surrendered to Japanese police or forcefully confiscated after serious battles. The Dahu Incident and 'Southern Barbarian' Incident were examples of such battles. Indigenous Peoples fought to keep their guns to subsist on hunting, to continue their ways of life as hunters and to protect themselves from hostile neighbors. After confiscation, they had to register and acquire guns and ammunitions at police stations and to report their uses when returned. For the ruling government, whether it was Japanese or the Nationalist, controlling the access to ammunitions for security reasons and to promote sedentary farming had been the main concern, whereas hunting rights had been a major issue in the struggle of Indigenous rights movement.

The proposed act of transitive justice aims at the authoritative regime of the Nationalist government and limits the effort of restorative justice. The President's Office promises to establish a "Committee on Truth and Reconciliation" to investigate and solve complex historical issues. However, unlike the organization under the proposed Act of Transitive Justice, members of the Committee of Truth and Reconciliation are part-time without pay and most importantly have no investigative power.

During the presidential election, President Tsai promised to apologize to Indigenous Peoples on August 1, the 21st anniversary of the name rectification (from mountain people to Indigenous Peoples). The official ceremony of apology was severely criticized in several ways, including that the President should go to villages to apologize instead of Indigenous representatives visiting the President's office. In addition, it was said that the Committee of Truth and Reconciliation has no real power. A small group of Indigenous people who had walked since early July around Taiwan, visiting Indigenous villages to bring messages to the President on August 1, voiced their different opinions at the Square while the official ceremony of apology took place inside the President's Office. The ceremony of apology at first did not receive much media attention, and the 'unthankful' reception of President Tsai's goodwill aroused commentaries from opinion leaders, which exposed the inherent marginality of Indigenous Peoples in Taiwan (Li, 2016).

The apology was perceived in the context of party politics. DPP is a party with a history more engaged in human rights issues, especially since some of its early leaders were once political prisoners. In the narrow context of party politics, President Tsai's apology was considered generous or unnecessary. Some commentators said that DPP has done no wrong and that the Chinese, and KMT should be blamed for the sufferings of the Indigenous Peoples and should apologize. These commentators ignored the migration of Han-Chinese since the early Ching dynasty, subsequent transfers of land from the Indigenous people to Han-Chinese, and finally the subjugation of the Indigenous Peoples to externally imposed state authority.

In the struggle for Taiwan independence from China, the localization and indigenization of early migrants and their descendant has gradually distinguished Taiwan from China. Along this line of thinking, Ching and the Nationalist government together with the Japanese are all external colonial rulers. This kind of independence discourse has ruled out the possibility for Indigenous Peoples that Han-migrants and their descendants are settlers and that Taiwan is a settler colonial society (Su, 2014). The name rectification of Indigenous Peoples in 1994 implies the special privileges reserved for the earliest living residents of the land, and at the same time recognizes Taiwan as a settler society. However, the implication of the category "Indigenous Peoples" has not been fully appreciated by the majority of Taiwanese. For decades Nationalists have represented outside, external, and bad colonists, it is intellectually and emotionally challenging for descendants of early migrants to think of themselves as colonists as in the Indigenous people's perspective.

For Indigenous Peoples to further assert their status and rights, it is important to explore the imagery of Taiwan as a bi-cultural or multi-cultural society as declared in the Amendments of Constitution. The Basic Law, which grew out of the United Nations Declaration of Indigenous Rights, has been regarded as the constitution for Indigenous Peoples. There have had important developments, such as the Protection Act for the Traditional Intellectual Creations of Indigenous Peoples parallel to laws related to intellectual property, the Education Act for Indigenous Peoples, and Regulations of Co-management of Natural Resources in Indigenous Areas.

However, many ministries of the government have not responded to principles prescribed in the Basic Law to amend relevant laws. In her apology on August 1st, President Tsai promised to make the Executive Yuan responsible for the inter-ministry collaboration and to facilitate trials of Indigenous autonomy. The President went on a tour to Atolan, an Amis village, to talk about official recognition of its traditional territory, then onto Orchid Island where nuclear waste was stored to promise to look into its historical background, removal, and compensation. President Tsai understood and admitted the suffering of Indigenous Peoples in the past four hundred years caused by external rulers and migrants. She was aware that to most people, her apology was unnecessary. This lack of understanding is exactly the reason that she needed to conduct an official apology. Her goodwill needs to materialize in difficult legal procedures that have to be supported by the majority of the Taiwanese voters in party politics.

Reference

(Chinese)
Awi Mona (蔡志偉)
2009. qi hou bian qian、sheng tai yong xu yu yuan zhu min zu she hui wen hua fa zhan : mo la ke feng zai de fan si (氣候變遷、生態永續與原住民族社會文化發展：莫拉克風災的反思), *Taiwan Indigenous Studies Review* 6, 27-54

Chang, Ying-hwa et. al. (章英華等)
2010. tai wan yuan zhu min de qian yi zi she hui jin ji di wei zhi bian qian yu xian kuan (台灣原住民的遷移及社會經濟地位之變遷與現況), in Government Policy and Social Development among Taiwanese Indigenous Peoples. Shu-min Huang & Ying-hwa Chang eds..Pp. 51-120. Taipei: Institute of Ethnology, Academic Sinica.

Chou, Hui-min (周惠民)
2010. tai wan she hui bian qian xia de yuan zhu min jiao yu : zheng ce de hui gu yu zhan wang (台灣社會變遷下的原住民族育：政策的回顧與展望) in Government Policy and Social Development among Taiwanese Indigenous Peoples. Shu-min Huang & Ying-hwa Chang eds..Pp. 259-296. Taipei: Institute of Ethnology, Academic Sinica.

Chou, Wan-yao (周婉窈)
1998. tai wan li shi tu shuo (si chien zhi 1945). (臺灣歷史圖說 史前至 1945) Taipei: Linking.

Council for Indigenous Peoples
2016a. http://www.apc.gov.tw/portal/getfile?source=79ADDDD9195D-B0E52610217BBF0B058FA9DAB2A97BBE1DD0E0C44C38ED 9E0AD26AFDA22BE291582A44D5EAC983117FF08F6B85B-5C9855EE23B91B9DF71659F0C&filename=83F7E35B21056CC200033F-4C65F5B7123D3CD606F1172413BD7076C11633C29B71CFEE5341DC-3880D0636733C6861689

Council for Indigenous Peoples
2016b. http://www.apc.gov.tw/portal/getfile?source=79ADDDD9195D-B0E52610217BBF0B058FA9DAB2A97BBE1DD0E0C44C38E-D9E0AD26AFDA22BE291582AF5343BD64AAAB1AAEAB-01F181859B6D53B91B9DF71659F0C&filename=83F7E35B21056C-C2870D865A60846592C60ED141A3AEC4633D3CD606F1172413F-5207C771EDBEB3FF1C28FC3FBB8058C

Editorial.
2013. PCT Preaches in the 'Amis Language, *Aboriginal Education World* 51, 42-47.

Hu, Chia-yu.
1998. Yi neng jia ju de tai wan yuan zhu min yan jiu yu wu zhi wen hua shou cang (伊能嘉矩的台灣原住民究與物質文化收藏), in Chia-yu Hu & Yi-lan Tsui eds. Studies on Ino's Collection at Department of Anthropology of National Taiwan University, Pp. 37-69. Taipei: Department of Anthropology of National Taiwan University.

Hsieh, Shih-chung.
1987. Ethnic Contacts, Stigmatized Identity, and Pan Taiwan Aboriginalism: A Study on Ethnic Change of Taiwan Aborigines. Taipei: *Independence Evening Post*.

Icyang, Parod (et al ed.)
2008. *Documentary Collection on the Indigenous Movement in Taiwan-Vol. 1&2*. New Taipei City: Academia Historica; Taipei: Council for Indigenous Peoples.

Huang, Shiun-Wey & Yih-ju Su. (黃宣衛、蘇如).
2008. Sakizaya's Name Rectification Campaign under the Perspective of Cultural Construction, *Journal of Archaeology and Anthropology* 68, 79-108.

Kuan, Da-wei. (官大偉).
2013. Indigenous Ecological Knowledge and Watershed Governance: A Case Study of the Human-river Relations in Mrqwang, Taiwan, *Journal of Geographical Science* 70, 60-105.

Kuan, Da-wei & Yi-ren Lin. (官大偉與林益仁).
2008. What Tradition? Whose Territory? A Critical Review to the Indigenous Traditional Territory Survey and the Translation of Spatial Knowledge in Marqwang Case, Taiwan. *Journal of Archaeology and Anthropology* 69, 109-141.

Kuan Hong-zhi. (官鴻志).
1987. wo ba tong ku xian gei nin men...: Tang Ying-shen jiu yuan xing dong shi mo (我把痛苦獻給您們……：湯英伸救援行動始末), *Ren jian Magazine* 20, 18-43.

Li, Xiao Feng. (李筱峰).
2016. yuan min xie lei shi qi shi 'dao qian' liao de (原民血淚史豈是「道歉」了得？) Originally published on 'Li Xiao Feng Column' of Liberty Times (2016.07.30) http://www.jimlee.org.tw/politics_detail.php?articleSN=9306

Lin, Yi-ren. (林益仁).
2015. ju mu wang shan si ma ku si ju mu shi jian er san shi (舉目望山司馬庫斯櫸木事件的二、三事) http://guavanthropology.tw/article/6421 http://guavanthropology.tw/(2015.03.02)

Liu, Chien-chia. (劉千嘉).
2009. Migration of Taiwan Aborigines: Clime-up or stumble in life course? Ph.D. dissertation, Department of Sociology, National Cheng-chi University.

Liu, Yi-chang & Ing-hai Pan.
1998. xu: qu yu yan jiu zai ping pu zu qun yan jiu shang de yi yi (序：區域研究在平埔族群研究上的意義), in Yi-chang Liu & Ing-hai Pan eds., ping pu zu qun de qu yu yan jiu lun wen ji. (平埔族群的區域研究論文集)
Nanto: Taiwan Historica.

Pan, Ing-hai. (潘英海).
1995. si hu shi yi---cong si hu zhi cun dao hu de xing yang cong jie (祀壺釋疑---從祀壺之村到壺的信仰叢結), Ing-hai Pan & Su-juan Jan eds., ping pu yan jiu lun wen ji (平埔研究論文集): 445-474. Taipei: Academic Sinica.

Pan, Chien-min. (潘謙銘).
2000. chi shan wan jin zhuang de dai zhi (赤山萬金庄的代誌), *Journal of Ping-tung History* 2, 104-122.

Shih, Cheng-feng. (施正峰).
2012. The Unrecognized Plains Indigenous Peoples in Taiwan: The Extinguishment and Restoration of Their Indigenous Status, *Journal of the Taiwan Indigenous Studies Association* 2(4), 111-136

Su, Jian-rong. (蘇建榮).
2014. Si fa ji guan dui shi yong gun ye yong di huo zhi yuan zhu min zi zhi lie qiang zhi jian jie fen xi (司法機關對使用工業用底火之原住民自製獵槍之見解分析), *Legal Aid Quarterly* 42, 19-24

Su, Bing. (史明).
2014. *Taiwan's 400 Year History: The Origins and Continuing Development of the Taiwanese Society and People.* Taipei: SMU Publishing.

Syaman Rapongan.
2014. *da hai fu meng* (大海浮夢). Taipei: Linking.

Tseng, Cheng-ming & Yuan-chao Tung.
1999. *A Collection of Archival Documents from Kavalan & Siraya*. Taipei: Department of Anthropology, National Taiwan University.

Wang, Yi-zhi. (王一芝).
2005. tai wan zui you li liang de shen ying hu de fu yong sheng ming wei yuan zhu min pu qu (台灣最有力量的聲音胡德夫 用生命為原住民譜曲), *Global Views Monthly* 225(3), 252-259

Yapasuyongu, Poiconu.
2012. The Myth and the Reality of the Indigenous Peoples' Sovereignty in Taiwan, *Journal of the Taiwan Indigenous Studies Association* 2(4), 1-26

Yu, Pei-hua. (余佩樺).
2016. Hong-jian Ting-hui: pei nan zu qing nian wei quan qiu yuan zhu min fa shen (卑南族青年為全球原住民發聲), *Common Wealth Magazine* 600 (2016- 06-21), 154-156.

(English)
Blust, Robert A.
1995. The position of the Formosan languages: Method and theory in Austronesian comparative linguistics. In *Austronesian Studies Relating to Taiwan*, ed. by Paul Jen-kuei Li, Cheng-hwa Tsang, Ying-kuei Huang, Dah-an Ho, and Chiu-yu Tseng, pp. 585-650. Symposium Series of the Institute of History and Philology, Academia Sinica No. 3. Taipei: Academia Sinica.

Chiu, Hsin-hui.
2008. *The Colonial 'Civilizing Process' in Dutch Formosa, 1624-1662*. Leiden & Boston: Brill.

Ministry of Education.
2014. http://edu.law.moe.gov.tw/EngLawContent.aspx?Type=E&id=163

Ross, Malcolm.
1992. The sound of Proto-Austronesian: An outsider's view of the Formosan evidence. *Oceanic Linguistics* 31, 23–64

Sámi of Norway, Sweden, and Finland

Dikka Storm

Tromsø University Museum
UiT The Arctic University of Norway

Acknowledgement:
To present this theme I thank Sharlotte Neely, for her initiative and great efforts collecting and presenting the articles, and Barbara Sjoholm, for her comments in a preliminary version.

In this chapter the focus of Sámi cultural history is from the period after the Second World War until today. During this period Sámi societies developed and expressed themselves in most fields of activity including the political, economic, social and cultural. The Sámi people gave voice to the perspective of themselves from the smallest local community to a unified nation of minority groups within the four countries of Finland, Norway, Russia, and Sweden. Most of the examples presented and referred to in this chapter are from Norway, but the examples reflect an historical development which is shared by all Sámi within their territories of the four countries they inhabit. The ethnic awakening is not only connected or limited to the local community but for a Sámi future it is also part of international connections and a global arena. From a condition of suppression by the national states, the Sámi people are today developing cultural, social, legal, and economic rights to their resources and land.

The Sámi are an Indigenous people. They have traditionally lived in a wide area which is divided by the four countries: Finland, Norway, Russia, and Sweden. The establishment of national states led to the division of the Sámi territory we know today. The border between Denmark-Norway and Sweden was drawn in 1751, between Finland and Sweden in 1852, and between Norway and Russia in 1826. The social organization of the Sámi communities were in *Siidas*, as a village, with families or households. Their economic livelihood was historically based on hunting, fishing, and an extensive exploitation of resources in the outlying fields. The hunting of the wild reindeer has been a cornerstone in Sámi life until modern times. Fishing in rivers, lakes, and at sea was and still is a part of the Sámi economy. Reindeer herding has played and still plays an important role both culturally and in the economy. How far back in history the Sámi have domesticated the reindeer is a question that researchers have been studying for a long time.

Until the 1950-60s the traditional livelihood was characterized by the combination of primary economies as farming, reindeer herding, animal husbandry, fishing, and land use of resources in the outlying fields. Only a minority of the Sámi were living as reindeer owners with reindeer herding as their primary economy. Use of resources included gathering of berries, hay, peat, etc.; fishing in rivers, lakes, and the sea; and hunting birds, fur-bearing animals, and sea mammals. Different parts of the economic livelihood were emphasized in varying degree – domestication of animals such as cows, sheep, and horses, cultivation of grass to fodder, and in olden times growing rye from the county of Romssa and southwards. For the majority of people the potato became a natural part of farming from the 19th century on. Handicrafts were part of the economy both for self-support and trade. The materials used were trees, roots, bone, horn, skin, and wool. Old handicrafts, such as sewing boats, are documented through archival source material and well known in early historical times by their "Norse" neighbors, the Vikings, who used sewn boats for sailing on their voyages. Research in a wide range of disciplines such as archaeology, history, language, cultural history, and social science the last forty years have produced detailed knowledge of settlement and economic livelihood of the Sámi origin in Fennoscandia. The information is filling out the picture of some subjects in the field, and gives new perspectives of prehistory, history, and society today.

A change in politics aimed at the Sámi people began in the period after the Second World War until today. In 1956 the Ministry of Church and Education appointed an official Committee to give an account of economic livelihood and cultural aspects for the Sámi population to develop within the Norwegian society. One of the results was an examination of the status of the social and cultural character. Since then Indigenous rights and cultural, social, and economic livelihood have developed both within the national state and also as part of a process which grew with revitalization of the rights of Indigenous Peoples around the World.

Economic and cultural organizations such as the *Sámi Searvi*, a local Sámi cultural organization, and *Norgga Boazusapmelaccaid Riikasearvi*, the National Sámi Reindeer Organization (1948), were founded in Norway after 1945. The last mentioned is one of the world's oldest Indigenous organizations. From the 1970s the local Sámi Searvis organized together and became a national organization. Their interests are of a cultural, social, and political character and based on local knowledge and participation. Norgga Boazusapmelaccaid Riikasearvi has been examining cultural and economic questions connected to the reindeer herding. These organizations have today developed a more political, economic, or cultural character. As a non-governmental organization, the Sámi Council was established in Kárášjohka 1956. The secretariat was located in Ohcejohka, Finland. The council was a result of the collaboration between the Sámi in Finland, Norway, and Sweden at the conference in Jokkmokk, 1953. The Sámi of Russia became full member in 1992. The Sámi Council has initiated cooperation with projects concerning Indigenous Peoples around the world.

The term Sapmi exist in each Sámi language, and has several meanings; the geographical region where the Sámi people traditionally live, the Sámi population, the Sámi language, and a Sámi person. A program of Sámi policy adopted at the Nordic Sámi Conference in Romssa in 1980 defines as a Sámi any person who has Sámi as his or her first language, or whose father, mother, or one of whose grandparents have Sámi as their first language; or considers himself or herself a Sámi; or lives entirely according to the rules of Sámi society; or who is recognized by the Sámi community as a Sámi; or who has a father or mother who satisfies the above-mentioned criteria. The Sámi Assembly – *the Samediggi* in Norway is localized in Kárášjohka and was inaugurated in 1989. The Sámi Parliament in Finland was established in 1973, reorganized in 1996, and located in Anár, and in Sweden it was established 1993 and located in Giron. The representatives are elected by direct ballot by the Sámi people who are registered in the Sámi electoral register. Those entitled to register are those who regard themselves as the above mentioned criteria. In Norway there are 13 constituencies which reflect the dispersal of Sámi settlement and also some internal cultural and linguistic variation of the Sámi.

The Sámi anthem, the *Sámi soga lávll*a, the Sámi People's Song, was approved in 1986 at the Nordic Sámi Conference in Åre, Sweden. The lyrics were written by the Sámi teacher and politician Isak Saba (1875-1921). The text was first published in the Sámi newspaper *Sagai Muitalægje* in 1906. Two melodies accompany the words, a traditional *Juoiggus*- a Sámi traditional melody, and the melody composed by Odd Sørli which was conveyed as the national melody at the Nordic Sámi conference in 1992. The Sámi flag was also adopted by the conference in Åre 1986. The flag was designed by the artist Astrid Båhl from Ivgobahta, Skibotn in Romssa, Norway. The inspiration is taken from the drum and from the poem "*Beaivvi bártnit*" – the Sons of the Sun, written by the Southern Sámi poet Anders Fjellner (1795-1876). In his poem Fjellner represent the Sámi as the son and the daughter of the Sun. The circle depicts the sun, red, and the moon, blue. At the Nordic Sámi Conference in Helsinki, Finland in 1992, the 6th of February was designated Sámi People's Day for all Sámi in Finland, Norway, Russia, and Sweden. The date refers to the first Sámi national meeting in Trondheim, Norway in 1917 where Sámi representatives from north and south of the Sámi areas in Sweden and Norway participated. The main themes of their discussions were economy and educational. In 1993, the Sámi People's National Day for the first time was celebrated officially, the same year the United Nations Office of World Indigenous People was officially opened in Kárášjohka.

Ethnic Identity Today: Means of Preservation

The Sámi languages belong to the Finnish-Ugric branch of the Uralic languages and are related to the Baltic-Finnish languages: Finnish, Estonian, and Hungarian. The Sámi languages comprise the areas of the northern parts of Norway, Sweden, Finland, and the Kola Peninsula in Russia. The Sámi languages include: (1) South, (2) Ume, (3) Pite, (4) Lule, (5) North, (6) Inari, (7) Skolt, (8) Kildin, (9) Ter, and (10) Akkala.

These languages are living languages and have survived in spite of harsh pressure from the national states. In Norway this process began with the Pietistic Mission at the start of the 18th century and continued with Norwegianization through the school system especially during the last part of the 19th century. All sorts of obstacles were set up to discourage the use, cultivation, and development of the Sámi languages. A language is a tool of communication between individuals and groups and conveys elements of philosophy, beliefs, social organization, and notions about the surrounding world. It is also the primary means of passing on the common fundamental customs and skills of Sámi people from generation to generation. The fact that the Sámi languages until recently had been an oral language underscores this point.

Sámi is as a language very rich in words and concepts relating to nature, animal life, the formation of terrain, snow, and other things which have been important in connecting to hunting or herding. This can best be demonstrated in fields where there is a connection to the terminology of traditional work, such as vocabulary covering reindeer herding, handicraft production, and any work related to the concepts of snow and natural places. Within these areas the use of the Sámi language is the best to express all the details of material, work, and skills. This can also be one of the explanations why the language has survived in spite of all governmental obstacles. One of the threats to the Sámi language is the change of life style. *Sámi giellalávdegoddi*, the Sámi Language Committee, appointed by the Sámi Conference in 1971, developed a Sámi Language Policy. The main task of the committee is the development of the cultural heritage which is connected to written and oral Sámi language.

Duodji is a common concept which covers traditions of handicrafts in a wide perspective including both the products themselves as well as the process from idea to the made product. *Duodji* is a concrete expression for a Sámi understanding of reality in time and space. Technology, material, and the aesthetic reflect a way of life adapted to the given natural conditions in the different geographical areas of Sámi settlement. The products were traditionally part of the way of life made for their own use, to trade, or to exchange and subject to taxation. In the period after 1945, the handicrafts of women were recognized as part of the economy, and a process of organizing the sale of products, offering expert advice, and teaching in the Sámi schools was started. The idea of *duodji* also covers intangible as well as material creative activity. Artists have their roots in the tradition of handicrafts, where they collect their inspiration in their artistic expressions.

Sámi artists representing different fields established *Sámi Dáiddačehpiid searvi*, the Sámi Artists Organization in 1979. The concept for art, *dáidda*, was introduced. Today Sámi authors, musicians, theatre workers, and artists have each their separate organization. The Sámi Artist Organization is an independent branch both of the national artist organization and a member of the International Association of Art. Art has been displayed and as such made Sámi pictorial art known both nationally and internationally. In the process of setting Sámi people and culture on the political agenda, art and culture have been playing important roles in the development with expressions through handicrafts, art, literature, and music. As an art print the map *Sabmi* published in 1975, shows Samiland in Fennoscandia without borders, with Sámi place-names. Hans Ragnar Mathisen, a Sámi artist, uses illustrations of places, cultural sites, symbols on material objects, and symbols from the old religion to tell the story of the Sámi and their use of the land. His work has resulted in a range of maps covering the Sámi settlement regions and areas mainly in Norway. Summing up collected information he presents a Sámi Atlas (Mathisen, 1996) of the World and historical maps of Sámi settlement areas in the North. His work is closely connected to earlier studies of Sámi documentation of place names.

Among the Sámi, the place informs about history and provides a cultural and social story of livelihood within the local community. In Sámi language place names and their description of places are like a guide including not only a route but the landscape seen on the route. The place-name is a spiritual sign of the place which is kept by oral tradition. Through a great effort during the last three decades, place names, which earlier were neglected and forbidden, are used and mapped. Studies have been taken up by Sámi researchers both at scientific institutions and locally at schools by "resource" persons. Place-names are protected by the Law of Place Names (18th of May 1990 nr 11 and revised 1993) in Norway. The law includes the Sámi and Finnish place-names in use and correct spelling in the local dialect.

Traditionally Sámi has been an oral culture, and today the oral tradition is partly alive in spite of the pressure and obstacles of the government and the church. The written literature in Sámi is connected to the process of christening beginning in the 18th century in Norway. From this period there are alphabets, school books, dictionaries, and holy writings in Sámi. Written literature telling stories not only for use of the authorities, started to be published around the turning of the century in 1900. From this period Sámi authors are describing the life of the Sámi. Johan Turi's (1854-1936) *Muittalus samiid birra*, Turi's book of Lapland (Turi, 1911), is the first book in Sámi and a poetic description of a dramatic period with illustrations. From this period there are also treasures like collections of Sámi folklore and fairytales. These were assembled through documentation studies and were printed both in Sámi and Norwegian. About 1970 Sámi literature changed to a fast growing and flourishing field with Sámi authors writing novels, short stories, and lyrics. In this field Nils-Aslak Valkeapää (1943-2001), a Sámi from Finland, started as a teacher and developed into a singer, musician, author, poet, and painter. He became the first Sámi to receive, in 1991, the Nordic Prize of Literature with the book, *Beaivi Áhčážan*, the Sun my father (Valkepää, 1988). He was the composer of the music to the Oscar nominated film *Ofelaš* - The Pathfinder - and also played a role in the film. He was responsible for the Sámi cultural presentation of the opening of the Olympic Winter games at Lillehammer in 1994. He was buried in Gáivuotna in the county of Romssa at the expense of the Norwegian State. Today his home "Lásságámmi" in Ivgubahtta is a center for researchers and artists.

Theater is a new medium in Sámi culture and has during a few decades developed as a cultural arena. The basis for this was in free groups such as *Dálvadis*, winter settlement area, Sweden, *Beaivváš*, the Sun, Norway, and *Rávgaš*, Ruff, Finland. In the South Sámi area *Åarjelhsamien Teatere* has been established. The performance is based on plays by local playwrights, traditions, or international plays with themes from comedy to tragedy, some directed to children and youth. The other new medium, film, is a growing arena to present cultural and political messages. Since Nils Gaup was nominated for an Oscar for the film *Ofelaš* (The Pathfinder), in 1988, new filmmakers are presenting their films at festivals, television, or through the film companies.

Information in the Sámi language through newspapers was one way of giving the opinions about the cases which were central for the Sámi people. Editing Sámi newspapers started during the last part of the 19th century. Some of them were sent out monthly for several decades. They were a way of giving voice to Sámi organizational questions, reindeer politics, school and language administration, and local, national, or international events. Some of the newspapers were in the Sámi language. Because of financial difficulties publishing stopped in the 1920s. The journal *The People of the Sámi's Own Journal - Samefolkets egen tidning* in Sweden started in 1919 and still comes out monthly in the Swedish language. Today newspapers and journals are edited in the Sámi language in Norway encompassing perspectives as diverse as religious, youth, or gendered perspective. Sámi news has been on the radio since 1946 in Norway, the first years only for short programs. The change happened in the 1970s when a Sámi radio station in Kárásjohká was established. Today daily news and programs are presented in the Sámi language to television viewers and radio listeners in Finland, Norway, and Sweden, in cooperation with the Nordic broadcasting companies.

The melody of *juiggus* is called *luohtti*, while the words in North Sámi are called *dajahusat*. The *juiggus* is a variety of expressions and varies from place to place, and both traditional and new expressions are flourishing today. The text of a *juiggus* is known from the middle of the 17th century. Old source material is to be found in archives in Helsinki, Uppsala, and Tromsø. In the 1950's the Radio of Sweden edited a collection of records from this material which today is available on CD. The Sámi publishers DAT and Idut have in the last decade edited CD's with traditional *juiggus*. In Sámi society traditional music and modern music meet in musical expression. Local Sámi cultural days and international festivals are important meeting places which are arranged in Sápmi. *Riddu - Riđđu*, Storm by the Coast, is one youth festival which has been arranged each summer for a period of three decades in the small community Gaivuotna, Norway. It has become an international festival and meeting place for Sámi culture and Indigenous People of the North.

Mari Boine, the international Sámi artist, singer, lyric writer, and composer gives concerts with her band around the world as well as locally on festivals in Sápmi. In 2003 she was awarded the Nordic Council Music Prize. According to the Nordic Music Committee: "Her work is characterised by its high artistic quality and she has put the Sámi music on the national, Nordic and international musical maps. She has managed to stick to the music's roots but also endow it with contemporary idiom that reaches out to an enormous public all over the world." Later in 2009, she was honored by the Royal Norwegian Order of St. Olav for her artistic diversity.

Sports have recruited persons who usually would not participate in Sámi activities. This is due to several reasons, but they have their roots in everyday life of Sapmi. The Sámi are well known in sports such as skiing, skating, and, today, football. A national Sámi football team (soccer) was established in 1985, and are recruiting players from Finland, Norway, and Sweden. They play against teams from other Indigenous groups all over the world.

Education is closely connected to the right to be educated in one's own mother tongue. The suppression of the Sámi language in school during the last three centuries has been closely connected to the history of colonization and creation of national states. An ongoing discussion has been lead by the state and the church about use of language as a tool to assimilate and/or christening the Sámi people. From last part of the 19th century, use of the Sámi language in school was prohibited. These strict instructions were in force until after World War II when a process of change started during the 1960-70s. The history of the Sámi schools, boarding schools, and pupils and their part in the history of assimilation is acknowledged by the Norwegian government. The use of Sámi as the first language in school has, since the 1950s, been a main political issue for Sámi organizations. In 1967 the Sámi language was allowed as an experiment in school, and from 1969 the Sámi language was acknowledged with a formal place as a subject in school. After a collective demand from two main Sámi organizations, a permanent official Sámi Educational Board was established in 1975. To carry out their intentions, a wide area of aims were set, so as to build up the competence of teachers, resources for Sámi children, translations as a means of instructions, new textbooks, language work, and terminology. The recruitment of teachers was central for these goals to succeed. Teaching at universities was important as well as at the local schools in the Sámi communities.

The law of the nine-year school, compulsory primary and secondary school in Norway, came in 1990. This created an opening for a Sámi Teacher Plan which was decided in the Storting, the Norwegian Parliament, in 1997 on the platform of the ILO-convention and the § 110 A of the Act of the Norwegian Constitution. "It was a milestone for development of Sámi culture and language as a natural part of the school system," Ole Henrik Magga expressed in summing up the development of the status of Sámi language around the millennium 2000. The means of instruction used in the compulsory primary and secondary schools are based on principles and directions for training of the Sámi school system. Textbooks and the means of instruction are closely connected to the linguistics. There is great effort across the national borders to develop common concepts within the same groups of language. This is based on the principle to strengthen Sámi identity of the pupil.

In spite of this positive strengthening, today there are areas were the Sámi language is threatened. In the southern Sámi area where few families used the language within the family, the boarding school was a positive offer. The pupils have the choice to use South Sámi language daily, which has had positive results. In Divtasvuotna in the Lule Sámi area they have through a revitalization project focused on language from Kindergarten on. Here knowledge of the Sámi language on the part of the parents is giving strength to the success. In other Sámi coastal areas, the need of programs of revitalization has led to the establishment of several Centres of Sámi Language.

Research in the Sámi language was carried out early on at the University of Oslo and is one of the reasons for priests who should work in Sámi areas. Today university studies have been developed in the Sámi language, culture and literature at the University of Romssa and at the *Sámi allaskuvla*, Sámi University College, established 1989 in Guovdageaidnu. Sámi researchers hold Masters and Ph.D's in the humanities, social and natural sciences, medicine, legal studies, and fishery studies. The development of Sámi knowledge in the diverse fields of archaeology, history, language, social anthropology, biology, medicine, and law has provided the opportunity to develop new perspectives and knowledge and understanding of the past, present, and future from a Sámi point of view. One of the main and very important changes was the transition of the Sámi language characterized as a foreign language to being characterized as a mother tongue. Likewise this change of focus is wanted in all disciplines through a demanding process of making new perspectives on the basis of Sámi traditional knowledge. The independent research institution *Sámi Instituht-ta*, the Nordic Sámi Institute, was in 2005 incorporated into *Sámi allaskuvla*. *Sámi Instituhtta, Guovdageaidnu* was established in 1973, and the aim of the institution was to strengthen and develop Sámi language, culture, and society. The staff included Sámi researchers from Finland, Sweden, and Norway. The activity was from the beginning mainly financed by the Nordic Council.

The health of Sámi people has been one of the main political issues since the 1950s and in different ways has been improved. These questions are closely connected to recruitment and education of Sámi medical personnel as doctors, nurses, and health visitors with knowledge of the Sámi language. Official information about health services was amongst the tasks. From the 1970s Sámi health and social workers have organized, and within their organizations they have stressed the situation of Sámi patients and clients. Sámi health and social issues were placed on the agenda in 1995 in an official plan for Sámi Health and Social Services, which was the basis for establishment of the Centre of Sámi Health Research in Kárášjohka in 1999. The goal of the centre is to carry out interdisciplinary research in subjects connected to Sámi health, and edit a journal in Sámi and Norwegian.

In the course of the three last decades, various Sámi local, regional, and national cultural institutions have been established. The institutions are centres where projects and studies are carrying out on the collection of traditional knowledge, oral and written, tradition and customs, objects, and archives. Development of cultural heritage from different perspectives is one of the main reasons for the institutions. The Sámi cultural policy is weighting the importance of the cultural centres, and looks at them as central arenas in the development of Sámi culture.

Sámi museums in Norway are organized as a branch of national museum organizations. There are about 15 cultural institutions with museum collections, archives, displays, and libraries from south to northeast just within Sámi territory in Norway. Two of these institutions have a special responsibility for Sámi art collections. Their functions are a meeting place for old and new generations, a place to take care of studies in oral tradition, and a place to house other activities such as workshops for handicrafts and offices of other related activities. *Sámi Museumsearvi*, the Sámi Museum Association, is a non-governmental organization for Sámi museums and adjoining museums in Norway with Sámi collections. The purpose of the association is to promote cooperation between members and contacts for institutions in Norway and neighboring countries. Physical remains more than 100 years old belonging to Sámi culture are automatically protected by the Cultural Heritage Act of 1978. This implies that Sámi sites and monuments more than 100 years old are protected in the same way as sites and monuments from prehistoric and mediaeval times, which includes all unattached objects and stray finds more than 100 years old. The Act is from 1994 and administered by the Sámediggi in cooperation with the Norwegian Ministry of Environment by the way of offices in four local cultural institutions localized to four Sámi communities from south to north. The main responsibility for collecting Sámi literature since 1990 is the *Sámi Sierrabibliotehkka*, Sámi Special Library, Kárášjohka which was established in 1983. A digital Sámi Bibliography became available in 1993 coordinated with the National Library. Printed matter and unpublished sources are to be delivered to the Sámi Archive, *Guovdageaidnu*, established in 1995 – a branch of the National Archives.

Sovereignty Issues and Relations with Government

The political system which has developed during the last four decades is from the perspective of the Norwegian experience. As the system continually develops, the strength of Sámi people is growing across the borders. During the period from 1945 until today, the rights of the Sámi as an ethnic and linguistic minority and as an Indigenous People was recognized. The general ideas of human worth and equal status of the cultures in the Universal Declaration on Human Rights and strengthened by the Article 27 of the International Covenant on Civil and Political Rights were fundamental in the process. This also applies to the ILO-convention no. 169 concerning Indigenous and Tribal People in Independent Countries, where the Sámi participation during the process of revision and replacement of convention no. 107 – was important in choosing a more current policy. The first country to ratify this document was Norway, something still not done by Sweden. Agenda 21 from the World Conference on Environment and Sustainable Development, in Brazil 1992 underlines the rights of Indigenous people to their resources. The ongoing work to make a Nordic Sámi convention should also be mentioned in this connection. Individuals and organizations started the process to put forward Sámi cultural and political issues in the period from 1945 on. The three Sámi sister organizations in Finland, Sweden, and Norway arranged a Nordic Sámi Conference in 1953 in Jokkmokk, Sweden. The main political issue was Sámi rights to land and water, language, and cultural rights. This was a first step on a wide range of national and international laws regulating the rights of the Sámi as an Indigenous People of Norway.

After the conflict of Sámi Rights to land use and resources initiated by plans of hydroelectric projects of the Alta River, the change of official governmental attitude to the Sámi People started a new, important process. A committee to study the legal rights of the Sámi people in Norway was appointed in 1980, and the first report was submitted in 1984 about the Legal Rights of the Sámi people. The proposals in the report resulted in a new statute, The Act of 12th June 1987 No. 56 relating to the Sámi people, and the inclusion of a new article in the Norwegian Constitution, Article 110A, which was adopted on 27th May 1988. Article 110 A says, "It is the responsibility of the authorities of the State to create conditions enabling the Sámi people to preserve and develop their language, culture and way of life". The obligation of the state implies a legal duty to support all basic elements necessary for the specific culture to live and develop including legal protection for the material foundations of the Sámi culture.

The Sámi Act of 1987 lays down administrative and language provisions in order to insure compliance with the Constitution. The *Sámediggi*, the Sámi Parliament, was established in 1987 and inaugurated in 1989 by King Olav V in Kárášjohka. The *Sámediggi* is a democratically elected body whose representatives are elected by and among the Sámi people, and Sámi language was recognized as an official language in Norway. The Sámi in Finland were acknowledged as an Indigenous People, and their legal rights were recognized in 1996 to protect and develop language and culture and to safeguard their cultural autonomy in the local communities as regards their language and culture. In Sweden the legislation referring to the Sámi is from 1976 and includes rights to protect and develop ethnic, linguistic, and religious minorities and the possibility to keep and develop their own culture and way of life. Internationally there are demands on Sweden that the questions of Sámi rights to land and resources, hunting, and fishing are solved. In spite of its consultancy role, the Sámi Assembly in Norway was from the beginning gradually moving toward administering all special state funding provided for Sámi activities concerning development of economic, educational, language, cultural, heritage, environmental, health, and social service.

The work of Sámi rights to land and water has been continuous since 1980. The preliminary work comprised a wide range of studies from customary law, local communities and regulations, national and international law to the Rights of Indigenous People published in reports. The new Act on land use and ownership in the County of Finnmark is now handled by the government at the *Storting* – the Norwegian Parliament. The Sámi Rights Committee submitted its second report on Sámi rights to land and natural resources in the County of Finnmark in 1997. The government is now following up on the report, and the Samediggi and the County of Finnmark are participating in the political process. A new Sámi Rights Committee was appointed 2001. Their mandate is to study the rights and management of land and natural resources in areas used by the Sámi people outside the County of Finnmark. The Committee's report was submitted in the middle of 2005. To follow up on the intentions of the principles in article of the Constitution, it implies a legal matter. To enhance the Sámi people's confidence in the courts, the *Storting* decided to establish a district court within the Sámi language administrative district, in which Sámi and Norwegian languages will have equal status. The court is located in the Deatnu municipality and was operative in 2004.

The Sámi Parliamentary Council was founded in 2000 as a joint organization of the Sámi Parliaments in Finland, Norway, and Sweden. The Sámi from Russia have observatory status in the Sámi Parliamentary Council. The council is to work with questions which affect the interests of Sámi across the borders and strengthen the cooperation between the Sámi people in the four countries. A special task is to coordinate the voice of the Sámi internationally. In Sámi Parliamentary Council they have on the agenda working with cases like education, research, handicrafts, other economic life, and coordination of the region of Barents, the Arctic Council, Interreg, and questions of Indigenous People within the United Nations. The United Nations works with questions of the Indigenous People which include the health of Indigenous People, especially within the World Health Organization.

In 2002 the composition of the expert group was decided that is to draw up a Nordic Sámi Convention. The group has been tasked with making a draft of a Nordic Sámi Convention among Finland, Sweden, and Norway. Important topics that the Sámi convention will include is the status of the Sámi people, the definition of "Sámi", self-determination, cooperation between the Sámi Parliaments and the states, language, the environment, the preservation of the cultural heritage, health, education, research, Sámi means of livelihood, culture, children, and youth. This process has again started after three years of inactivity. To promote, protect and coordinate Sámi church life within the Norwegian Protestant Church, the Sámi Church Council was established in Norway 1992. The agenda includes all cases relating to Sámi church life. The Council wants to contribute and strengthen Sámi church life across the borders in the Nordic countries and Russia. The council is cooperating through the World Councils of Churches with Indigenous Peoples all around the world, and the focus of the work is the rights of Indigenous Peoples. Through Sámi projects they are participating in solidarity work with other Indigenous groups and peoples around the world organized through the Sámi Council or other organizations or institutions.

Outlook for the Future
The World Council of Indigenous People was established in Port Alberni 1975, and the organization acquired consultative status as an Indigenous organiza-

tion in the United Nations. Through their active support during the 1980s, Sámi representatives contributed in having the World Council of Indigenous People recognized as a representative organization for the Indigenous People around the world. Aslak Nils Sara was appointed by the Nordic Sámi Council to represent the Sámi from the outset.

Sámi representation was important both in giving birth to the idea and later in appointing the first leader of the Permanent Forum of Indigenous Issues. In view of the increasing importance of issues affecting Indigenous Peoples, the former president of the *Samediggi* in Sweden, Lars-Anders Baer, proposed in 1993 at a session of the Commission of Human Rights that the system in the United Nations should be strengthened by an advisory body. In April 2000, the Commission on Human Rights adopted a resolution to establish the Permanent Forum on Indigenous Issues during the first International Decade of the World's Indigenous Peoples. Three months later, the Economic and Social Council endorsed the resolution, and the Permanent Forum came into formal existence. The first meeting of the Permanent Forum was held in May 2002, and annual meetings will take place either in New York or Geneva. Ole Henrik Magga, the first president of the *Samediggi* in Norway in 1989, was chosen to represent both the Sámi and Inuit as the first Chair of the Permanent Forum of Indigenous Issues from 2002. The Permanent Forum is an advisory body to the Economic and Social Council, with a mandate to discuss Indigenous issues related to economic and social development, culture, the environment, education, and health, as well as human rights. To increase the general public's knowledge of Indigenous People's rights in Norway, *Gáldu* - the Resource Centre for the Rights of Indigenous People - was established in Guovdageaidnu in 2002. The aims are to create a professional network dealing with Indigenous issues with other institutions both in Norway and in other countries. Other important tasks include documenting the rights of Indigenous Peoples and disseminating information.

The change of society, knowledge, and political systems make visible the social and cultural role of women and men that are central in the process of development. The traditional tasks of women have been taking care of and bringing up children, education, traditional handicrafts, home care, and taking care of ill and old people. These tasks are to be organized in new systems of social, cultural, and political development. After the Women's Conference of the Nordic Council in 1988, the woman's organization *Sáráhkká* was established, and was central in founding the World Council of Indigenous Women in 1989. The aim for these organizations is to underline that Indigenous women have other concerns than men, and that modernization of Indigenous People's cultural, social, and political changes often destroys the system of common law and traditions of women. The *Sámi Nisson Forum*, the Sámi Women Forum has existed since 1993, and through the journal *Gába* - a skilful, able woman, published in Sámi and Norwegian, they initiate and develop Sámi women local community projects. In the matter of the reindeer herding, it is a growing interest to attend to a gendered perspective with regard to recruitment and the economy of herding. Today the management of reindeer herding considers, together with the Ministry of Agriculture, how the United Nation's Convention on Women can be implemented into the Act of Reindeer Herding.

Closing Remark

The process of casting away the suppression of modern nations and creating a Sámi Nation of an Indigenous People in the 21th century has involved the creativity, knowledge, and political skills of each participant. Climate change, which is challenging the Indigenous Peoples, is met by the knowledge based on the individual's – his or her local cultural knowledge, oral traditions, customs, and the assurance based on human rights. The contribution of the Sámi people and their representatives to the economic and cultural life of their states and the world community has been fundamental in the fields of economic and social development, culture, the environment, education, health, and human rights. The process has showed the strength of solidarity with other Indigenous People of the world community.

References

10-jagi vuoddoskuvlla Sami Oahppotplánat. Oslo: Gonagaslaš girko-, oahpahus- ja dutkandepartementa 1997. / Det samiske læreplanverket for den 10-årige grunnskolen. Oslo: Det Kongelige Kirke-, Utdannings- og Forskningsdepartement 1997.

Act of 12th June 1987 No 56 Relating to the Sami people.

Act of 18th May 1990 No 11 Place names (Om Stadnamn).

Act of 9 June no. 50 concerning Cultural Heritage, entered into force 15th February 1979, revised 2003, Ministry and Environment.

Bjørklund, Ivar, with Terje Brantenberg, Harald Eidheim, Johan Albert Kalstad and Dikka Storm.
2000. *Sápmi - Becoming a Nation: The Emergence of a Sami National Community*. Tromsø: Tromsø University Museum. Online resource: http://sapmi.uit.no/sapmi/ExhibitionStart.do?language=norsk - accessed June 27, 2013.

Convention (No. 169) concerning Indigenous and Tribal Peoples in Independent Countries. Adopted on 27 June 1989 by General Conference of the International Labour Organisation at its seventy-sixth session. Entry into force 5 September 1991.

Dunfjeld, Maja.
2006. *Tjaalehtjimmie. Form og innhold i sørsamisk ornamentikk*. Snåsa: Samien Sijte.

Gaski, Harald. (ed.)
1997. *Sami Culture in a New Era. The Norwegian Sami Experience*. Kárášjohka: Dávvi Girji OS.

Gaski, Harald and Lena Kappfjell.
2002. *Samisk kultur i Norden – en perspektiverende rapport. Nordisk Kulturpolitik under Forandring*. København: Nordisk Kultur Institut.

Hansen, Lars Ivar and Bjørnar Olsen.
2004. *Samenes historie fram til 1750*. Oslo: Cappelen Akademisk Forlag.

Hicks, Christian Jakob Burmeister.
2000. *Historical Synopsis of the Sami/United Nations Relationship*. Fairbanks: The Arctic Institute.

Hinsch, Luce, with Hans-Emil Lidén, Dag Myklebust and Stephan Tschudi-Madsen. (eds.).
1987. *Norway: A Cultural Heritage. Monuments and Sites*. Oslo: Universitetsforlaget.

Jentoft, Svein, with Henry Minde and Ragnar Nilsen. (eds.).
2003. *Indigenous Peoples*. Resources Management and Global Rights. Delft: Eburon.

Nickul, Karl, with Asbjørn Nesheim and Israel Ruong. (eds.).
1957. *Sámiid Dilit. Speeches at the Nordic Sámi Conference in Jokkmokk 1953*. Oslo: Merkur Boktrykkeri.

Magga, Ole Henrik.
1998. *Cultural Rights and Indigenous Peoples: The Sami Experience in World Culture Report – Culture, Creativity and Markets*. Unesco: Unesco Publishing. 76-84

Magga, Ole Henrik.
2000. Samebevegelsen og det samiske språket. Theme Issue "Becoming a Nation". *Ottar – Populærvitenskapelig tidsskrift fra Tromsø University Museum*, nr 4 (232), 39-48.

Mathisen, Hans Ragnar, with Anders Henriksen and Samuli Aikio.
1996. *Sámi Atlas*. Geográfalaš ja historiálaš kárttat. Romssavárdu: Keviselie.

Minde, Henry.
2000. Samesaken som ble en urfolkssak. Theme Issue "Becoming a Nation". *Ottar – Populærvitenskapelig tidsskrift fra Tromsø University Museum*, nr 4 (232), 27-38.

Official Norwegian Report.
1984: 18. *Legal Rights of the Saami People*. Oslo-Bergen-Tromsø: Published by Universitetsforlaget.

Official Norwegian Report.
1995: 6. *Plan of Sami Health- and Social Services to the Sami Population in Norway*, Oslo: Statens Forvaltningstjeneste.

Sápmi – Becoming a nation,
N.d. *About the Sápmi – Becoming a nation* http://sapmi.uit.no/sapmi/ExhibitionStart.do?language=norsk accessed June 27, 2013

Sámediggi / Sametinget – The Sámi Parliament in Norway.
N.d. *About Sámediggi in Norway* http://www.samediggi.no accessed June 27, 2013

Sametinget - The Sámi Parliament in Sweden.
N.d. *About Sámediggi in Sweden* http://www.samediggi.se accessed June 27, 2013

Sámediggi – The Saami Parliament / The Finnish Saami Parliament.
N.d. *About Samediggi in Finland* http://www.samediggi.fi/ accessed June 27, 2013

The Sami: The Indigenous People of Norway.
1995. The Norwegian Ministry of Local Government and Labour, Oslo: Department of Sami Affairs.

Turi, Johan.
[1931] 1966. *Turi's Book of Lappland*. Edited by Emilie Demant Hatt, London: Jonathan Cape. Reprint Elizabeth Gee Nash ed. Anthropological publications, Oosterhout: N.B.

Valkeapää, Nils-Aslak
1988. *Beaivi, Áhcázan*. Guovdageaidnu: DAT.

Basques of Spain and France: The Native Europeans

Xabier Irujo

University of Nevada, Reno

Hither comes the Basque voiturier, with his long wagon drawn by three horses, wearing the Béarnaise beret; but you will easily tell the Béarnaise from the Basque—the sprightly, handsome little man of the plain, ready of tongue, and of hand as well —from the son of the mountain, with his rapid stride and huge limbs, a skillful farmer, and proud of the family whose name he bears. To find men like the Basque, you must search among the Celts of Brittany, of Scotland, or of Ireland. The Basque, eldest of the Celtic races, immovably fixed in the corner of the Pyrenees, has seen all the nations pass in review before him—Carthaginians, Celts, Romans, Goths, and Saracens. He regards with pity our recent genealogies. A Montmorency said to one of them: "Do you know that we date a thousand years back?" "We," was the rejoinder, "have left off dating."[1]

And that is the fact: Basques do not date. The origin of the Basques and their ancestors is lost in the midst of time and remains a mystery to this day.

We do know that this part of the world that we now call the Basque Country, enclosed in hundreds of deep and narrow valleys down each of which cold streams of fresh water are constantly pouring water into the North Atlantic, has been inhabited ever since, when 40,000 years ago the first humans visiting Europe decided to settle in this green and foggy region of the Pyrenean mountains. One of this forerunners of the Upper Paleolithic descended into a silent and arcane cave that we call Altxerri and started painting at the light of a torch. The result was an exquisite bison painted in red, one of the few and very rare examples of Aurignacian art in Europe, and one of the oldest too.[2]

During centuries and even millennia these Proto-Basque pilgrims lived isolated from the rest of the world, surrounded by the massive and insuperable mountains of ice that governed Europe during the ice age. However, while the Würm glacial period closed Europe from the East, it might have opened the gates of the western hemisphere to the inhabitants of this part of the world as suggested by archaeologists Dennis Stanford and Bruce Bradley. People with Solutrean tool-technology could have reached the eastern cost of the Americas across the Atlantic Ice about 22,000 to 17,000 years ago.[3]

And the glacial white closed the gates of Europe for further 20 millennia when about 1,200 years ago the first Indo-European explorers arrived in the old continent. They were the Celts, a persevering nation of warriors coming

1. Michelet, Jules, *History of France from the Earliest Period to the Present Time*, D. Appleton & Company, New York, 1851, vol. 1, pp. 161-162.
2. González-Sainz, César et alia, "Not only Chauvet: Dating Aurignacian rock art in Altxerri B Cave", *Journal of Human Evolution*, vol. 65, 4, October 2013, pp. 457-464.
3. Stanford, Dennis Jand Bruce A Bradley, *Across Atlantic Ice: The Origin of America's Clovis Culture*, University of California Press, Berkeley, 2012.

in Europe from the East with powerful weapons made of bronze. By then the Proto-Basque culture had flourished, developed and transformed itself for 37 white and old millennia, time to adapt and readapt, develop habits, grow a culture and produce a language. The current Basque language is the result of that all-time-embracing cultural evolution.

After the Celts, Romans, Vandals, Alans, Suevi, Visigoths, Umayyad, Abbasid, Almoravids, Frankish... and a countless list of other cultures have stepped the land of the Basques. By the 7th century the Basque Country, then called Vasconia, occupied a territory that stretched from the river Loire in the north to the river Ebro in the south. By the end of the 8th century Vasconia saw its territory reduced to that between the river Garonne in the north to the river Ebro in the south. By the 10th century the territory of the Basque Country was basically the one it is today, a portion of land extended between the river Aturri in the north and the river Ebro in the south.

The Basque culture encloses eight treasures, among them, the most precious ones are the trunk-line family and social structure founded on an equalitarian production system (*auzolan* or cooperativism) and grounded on a proto-democratic political system (*foruak*) and, the language (*Euskara*). From the Pre-proto-Basque to the Basque language, this 'strange and powerful language' has been passing from lip to lip all along millennia and thus it is today the only living eyewitness of the European prehistory, the last stand of the prehistoric European culture.[4] As archeologist and anthropologist Joxe M. Barandiaran once wrote, "Europe as a whole should preserve Basque as the only living treasure of its millenary past."[5] Yet, this linguistic isolate, the only breathing Pre-Indo-European language in Contemporary Europe, has been in the brink of extinction since 1789.

Native nations all over the human biosphere share a sundry source of cultural values. Being all human, all cultures share that deeply genuine and sincere part of our anthropological universe and thus we, peoples of the world, are united in diversity, because there is a common soil, a joint denominator in all our cultural expressions, no matter how far our ecospheres are from each other. However, as history of the last two centuries reveals to us, Native nations have shared, above all and over all, sorrow, agony and distress. And this pain persists in us all.

In June 1782 Johann Formey, secretary of the Berlin Academy of Sciences, held a philosophical contest around a question: "What facts have turn the

---

4.   Zaldua, Iban, *This Strange and Powerful Language*, Center for Basque Studies Press, Reno, 2005. Hualde, José I., *History of the Basque Language*, John Benjamins Publishing, Philadelphia (Pa.), 1995.

5.   Baradiaran, Jose Miguel, *Selected Writings of José Miguel de Barandiarán: Basque Prehistory and Ethnography*, Center for Basque Studies Press, Reno, 2009, p. 37.

French language into a universal language?" Antoine de Rivarol won the contest with a speech entitled *On the Universality of the French Language* that was published in 1784.[6] The author argued that the French deserved the title of 'universal language' in virtue of its 'inner genius' or spirit, which endowed the language of extraordinary clarity, expressivity, rigor and, rationality. It was Rivarol who coined the expression "If something is not clear, is not French."[7] In short, French was the language of Enlightenment and, as a natural consequence, the French speaker the vehicle of progress. Furthermore, it was not possible to be an enlightened, sophisticated and well-educated person but speaking French. This assessment was shared by several authors of the time who (in different languages) defended based on this or that criterion the adequacy of their own languages and their superiority over the rest others.

This book that was not translated into English, nor into any of the other dominant European languages of the time, had an exponential impact at both philosophical and political level. The prejudices poured into Rivarol's discourse rapidly reached the European legislative chambers and in next to no time became the law. On May 9, 1794 Henri Gregoire defended before the revolutionary Convention in Paris that under the monarchy the French language had hardly generated a correct political vocabulary, however, the Revolution had turn French in the most appropriate language to express the ideals of the Jacobin ideology, since the rest of the languages spoken in the Republic were but "vulgar and indelicate jargons without specific syntax, because language is always the measure of the genius of a nation."[8] And the convention unanimously approved the decree on the need to create a new grammar and a new French vocabulary and gave this new language the official name of "French" and the title of "the language of freedom."[9]

After becoming the law, prejudices soon were spread through the use of force and cannons all over Europe defended in prose their own rights, and words.

One of the most glaring promoters of the language policy in fashion was Bertrand de Barère, a member of the 'Public Health Committee' of the French National Convention (*Comité de salut public*).[10] The first of August of 1793 Barère took the floor before the legislative Convention and, under the slogan

---

6.   Rivarol, Antoine de, Dissertations Sur L'Universalité de la Langue Françoise, Decker, Berlin, 1784.

7.   "Ce qui n'est pas claire, n'est pas française". Ibid., p. 57.

8.   Grégoire, Henri-Baptiste, *Rapports de Henri Grégoire, ancien évêque de Blois, sur la bibliographie, la destruction des patois et les excès du vandalisme, faits à la convention du 22 germinal an 2 au 24 frimaire an III*, A. Massif/Delarocque, Caen & Paris, 1867, pp. 17-18.

9.   "Langue de la liberté."

10. Usually translated to English as 'Committee of Public Safety'.

"We must destroy the Vendee!," persuaded the assembly to send an army composed of "Commissioners of a pronounced patriotism" to loot and burn that territory, even ordering to make available to these troops the necessary amount of fuel "to destroy forests, farm fields and livestock."[11] And the secretary of war provided "all kinds of combustible materials to burn forests, scrubland and thickets."[12] On September 5 in order to set a methodical campaign of material destruction and extermination, Barère harangued the assembly to establish a dictatorship of terror (*a terror agenda*) through the creation of special executive tribunals, "to make disappear in an instant royalists and moderates."[13] And the assembly approved by acclamation the decree that anyone could be arrested, sentenced and executed summarily, without further evidence that the will of a revolutionary advocate. Barère gained thus the title of 'The Anacreon of the Guillotine' for his 'poetical' use of the speech to spread terror among the ones who did not speak like him.

On 1 and 10 October 1793 Barère urged the assembly of the obligation of spreading terror as a "political medicine" to exterminate all enemies of the Republic.[14] Yet again on February 12, 1794 Barère delivered a new speech on the need of "pacifying" the Vendee and remove the last vestiges of the rebellion.[15] Following orders, the troops François Joseph Westermann and the 'Infernal Columns' of General Louis M. Turreau, murdered between 20,000 and 50,000 civilians, mainly elderly, women and children, between late January and mid-May 1794. Meanwhile, Jean-Baptiste Carrier, delegate of the revolutionary government in Nantes, undertook the killing of around 9,000 civilians between mid-November 1793 and the end of February 1794. Many of these women and children and a large group of priests and nuns, were killed by drowning them in sinking barges on the river Loire. Thousands were shot at the Gigant pits and others were killed by abuse, disease, cold and starvation.

Since the beginning of 1793 until the spring of 1796, between 117,000 to 200.000 and 400,000 people died or disappeared in the Vendee, which then had a population of about 815,000 people.[16] On his return to Paris, Carrier

---

11. Discourse of Bertrand de Barère before the French National Assembly in Paris. *Réimpression de l'ancien Moniteur*, Typographie de Henri Plon, Paris, 1860, vol. 17, pp. 338-341.

12. Ibid.

13. "Plaçons la terreur à l'ordre du jour. C'est ainsi que disparaîtront en un instant et les royalistes et les modérés, et la tourbe contre-révolutionnaire qui vous agile." *Gazette Nationale ou Le Moniteur Universel*, No. 251, dimanche 8 septembre 1793, l'an 2 de la *République Française*, Sunday, September 8, 1793, pp. 3-5.

14. Rapport sur la Vendée, fait au nom du Comité de salut public, dans la séance du 1er octobre 1793. *Réimpression de l'ancien Moniteur*, Bureau Central, Paris, 1841, vol. 18, pp. 50-54.

15. Journal des débats et des décrets, No. 512, Paris, 1794, pp. 361-374.

16. Babeuf, Gracchus, *Du Système de dépopulation, ou la vie et les crimes de Carrier, son*

was appointed Secretary of the National Convention and Turreau's name is inscribed in stone in the *Arc de Triomphe de l'Etoile in Paris*. A commonplace to episodes of genocide.

Vendeans were exterminated because they were not *French, French* in the sense required and imposed by the legislative convention led by Maximilien Robespierre. The revolutionary government in Paris also forced mass migration of nationals outside their territory in 1794. Barère sparked a campaign of hatred in the Basque Country when on January 27, 1794 stated that the Basque people were a band of fanatics whose culture and language had to be eradicated (*le fanatisme parle le basque*).[17] Less than two months later the Convention organized the deportation of more than 4,000 civilians, and all inhabitants of the municipalities of Sara, Itsaso and Azkain were mobilized. The displaced ones were forbidden to take any food or warm clothes with them and were concentrated in several churches in the Landes where, separating family units, had to face extreme situations as a result of what more than half of them perished.[18]

Members of the Public Health Committee soon realized that the destruction of a nation's collective identity was not possible by the sole means of violence and oppression. Once the rebellion was crushed and the Vendée 'pacified', Barère -inspired by Gregoire and under the political leadership of Maximilien Robespierre, Georges Danton, Jean-Paul Marat and Louis Antoine de Saint-Just, all members of the Public Health Committee- set in motion the mechanisms of cultural genocide aimed to destroy "these instruments of prejudice and error",[19] that is, all languages spoken in the Republic not being the official and revolutionary French language. The decree of 20 July, 1794 (2 Thermidor Year II) on the French language imposed French as the sole language of administration and chased the rest of the other languages that were -and sometimes still are- referred to as "regional patois" and "local jargons." 1794 will be known as the year of the "Linguistic terror" (*terreur linguistique*).[20]

Barère realized that the only way to prevent insurrections like those of the

---

procès et celui du Comité révolutionnaire de Nantes, Imprimerie de Franklin, Paris, 1794.

17. *Gazette Nationale ou Le Moniteur Universel*, No. 129, nonidi, 9 pluviose, l'an 2e (Mardi 28 janvier 1794, vieux style), Tuesday, January 28, 1794, 3a series, vol. 6, pp. 5-8. See also, *Recueil de lois et règlemens concernant l'instruction publique, depuis l'Edit de Henri IV en 1598 jusqu'à ce jour*, Brunot-Labbe, Paris, 1814, vol. 1, pp. 22-26.

18. Goyhenetxe, Eukeni, *Historia de Iparralde: Desde los orígenes a nuestros días*, Txertoa, Donostia, 1985, p. 84. Ver asimismo, Letamendia, Francisco, *Los vascos: Ayer, hoy y mañana*, Mugalde, Hendaia, 1977, p. 102. Y, Bazan, Iñaki et al., *De Túbal a Aitor: Historia de Vasconia*, La Esfera de los Libros, Madrid, 2002, p. 359.

19. *Gazette Nationale ou Le Moniteur Universel*, No. 129, nonidi, 9 pluviose, l'an 2e (Mardi 28 janvier 1794, vieux style), Tuesday, January 28, 1794, 3a series, vol. 6, pp. 5-8.

20. Schiffman, Harold, *Linguistic Culture and Language Policy*, Routledge, London and New York, 2002, pp. 93-114.

Vendée and the Basque Country was by generating and enacting a public system of 'production of French citizens', what he called 'the Mars Schools' and Grégoire named 'Hospitals of the human spirit'. The basic idea defended by Barère in his speech to the National Convention on January 28, 1794 was that it was necessary to "forge revolutionary spirits at public schools."[21] French, history of France, 'correct political ideology' and basic military training for boys was to be taught. The new system of education had to be organized regimentally, controlled from the Ministry of the Interior. New schools would be free of charge to students from 3 to 14 years of age but compulsory school attendance was imposed. Students would no longer belong to their families or their Gods but, by becoming citizens of the Republic, would be educated with no other affiliation but that indebted to the revolutionary ideal and no greater glory than to serve the country at war (or through the exercise of the right to pay taxes.)

Only citizens accredited by the state could -and still can- become teachers of the public schools. Special schools for the training of teachers were generated under the name of 'normal school'. Initially, the only requirement to access these schools was a certificate of good conduct and loyalty to revolutionary ideals. Parents that did not take their children to schools would be fined and punished, children who spoke a language other than French at schools would be punished, teachers who used a language other than French in the classroom would be punished or dismissed. The destruction of all languages and cultures other that the official of the state was necessary 'in the name of civilization and revolution,' moreover, it was 'a patriotic duty.'[22]

The ideological and programmatic foundation of the language policy of the French republic were settled between June 1793 and December 1794, a period of time in which no less than twenty legal texts that seriously affected the existence of the languages spoken in the territory of the state were passed. Following the adoption of the so-called 1794 autumn decrees the French language was definitively imposed as the only language of state and thus henceforth the only language holding the legal title of *langue française*, a political term that refers to its non-official status of symbol of the national unity (*symbole de l'unité nationale*). It is significant that these legal norms, which became the standard guidelines of the language policy for a large number of European countries, were designed, drafted, approved and executed on behalf of a constitution and a *Corpus juris* or body of law that had been suppressed by a dictatorial and terrorist government (genocidal in essence) in the historical context of the "Reign of Terror" (*La Terreur*). In sum, legal standards generated and passed in transgression of the most basic human rights.

---

21. *Ibid.*
22. *Ibid.*

Other authors had argued that languages are the image of the 'genius of nations' and, therefore, that there are languages like Spanish or French that may be considered 'languages of culture' in opposition to others, such as Basque, Breton or Catalan that simply were not. More than a century after Barère's and Gregoire's inspired speeches, the acclaimed philosopher Miguel Unamuno expressed and put in writing that "I have believed for a long time that Basque, being an interesting subject of study, lacks the intrinsic conditions to serve as a mean of expression for people fully immersed into the modern spiritual life."[23] Unamuno defended the idea that Spanish was a 'superior' language because "it is a more complete, more integrated and more analytical language and, fits better with the level of culture that we have reached."[24] Furthermore, the author catalogued the status of all languages in two groups, that is, 'languages of culture' and 'rustic languages'. Unamuno also expressed that a 'rustic language' could never become an 'instrument of civilization' but he never specified what 'language of culture' or 'instrument of civilization' means in this context. A second acclaimed writer, Pio Baroja, added more thoughts in this regard stating that "only a small number of crackpots, and a large number of Basque Carlist disguised as philologists who believe that the whole truth of the world is locked in the Catechism have tried to show that Basque is a language that can be transformed into a literary and scientific language."[25]

In the view of these authors there were 'superior' and 'inferior' nations, cultures and languages because it is "very rational to assume that the language of a people that is superior in thought and culture to another is, therefore, superior to the language of this people."[26] The conclusion was thus obvious: to impose French or Spanish in schools and in all areas of the public administration was not only a cultural imperative, but a legal constraint, so that as for Unamuno and other authors to abolish and extinguish cultures and languages became a 'patriotic duty', a 'moral imperative' and a 'political necessity'. Unamuno compared the Basque language with a disease that was necessary to remove *bone fides*, for the sake of humanity and civilization, in the benefit of the Basque speakers themselves. Once he ironically commented that he had received "a letter from Doctor Joaquín Costa who lamented that Basque -being son interesting for the study of the Iberian antiquities- was disappearing. I had to answer to him the following: 'It's fine; but I won't be keeping what I think it's a disease to satisfy a pathologist.'"[27] Betrand of Barère had expressed the same

23. Unamuno, Miguel, "La cuestión del vascuence." In, Unamuno, Miguel, *Ensayos*, Residencia de Estudiantes, Madrid, vol. 3, pp. 191-237.
24. Unamuno, Miguel, *Revista de Vizcaya*, Bilbao, febrero 15, 1886.
25. Baroja, Pío, *El Imparcial*, agosto 31, 1901.
26. Unamuno, Miguel, "La cuestión del vascuence". In, Unamuno, Miguel, *Ensayos*, Salamanca, 1902, p. 382.
27. Unamuno, Miguel, *Discurso de Unamuno a propósito de la oficialidad del castellano,*

ideas from his podium at the French Convention on Tuesday, January 28, 1794 when he stated that "the language called low-Breton, the Basque language and, the German and Italian languages have perpetuated the reign of fanaticism and superstition, ensuring the domination of priests, nobles and professionals, preventing the revolution penetrate in nine major departments [of the Republic] and perhaps helping the enemies of France... federalism and superstition speak low-Breton, migration and hatred for the Republic speak German, counter-revolution speaks Italian and fanaticism speaks Basque. Let's destroy these instruments of prejudice and error."[28]

These ideas and the subsequent strategies soon reached the shores of North America. It was the head of the Carlisle school for Indians, Captain Pratt, who said in substance, "We accept the watch-word. There is no good Indian but a dead Indian. Let us by education and patient effort kill the Indian in him, and save the man."[29] In the words of Reverend A. C. Whitmer, "the Indians are human beings, needing redemption, and therefore should have the gospel. Strange that any one should say the Indian has no soul! Of course they are ignorant, superstitious, having odd notions and customs, with a way of life very different from ours; but all this equally true of the Chinese, Africans, and others. Indeed all this was true of our own fathers in Europe not many centuries ago. It seems a wicked slur upon the Creator to say that the only good Indian is a dead one. Give him a chance, treat him as human, do for him what has been done for the white man and for the black man, and see what he will become! The proof of all this is before us. Gray Cloud, once a chief among the Dakotas, is now a most useful Christian minister among his people."[30]

The logic laying behind this idea is substantially the same that enlightened Barère's discourses at the French National Convention. An opinion and a program grounded on three basic points:

1. 'Indias' are uncivilized people speaking under-civilized languages.
2. 'Indians' must be civilized by 'educating' them in civilized values and by teaching them a civilized language, aka, 'a language of culture.'

Diario de Sesiones del Congreso español, Septiembre 18, 1931.

28. *Gazette Nationale ou Le Moniteur Universel*, No. 129, nonidi, 9 pluviose, l'an 2e (Mardi 28 janvier 1794, vieux style), Tuesday, January 28, 1794, 3a series, vol. 6, pp. 5-8. See also, *Recueil de lois et règlemens concernant l'instruction publique, depuis l'Edit de Henri IV en 1598 jusqu'à ce jour*, Brunot-Labbe, Paris, 1814, vol. 1, pp. 22-26.

29. "Annual Report of the Board of Indian Commissioners", Washington D.C., February 15, 1885. In, Annual Report of the Department of the Interior, Washington D.C., 1885, vol. 1, p. 775.

30. Whitmer, A. C., "Missions to the Indians". In, *The Gospel in All Lands. An Illustrated Monthly Missionary Journal*, Methodist Episcopal Church Missionary Society, 1885, vol. 11, pp. 305-307.

3. This we will do bona fides, for the good of the 'Indians' themselves and for the good of the human kind.

This opinion also laid on financial calculations. According to Rev. Whitmer, the Indian had been badly treated by the U.S. Government that had, in the main, followed 'the killing policy', a strategy that had been "not only cruel but also costly." According to the author, for forty years the U.S. Government had spent a yearly average of $10,000,000 on Indian wars in addition to almost as much for keeping the Indians in reservations. From 1872 to 1882 the U.S. Government had spent $223,000,000 in wars, besides $50,000,000 for their support or a yearly average of more than $27,000,000. "These are reliable official figures. I need hardly add that this policy has been fruitless of good. The Indians have not been helped, blessed, lifted up, but continue idle, thriftless, ignorant and wicked, because the Government failed to bring out the manhood that is in them."

In the view of the results the U.S. Government set off a new policy, or rather "an experiment" with what we may call the educational policy. "The peace policy began in the time of President Grant, who sent out to the Indian stations agents that were nominated and thus recommended by Churches and Missionary Societies. Ever since a growing interest has been taken in this form of the Indian question, and the Government is now giving it a fair trial. At different times of late years the Commissioner of Indian Affairs and the Secretary of the Interior have urged this peace policy, this educational plan, and the Government now spends $500,000 yearly upon it. It says it cannot do more (as men often say about alms-giving), bat this is only one twentieth of the yearly cost of Indian wars. Why so little for peace and so much for war? Would not millions have been saved if the Indian had long ago received the gospel instead of bullets? It costs the Government 11,000,000 to kill an Indian. The Church can save him for $1,000!"

In sum, cultural genocide was –and still is- far more effective, inexpensive and expeditious than physical genocide or extermination. Here a good example of this faith. Under the title of "A Good Way to Make Good Indians" the *Red Man*, 'a real progressive and meritorious journal published at Carlisle (Pa.),' printed an article 'in the interest of the red man', 'a pleasing and convincing way of telling the truth on the Indian question that show how pertinently it talks:'

1. "If we do not educate Indian children to our civilized life their parents will continue to educate them to savagery".
2. "Indian tribes, languages and reservations are combinations against the first law announced to man at creation, directing him to be fruitful, multiply and replenish the earth."
3. "The day of real progress for the Indians will begin when each Indian becomes an individual and an organized unit in himself to make the

most of himself that he can."

4. "One of the greatest hindrances to the Indian in his transit from barbarism to civilization is his entire exclusion from the experiences of practical civilized life."

5. "A great general has said that *the only good Indian is a dead Indian*. The friends of the Indian everywhere ought to unite in hearty thanks to the general for the remark, because it has been the text and inspiration of more help for, and speech in behalf of the Indian than any other words ever uttered on the subject, and it is becoming evident everywhere that the Indian will never be good until *his Indian is all dead* - speech, habits, customs, beliefs, and all else of his old life which clings to him to hinder the new."

If this is not good sense, and does not indicate the right way to make good Indians, then there is no good in humanity anywhere. The Red Man is a bright champion of a noble cause.[31]

Raphael Lemkin, Polish lawyer of Jewish origin, coined for the first time the word 'genocide' in 1944. According to Lemkin, "genocide does not necessarily mean the immediate destruction of a nation, except when accomplished by mass killings of all members of a nation. It is intended rather to signify a coordinated plan of different actions aiming at the destruction of essential foundations of the life of national groups, with the aim of annihilating the groups themselves. [...] The objectives of such a plan would be disintegration of the political and social institutions, of culture, language, national feelings, religion, and the economic existence of national groups, and the destruction of the personal security, liberty, health, dignity, and even the lives of the individuals belonging to such groups. Genocide is directed against the national group as an entity, and the actions involved are directed against individuals, not in their individual capacity, but as members of the national group."[32] The aim of the genocidal agent is not thus the extermination of all the people belonging to a given nation but to destroy the nation itself, what Lemkin described as the 'national patter' of the nation, that is, the 'way of life' or 'culture' of a human group or nation.

As described by Lemkin, all campaigns of genocide have two phases. During the first stage of the campaign the genocidal agent destroys the national pattern of the oppressed group while in the second phase the agent imposes its

---

31. *The Now and Then. Devoted to History, Amusement, Instruction, Advancement*, Muncy (Pa.), Nov.-Dec. 1889, vol. 2, p. 133.

32. Lemkin, Raphael, *Axis Rule in Occupied Europe: Laws of Occupation, Analysis of Government, Proposals for Redress*, Carnegie Endowment for International Peace, Washington D.C., 1944, p. 79.

own national pattern on the victims. "This imposition, in turn, may be made upon the oppressed population which is allowed to remain, or upon the territory alone, after removal of the population and the colonization of the area by the oppressor's own nationals."[33]

Lemkin first coined the word 'genocide' in 1944 but the concept is much older and the performance of genocidal campaigns is as ancient as humanity. 'Depopulation' or 'denationalization' were some of the terms used in the past to describe the destruction of the national pattern of a human group. In view of the crimes committed by Carrier and other members of the Revolutionary army at the Vendée, Gracchus Babeuf was one of the first authors describing the crime of 'depopulation' in his book *On the Systems of Depopulation, or the Life and Crimes of Carrier*, first published in Paris in 1794.[34] The first author to register a case of 'depopulation' or 'denationalization' in the Basque Country was Charles F. Henningsen in his book *The Most Striking Events of a Twelvemonth's Campaign with Zumalacarregui* first published in London in 1838. In view of the author the Basques as the Vendeans could only be submitted "by the extermination of the male population, the transplanting of families, burning of harvests, and destroying every human habitation, as was attempted by the French Convention in La Vendée. But to effect all this ill a country like the present seat of war, which baffled the genius of Napoleon with all his legions, and where every arbitrary act, instead of striking terror, arms fresh masses of its population, would require, I apprehend, a larger army than was ever marshalled under any man since the days of Xerxes. It would, moreover, be forced to feed upon itself, like a swarm of lemmings, when its work was done."[35]

Cultural genocide is an essential part of any campaign of genocide, involving the destruction of the most distinctive and representative features of a nation by "destroying the specific characteristics of the group by (a) forcible transfer of children to another human group; or (b) forced and systematic exile of individuals representing the culture of a group; or (c) prohibition of the use of the national language even in private intercourse; or (d) systematic destruction of books printed in the national language or of religious works or prohibition of new publications; or (e) systematic destruction of historical or religious monuments or their diversion to alien uses, destruction or dispersion of doc- uments and objects of historical, artistic, or religious value and of objects used in religious worship."[36]

---

33. *Ibid.*
34. Babeuf, Gracchus, *Du Système de dépopulation, ou la vie et les crimes de Carrier, son procès et celui du Comité révolutionnaire de Nantes*, Imprimerie de Franklin, Paris, 1794.
35. Henningsen, Charles F., *Doce meses de campaña con Zumalakarregi durante la guerra en Navarra y Provincias Vascongadas / The Most Striking Events of a Twelvemonth's Campaign with Zumalacarregui in Navarre and the Basque Provinces*, Zumalakarregi Museoa, Ormaiztegi [bilingual edition], 2015, pp. 47-48.

There is no more effective strategy to destroy a language and thus the collective identity of a nation that the imposition of a monolingual system of education, the implementation of a monolingual administration, including a monolingual organization of the four branches of government and, the establishment of a monolingual system of justice administration. One fact corroborates this idea: the increasing evolution of the number of speakers of French, Spanish and Basque in the Basque Country from 1789 to day, and the decreasing evolution of the number of speakers of the Basque language for the same period. Another fact: there are 24 official and working languages in the 28 states that conform the European Union today. According to the data of the UNESCO for 2013, there are 114 languages and language varieties in danger of extinction in these 28 states: all except the referred 24 official and working languages.[37]

Pain unites us, Native nations of the world. According to the figures of the UNESCO, there are 5 endangered languages in the Spanish state; there are 26 endangered languages in the French state and there are 191 languages are endangered in the United States.[38]

I have been teaching genocide studies for a long time. Some years ago a student came to speak to me after the last session of the semester. He had a Basque surname so I asked him if he was of Basque origin. He told me the following: "I am a Paiute but I do not speak the language. My mother still speaks a bit. I do not worship Paiute Gods because they are long gone and there is little left of our ancestral religion; I do not eat Paiute and I do not play Paiute sports; I do not dress Paiute and I even have a Basque surname. So, answer this to me professor, how may I be a Paiute?" I was shocked: "I do not have an answer for such a difficult question but I can tell you that you have the 'will to be' a Paiute and this is a treasure that you keep in your soul. You may not be a Paiute in the way your ancestors were but you have to find your own way of being a Paiute today and tomorrow."

As the Montmorencys, many have lost their temper in disputes with the Basques and other nations all over the world, but in Unamuno's own words, that is the fact: We do not date, and we know who we are and who we want to be."[39]

---

36. *First Draft of the Convention on the Prevention and Punishment of the Crime of Genocide.* Prepared by the UN Secretariat, [May] 1947 [UN Doc. E/447].

37. UNESCO Atlas of the World's Languages in Danger: http://www.unesco.org/culture/languages-atlas/index.php

38. *Ibid.*

39. Unamuno, Miguel, *Our Lord Don Quixote: The Life of Don Quixote and Sancho*, Princeton University Press, Princeton, 1967, pp. 63-64. Taken from, Michelet, Jules, *History of France from the Earliest Period to the Present Time*, D. Appleton & Company, New York, 1851, vol. 1, pp. 161-162.

References

Arnold, Matthew.
1861. *The Popular Education of France: With Notices of that of Holland and Switzerland*, Longman, London.

Babeuf, Gracchus.
1794. *Du Système de dépopulation, ou la vie et les crimes de Carrier, son procès et celui du Comité révolutionnaire de Nantes*, Imprimerie de Franklin, Paris.

Baradiaran, Jose Miguel.
2009. *Selected Writings of José Miguel de Barandiarán: Basque Prehistory and Ethnography*, Center for Basque Studies Press, Reno.

Certeau, Michel de; Julia, Dominique; Revel, Jacques.
2002. *Une politique de la langue. La Révolution française et les patois. L'enquête de Grégoire*, Gallimard, Paris.

Chaliand, Gérard.
1985. *Les Minorités à l'âge de l'État-nation*, Fayard, Paris.

Chanet, Jean-François; Ozouf, Mona.
1996. *L'école républicaine et les petites patries*, Aubier, Paris.

Gazier, A. (ed.)
1969. *Lettres à Grégoire sur les Patois de France (1790-1794). Documents inédits sur la langue, les mœurs et l'état des esprits dans les diverses régions de la France, au début de la Révolution*, Slatkine Reprints, Genève.

Gréard, Octave.
1875. *La législation de l'instruction primaire en France depuis 1789 jusqu'à nos jours: Recueil des lois, décrets, ordonnances, arrêtés, règlements, décisions, avis, projets de lois, suivi d'une table analytique et précédé d'une introduction historique*, Ministère de l'éducation nationale, C. de Mourgues fréres, Paris.

Grégoire, Henri-Baptiste.
1867. *Rapports de Henri Grégoire, ancien évêque de Blois, sur la bibliographie, la destruction des patois et les excès du vandalisme, faits à la convention du 22 germinal an 2 au 24 frimaire an III*, A. Massif/Delarocque, Caen & Paris.

Hualde, José I.
1995. *History of the Basque Language*, John Benjamins Publishing, Philadelphia.

Irujo, Xabier.
2015. *Genocidio en Euskal Herria (1936-1945)*, Nabarralde, Iruñea.

Irujo, Xabier and Iñigo Urrutia.
2009. *A Legal History of the Basque Language (1789-2009)*, Eusko Ikaskuntza/ Society for Basque Studies, Donostia.

Irujo, Xabier and Viola Miglio (eds.).
2013. *Language Rights and Cultural Diversity*, Center for Basque Studies - University of Nevada, Reno.

Kline, Michael B.; Mellerski, Nancy C.
2004. *Issues in the French-speaking world*, Greenwood Publishing Group, Westport.

Lodge, R. Anthony.
1993. *French, from dialect to standard*, Routledge, London & New York.

Orpustan, Jean-Baptiste.
1991. *1789 et les Basques: histoire, langue et littérature. Colloque de Bayonne, 30 juin-1er juillet 1989, Département interuniversitaire d'études basques de Bayonne*, Presses Université de Bordeaux, Bordeaux.

Ostler, Nicholas.
2005. *Empires of the word: a language history of the world*, HarperCollins, New York.

Rivarol, Antoine de.
1784. *Dissertations Sur L'Universalité de la Langue Françoise*, Decker, Berlin.

Schlieben-Lange.
1996. Brigitte; Le Gal, Christine, I*déologie, révolution et uniformité de la langue*, Editions Mardaga, Liège.

Sepinwall, Alyssa G.
2005. *The Abbé Grégoire and the French Revolution: the making of modern universalism*, University of California Press, Berkeley.

Schiffman, Harold.
2002. *Linguistic Culture and Language Policy*, Routledge, London and New York.

Torrealdai, Juan M.
1998. *El libro negro del euskera*, Ttartalo, Donostia.

Totoricagüena, G., Urrutia, I., (eds.).
2008. *The legal status of the Basque language today: one language, three administrations, seven different geographies and a diaspora*, Eusko Ikaskuntza, Donostia.

Unamuno, Miguel.
"La cuestión del vascuence." In, Unamuno, Miguel, *Ensayos*, Residencia de Estudiantes, Madrid, vol. 3, pp. 191-237.

Whitmer, A. C.
1885. "Missions to the Indians". In, *The Gospel in All Lands. An Illustrated Monthly Missionary Journal*, Methodist Episcopal Church Missionary Society, vol. 11, pp. 305-307.

Zaldua, Iban.
2005. *This Strange and Powerful Language*, Center for Basque Studies Press, Reno.

Bretons of France

Michael J. Simonton

Northern Kentucky University

The Argument

The Peninsula of Brittany (*Bretagne*, or in their own *Breton* language, *Breizh*) lies at the northwestern tip of continental France; the provincial capital is the city of Rennes. The modern *départements* of Brittany include *Côtes-d'Armor* (also known as *Côtes-du Nord*), *Morbihan, Ille-et-Vilaine*, and *Finistère*; the *département of Finistère*, at the tip of Brittany, is one of the westernmost points in continental Europe. Brittany may be thought of politically in three different ways: as a modern French administrative region, as a province, and as a duchy. The modern administrative unit is coterminous with neither the province nor the duchy, some of which lies in the *département Loire-Atlantique* (including the old ducal capital, Nantes, the largest city in Brittany – although Rennes is the largest city in the modern administrative region, followed by Brest). For this reason some would argue that the *département Loire-Atlantique* should be a fifth *département* of Brittany, rather than be part of the *Pays de la Loire region*, and the *département Loire-Atlantique* has had representatives in the Cultural Council of Brittany (McDonald, 1989, p. 329).

One might question why a chapter on a European people would be included a book about the fourth world. Some might wonder why Europe would be included in anthropology at all – after all, do anthropologists not study 'the Other'? Susan Parman argues that 'Other' includes 'Celts, Lapps [Saami], Basques, gypsies, peasants, [and] nomadic pastoralists...' (1998, p. 173). Studies of the European 'Other' hardly are new in anthropology; in fact, in the 1930s Harvard University's Anthropology Department conducted a major, three subfield study of Ireland, in which the Social Anthropology team was led by W. Lloyd Warner, with by Conrad M. Arensberg, and later with the addition of Solon T, Kimball. Harvard Anthropology led the way with Little Community studies, in the vein of Robert Redfield (1960), with the publication of Arensberg's and Kimball's *Family and Community in Ireland* (1940). Arnold van Gennep argued that in Europe 'we are left with a variety of groups which do not want to be assimilated to each other or to be absorbed by a single one of them' (Llobera, 1994, p. 96). These are the people that Europeanist anthropologists normally study, rather than the inhabitants of London, Paris, Rome, or Berlin. As we wrote recently in a chapter on Europe in *Twenty First Century Anthropology*:

> We would argue that the European culture area is as worthy of study as any other culture area, and this is especially so as the foci of anthropology have changed over time from isolated, technologically and politically simple societies to more urban and interethnic studies than was the case prior to the Second World War. With as many anthropologists who study behaviors in the modern United States of America as there are today, it is illogical to hold on to the belief that anthropologists should not study Europe as well.... There is a prejudice in anthropology against European studies: Susan Parman writes that some scholars consider the anthropol-

ogy of Europe to be a self-contradictory phrase; that anthropologists are supposed to study 'the other,' that is, people in leopard skins or Tibetan nomads; to study Europe, she writes, is considered problematic. Parman wryly has quoted John C. Messenger Jr.'s assertion that Europeanists sometimes are considered people who study those with particularly interesting local vintages. Nonetheless, Europe is as worthy a province of anthropological research as any other culture area, and just because one has studied what Robert Redfield called 'the Great Tradition' of Europe in school does not mean that he or she has the least familiarity with the various 'Little Traditions,' be they Inis Beag, Kippel, Vasilika, Locorotondo, Hal-Farrug, or Cairn, extant in Europe any more than having taken a Spanish language class and having visited Mexico city automatically makes one familiar with rural Tarascan or Zapotec folk culture on the western side of the Atlantic. (Simonton, 2010, p. 716-717)

It is for these reasons[1] – to show that Europe is as much a part of the anthropological world as other places - that Eric Wolf wrote *Europe and the People without History* (1982); European folk cultures can be as different from their Great Traditions as can be the folk cultures in any other country, and it is not insignificant in this regard that Ferdinand Tönnies' terms *gemeinschaft* and *gesellschaft* first were applied to European traditions (1887). No less an anthropological personage than George Peter Murdock 'viewed Europe as the key area for future anthropological research and that he urged students… toward a path of European ethnography and ethnology' (Shutes, 1998, p. 158). As early as 1898 *The Journal of the Anthropological Institute of Great Britain and Ireland* published an article *On the Anthropology of Brittany* (Topinard, 1898, p. 96-103), to which an editorial note describes it as a valuable contribution to anthropology. Thus the foregoing leads us to conclude without question that the Celts of Brittany are worthy subjects of study in Anthropology; they *are* the 'Other'.

Brief History of Contact
The earliest recorded account of contact with Brittany comes from the travelling geographer Pytheas the Massaliot, in the fourth century BCE, although there may be references to Brittany in the older Massaliot periplus, which has been lost (Cunliffe, 2002, p. viii, 41-44). Pytheas recorded latitudinal readings on the peninsula prior to circumnavigating the island of Britain. Before the peninsula became known as Brittany, the province in Transalpine Gaul was part of the Roman *Tractus Armoricanus*, or Armorica (Smith, 1992, p. 10).

---

1.   Among others, i.e., his main thesis was to show global interconnectedness prior to the modern era.

Caius Julius Caesar claims in Book III, Chapter VIII of his Commentaries on the Gallic War, with regard to the Armoricans, that:

The influence of this state is by far the most considerable of any of the countries on the whole sea-coast, because the Venĕti [the dominant tribe] both have a very great number of ships, with which they have been accustomed to sail to Britain and [thus] excel the rest in their knowledge and experience of nautical affaires; and as only a few ports lie scattered along that stormy and open sea, of which they are in possession, they hold as tributaries almost all those who are accustomed to traffic that sea. (Caesar, 1896, p. 69).[2]

The connections between Armorica and the island of Britain being clearly stated by Caesar, nonetheless, Armorica did not become Brittany until the Roman Empire began to withdraw from its northern provinces in the fifth and sixth centuries, leaving them undefended from invasions by the 'Others' of *their* day:

L'anthropologie de la Bretagne et l'anthropologie de l'Angleterre se touchent par un autre point. La race historique qui a changé le nom *d'Armorique* en celui de *Bretagne* est celle qui a règné en Angleterre du 2ème ou 3ème siècle avant J. C. au 4ème siecle après, et qui alors a été refoulée par le Anglo-Saxons en partie dans le Pays de Galles, en partie dans la Cornouaille, d'où l'émigration bretonne est partie pour l'Armorique. (Topinard, 1898, p. 97)[3]

As Britain was invaded and colonized by Saxons, Angles, and Jutes from the east, and by the Irish from the west, refugees from the British regions of Wales and Cornwall fled to Armorica in Roman Gaul between the fifth and seventh centuries CE for succor (Cunliffe, 2003, p. 50-51), slightly later than Topinard indicates, above. Based on forensic linguistics, it appears that the new rulers of Armorica were chieftains from eastern Wales, but that the majority of the settlers were Cornish. The colonization appears to have been orderly, planned, and resulted in three main kingdoms: Domnonia, Cornouaille, and Bro Erech

---

2. In the modern era, the most famous Armorican of Caesar's time is the cartoon character, Astérix the Gaul, whose exploits against the Romans are popular entertainment fare for readers internationally.

3. The anthropology of Brittany and the anthropology of England touch on another point. The historical race that changed the name from Armorica to Brittany is that who prevailed in England from the 2nd or 3rd century before J.C. to the 4th century after, and who thereafter being driven back by the Anglo-Saxons, left from Wales and left from Cornwall, from whence the Bretons emigrated to Armorica [our translation].

(Chadwick, 1971, p. 81). Although the Natives appear to have accepted the newcomers, Gregory of Tours, describes battles between the *Bretons* and the Germanic Franks, who believed that the region was their inheritance from the Romans (Chadwick, 1971, p. 82).

Because Armorica was settled by so many British refugees, known as *Britanni*, Armorica took their name and became known as *Britannia*, from which we get its modern English name, 'Brittany' (Cunliffe, 2003, p. 103-105; Timm, 1973, p. 284-285). *Britannia* (in modern French Bretagne) had become the standard Latin usage by the time that Gregory of Tours, Venantius Fortunatus, and Marius of Avenches wrote in the sixth century, although the inhabitants of *Britannia* referred to themselves at *Letavii* (Smith, 1992, p. 12-13).[4] Pressure from the Frankish Carolingians caused the several petty kingdoms of Brittany to coalesce into a single, more or less independent duchy, a 'territorial principality' that endured through the Middle Ages, despite Frankish attempts at hegemony, in large part thanks to the *Bretons* widely regarded light cavalry (Smith, 1992, p. 3-4, 18-20).

In 826 Louis the Pious, son of Charlemagne, chose the native-born Breton aristocrat Nominoë to be his deputy, but Nominoë saw his chance in the Carolingian succession struggles between Louis' sons, and, leading the *Breton* knights, defeated Charles the Bald on 22 November, 848. Charles recognized Nominoë as duke, nonetheless, 'Nominoë was consecrated king of the Bretons by an envoy of the pope', and later was given the title of sovereign lord of Brittany by the holy Roman Emperor, making him 'the father of his country' (Reece, 1977, p. 7-8).

Viking and Norman raids caused the Frankish Kings to be more concerned with self defense than with consolidating any gains in the duchy. The *Bretons* were left, more or less, to their own devices, even to the point that Alain I used the title *rex* in the late ninth century, implying that the duchy was being considered a client kingdom, and Alain a dependent king. But the Viking menace led Alain to strengthen relations with the West Saxon kings of Britain (Smith, 1992, p. 189-197). Following the expulsion of the Normans by 937, Alain Barbetorte (Alain II) did not assume the title of king, and only retained the title of duke (this may be because of a childhood acquaintance while both Alain II and Louis IV were fostered at the court of Athelstan in England).

Despite this, Breton dukes and French kings chose to ignore each other until 1154, when Henry II of England, who also was duke of Aquitaine and

---

4. Arguably, for this reason the Breton language more likely resembles Welsh and Cornish than it does old Gaulish (except, perhaps, in the eastern part of the province). Ironically, the last Cornish speaker died in 1777, but Cornish (Revised Cornish) has been restored from written sources, with some of the holes patched from *Breton* (Cunliffe, 2003, p. 129-130).

Guyenne, and count of Anjou and Touraine, became duke of Normandy and spread his rule over Brittany (Reece, 1977, p. 10-11). The peninsula went back and forth between England and France until 1453, by when the English were expelled from everywhere on the mainland except Calais, although this did not secure Brittany for the French crown until 28 July, 1488, when Charles VIII defeated François II, the last Breton duke.

Following military occupation by the French, François II's successor, his daughter, Duchess Anne, formally capitulated and married Charles VIII in 1491, becoming queen of France (Reece, 1977, p. 14).[5] After the death of Charles, Anne also married his successor, Louis XII. Anne's ducal successor (and daughter), Claude, married Louis's successor, François I of France in 1513 and transferred the rights of *Breton* succession (some would say illegally), to the *dauphin*, after which François I united the crowns of Brittany and France. After 1536 he and the subsequent monarchs regarded Brittany as a province of France, although with a separate administration and relative autonomy until the Revolution 250 years later (Reece, 1977, p. 14-17). Nonetheless, in 1909 Henry Jenner, writing in the *Celtic Review*, claimed that 'The Heiress of Line of the ancient Ducal House of Brittany can be no other than her Royal Highness Princess Maria Theresa of Modena, Princess Louis of Bavaria' (1909, p. 54-55), whose pedigree would make her the heir to 'Celtia', 'Saxondom', and Normandy.

Ethnic Identity Today: Means of Preservation

Lois Kuter's excellent article, *Labeling People: Who are the Bretons? in Anthropological Quarterly* (1985) explores the different levels of identity in what it means to be *Breton*, who is more *Breton* than whom, and what makes someone *Breton* or French. The *Gallo* in the eastern, more French part of the peninsula accept that the westerners are the 'real Bretons'. The *Gallo* are more likely to rely on external expectations of what a *Breton should* be like for their clues as to how to express their cultural identity (Kuter, 1985, p. 18). Nonetheless, the Gallo are *Bretons*. What, then, constitutes ethnicity?

Ellen Badone argues that, although ethnicity has become an important theme in anthropology, self identification, or 'local identity' – identification with a particular locality, has not been a major theme, losing out in favor of borderland studies which focus on the relationship of ethnic boundaries with their larger nation-states, of which they are a part (Badone, 1987, p. 161-162). She identifies different levels of identity within Brittany (as does Kuter, above): linguistic, by Roman Catholic diocese, by local region, or *pays*, such as the

---

5. Anne often is represented as the symbol of Breton independence because of her resistance to the French, although she was only a teenager, prior to her marriage to Charles. Anne is considered a saint in Brittany.

Bigouden in Kernev (see below), by parish or commune, and by the least in-clusive level, *quartier*, or neighborhood within the parish (Badone, 1987, p. 163-164). The local *mentalité* may be the result of subsistence technology, local topography, return migration that can result in a 'greying' of the population, or the result of esoteric-exoteric folklore, that is, beliefs about themselves ver-sus beliefs about others – jokes, stories, rhymes, names, or turns of phrase, which serve as boundary maintenance devices and models for how to deal with others (Badone, 1987, p. 167-168). This was especially the case prior to road improvements in the 1960s, when rural isolation led people to rely on accumulated folk knowledge about the world. One such well known intra re-gional demarcation prior to the 1980s was by women's *coiffes*, or starched lace head coverings, embroidered velvet dress clothing, as well as by local speech (Badone, 1987, p. 171-172). 'The borders that the peasants knew best were symbolized by, say, a Bigouden waistcoat as distinguished from a Ploaré waist-coat, although the Bigouden and the Ploaré were merely a few leagues apart' (Hélias, 1978, p. 319).

Perhaps there is no one so identified with Breton cultural identity in the twentieth century as is Pierre-Jakez Hélias, Professor of Celtic at the University of Rennes, whose 1975 novelized autobiography, *Le Cheval d'Orgueil* (pub-lished in English as *The Horse of Pride: Life in a Breton Village* in 1978) com-prises a comprehensive ethnography of the Breton peasantry from Bigouden in the first half of the twentieth century.[6] Jeanine Picard describes the book 'As a semi-scientific inventory of a disappearing civilization' and 'As a work of eth-nology. This term [ethnology] traditionally used in France to define the disci-pline concerned with anthropological studies carried out in rural France, en-compasses social history and folklore of traditional peasant cultures' (Picard, 1999, p. 2). The title of Hélias' book comes from his grandfather's assertion that 'Since I am too poor to buy any other horse, at least the Horse of Pride will have a stall in my stable' (1978, p. v). Laurence Wylie, known for his ethnogra-phy of southern France, *Village in the Vaucluse* (1974), describes *The Horse of Pride* as 'an epic of peasant life in Brittany during the first half of this century. It is also an ethnographic description of a culture that has all but disappeared... *It is a case study in the quarrel over ethnicity*' [emphasis added] (1978, p.xi).

John K. Cox describes nationalism as a sense of belonging which links peo-ple through shared characteristics of language, history, customs or cultural traditions, and religion. When this feeling becomes political it can lead to ef-forts toward self-determination, or the perceived right to self-rule (1998, p. 29). Linguistic pride is a strong marker of ethnicity, and in the rebellious prov-

---

6.   Caveat: Xavier Grall wrote a scathing riposte to Le Cheval d'Orgueil entitled Le Cheval couché, in which he skewers Hélias for a backward-looking mummification of Breton culture and a political sellout (Picard, 1999, p. 59-66).

ince of Brittany the *Breton* language became a symbol of nationalism. Thus it was perceived to be a threat to French unity.

Brittany has been noted throughout history for its cultural and linguistic distinctiveness; it is relatively isolated geographically, and linguistic criteria divide the region into two sub-regions, Upper and Lower Brittany. Lower Brittany, in the west, is linguistically *Breton*, while Upper Brittany, in the east, is linguistically French and *Gallo*, a *Breton patois* (Badone, 1989, p. 1). *Breton* linguistic ambiguity not only was found with French, but with the Latin and Greek that the peasants heard in church, as well: Hélias relates how *Kyrie eleison*, 'Lord have mercy', was mistaken for the *Breton* 'Kirri eleiz 'so', 'there are lots of wagons', although none were in sight of the congregation. Likewise, he illustrates that Pontius Pilate must have knocked Christ to the ground, they believed, because *pilad* is *Breton* for 'to knock over' (1978, p. 92-93).

Hélias, a native speaker of *Breton*, was forced to swallow his ethnic pride to obtain a scholarship to a French speaking *lycée* in Quimper, where he and his companions, still struggling with book French, felt themselves to be on foreign ground 'For seven years, condemned to speaking and listening in French without stop... We were punished for speaking *Breton*. Besides, no one seemed to remember that we had been transplanted, that *we were immigrants living in a civilization foreign to our own*' [emphasis added] (1978, p. 304-305).[7]

Besides language, religion too can be seen as a source of ethnic identity, especially when the priests speak their congregation's own language, in this case *Breton* – even if the dialect used came from a different region (Hélias, 1978, p. 91), and the annual cycle of the *Breton* peasants revolved around the Roman Catholic calendar. Nonetheless, the ancient Celtic religion, what Hélias refers to as the 'Cult of the dead', persisted syncretistically within Roman Catholicism (1978, p. 104). This appears to be especially the case with the *Ankou* and death imagery, as described for Lower Brittany by Ellen Badone in *The Appointed Hour: Death, Worldview and Social Change in Brittany* (1989), and the following section is abstracted from that book:

> The Breton fixation with death and the dead has been remarked upon by a number of observers and collectors of Breton deathlore since the 19th century, when the region's people believed that the souls of the dead continued to lead everyday lives, just as they had when they were alive, in a community called Anaon.[8] Death is personified as a skeletal figure known as the Ankou, which is dressed in a shroud and holds a scythe in its hand.

---

7. Ironically, in the cinematic version of The Horse of Pride, the Bretons are speaking French. There is a rather bemusing scene in which Hélias, as a boy, is told – in French - that he must go to school to learn to speak French.
8. This is parallel to the Welsh Underworld, *Annwn*, which Miranda Green describes as

Badone reports that many of her subjects believe that the process of death commences when they retire and return to the community into which they had been born, and where they will stay after they have died. This is accepted and advance preparations are made for their funerary rituals to reduce fear by making it familiar. Although the process of death may be frightening, low birthrates and high mortality rates make the state of death an accepted fact: death is preferable to suffering. Hélias (1978) tells several stories of individuals who actively sought death to escape the World Bitch (*la Chienne du Monde*), that pursues people to bring them insurmountable and unending troubles.

Because of the migration of young people to large cities and retirees' return migration, people pass through all the major rites of passage, such as the Roman Catholic sacraments, with members of their own age cohort, including death, which involves a series of rites, some of which entail what Badone considers to be denial of death's finality. Badone's analysis recurs to Arnold van Gennep's rites of separation, rites of transition, and rites of incorporation from his book, *The Rites of Passage* (*Les Rites des Passages*) (1988).[9] The sacrament of extreme unction is a rite of separation of the dying person from the community of the living. The individual's death brings on a liminal period from the passing away to the burial. The funeral itself is the rite of transition and the interment is the rite of incorporation into the community of the dead.

Because Roman Catholics believe that one's lesser sins during life can be redressed after death by suffering in Purgatory, those left behind will offer masses and services as a social obligation for the souls of the departed to lessen their periods of suffering prior to entering into heaven, and lists of mourners who have contributes masses are read at the funerals (this practice is disappearing), demonstrating that the social networks formed in life are not extinguished at death. Masses for the dead include the *messe de huitanine* after one week and the *messe d'anniversaire* one year after a death to ensure that the memory of the dead continue in the minds of those left behind and to reinforce the entry of the deceased into *Anaon*.

In rural Brittany the transition of the dead from the living realm into *Anaon* reaches an intersection at the cemetery, and those who have died continue an existence there in body and soul, neither condemned to hell nor exalted in heaven, but sleeping where they can be visited by the living. This is an ancient,

---

being similar to earthly life (1993, p. 12), and we can see the obvious historical reasons for the connection above. Interestingly, Bronislaw Malinowski reported a similar belief in the *baloma* spirits on the island of Tuma in the Trobriand Islands (1992).

9. Hélias describes a rite of passage that involves changing one's clothing style as the trouser ceremony: small boys, who had been dressed the same as girls until the age of five or six, became little men when they acquired their first pair of trousers, following which a feast was given for close relatives (1978, p. 49-51). This parallels Conrad Arensberg's description from County Clare, Ireland, but without the feast (1988, p. 64).

pre-Christian belief which is definitive of the *Breton* variety of Roman Catholicism, and its roots can be traced folkloristically back to Celtic religion, as can the *Ankou*, the personification of Death. This syncretism of Celtic and Roman Catholic beliefs can be found in three festivals, all associated with death: All Saints' Day, which comes from the Celtic *Samhain*, the start of winter; the midsummer feast of Saint John corresponds to the Celtic solstice practices; and Palm Sunday, in which boxwood is substituted for palms and placed in fields to guarantee good harvests, and in barns for good fortune. The syncretism of Celtic and Roman Catholic beliefs also can be found 'Calvaries', large, graphic, raised monuments depicturing the death of Jesus Christ in brutal detail.

Until the mid to later twentieth century, Catholicism in Brittany focused on the afterlife and salvation (by specific ritual observations, such as observing the sacraments and praying the Rosary) versus damnation. One way to salvation was by participating in *pardons*, processions and church services on saints' feast days. The name, *pardon*, comes from the indulgences granted to the attendees. Proper observances can lead to happiness in the next world, which would make up for poverty and suffering in this world. Ritual performance in Latin added to its sacrality.

The nineteenth century *Breton* view resembles modern beliefs in parallel universes occupying the same time and space, but in different dimensions – in this case the dimension of time: the living had the diurnal world; the dead had the nocturnal world. Good people were locked in their houses when the dead walked the earth. Secularization in the twentieth century has rationalized many of these old beliefs, but contemporary *Breton* ethos recurs to these ancient, syncretized beliefs, and even modern witches use Catholic terminology when practicing sorcery.

Breton culture has made some adjustments, in addition to forced language change, in order to syncretize with the larger, dominant French culture, such as exchanging the traditional bombard for the oboe in musical performances. Other adjustments were made within the modern, swelling, non-Western 'Celtic sea' that flows, ignored by many in academia, below the surface of Western Culture,[10] among which is the growing replacement of the Breton bagpipes with the larger Scottish highland pipes.

Despite Simon James' arguments that (at least in Britain and Ireland) the term 'Celt' was not even in common usage until after 1700 (1999, p. 33), and

---

10. We introduce and use the term 'Celtic sea', with a lower case 's', not to refer to the body of water between Brittany, Ireland, and Cornwall, but to the Celtic Movement for recognition as being distinct from the Great Traditions of Europe, of which they often mistakenly are considered to be a part. We refer to it as 'non-Western' because Western culture traces its European, as distinct from its Biblical, origins to the Greeks and Romans. The Greeks' and Romans' opposites, their Celtic enemies, therefore are non-Western.

it entered usage as part of what Cunliffe refers to as eighteenth and nineteenth century 'Celtomania' (2003, p. 117-121), we would argue that, in the modern era, the disparate inheritors of the Celtic tradition are *recovering* their distinct cultural identity, not just inventing it. Cunliffe concurs: 'The past does not have to be reinvented but simply called to mind' (2003, p. 135). Patrick Galliou, of the *Centre de Recherche Bretonne et Celtique, Université de Bretagne Occidentale*, in Brest, clearly is of the opinion that:

> ...Armorica was part of a complex network of technical and stylistic influences interlinking the major 'cultural' zones of Celtic Europe, which developed to a substantial extent in the early phases of the La Tène period. ...It would, however, be wrong to restrict the 'Celticisation' of the Armorican peninsula to the mere side-effects of long distance 'trade' connections, since it is now certain that the spiritual world of the local Iron Age communities was closely similar to that of other Celtic tribes... Armorica was fully integrated into the Celtic world by a long and complex process combining internal social changes with cultural interchange. (Galliou, 1995, p. 19)

Celticism in France received a cultural and archeological B-12 shot from the efforts of Napoleon III in the mid nineteenth century to trace the Gauls' campaigns against Caesar in the first century BCE. The Breton reaction was that they were the only true Celts in France, because only their peninsula had not been settled by the invading Germanic Franks, Burgundians, and Visigoths (Cunliffe, 2003, p. 125-126). Thus the first Interceltic Congress was held at Saint-Brieuc in Brittany in 1867, to which Vicomte Hersart de La Villemarqué issued invitations to delegates from Cornwall, Ireland, Wales, and Scotland, while the French government 'Was actively suppressing Breton Culture and language (Cunliffe, 2003, p. 126).

The 'Celtic sea' also washes onto Brittany in the form of a series of local Celtic folk festivals. Hélias argues that the most important of all were The Great Fêtes of Cornouille, which were founded in Quimper in 1948 and swelled to several thousand 'Dancers, musicians, and singers giving regular performances and drawing crowds estimated by the police at over a hundred thousand', as well as the Brest Bagpipe Festival (1978, p. 328). Cunliffe also cites *La nuit de la saucisse* (The Night of the Sausage – which combines traditional *Breton* music and food) in Plestin, Côtes-d'Armor every July. This is followed two weeks later by the *fête folklorique* in the commune of Ploulec'h, which combines an afternoon exhibition of folkloristic village life with evening meals and folk dancing and singing. According to Cunliffe, the Brest Bagpipes Festival has been eclipsed by the Interceltique Festival held in L'Orient held every August, and which draws over half a million visitors per year to performances by groups from all the Celtic-speaking regions (2003, p. 133-135). The interested reader may see scenes from some of these festivals on the internet at http://www.antourtan.org/#

which also is an excellent guide to the events.

Sovereignty Issues and Relations with National (and Local) Government(s)

Michael Orwicz argues that *Breton* religious practices were indispensable to political schemes by the Opportunist and Conservative parties in the late nineteenth century: the Roman Catholic Church's acceptance or denial of the parties was critical to the mobilization of the rural vote. Anticlerical legislation in late nineteenth century France led many peasants to abandon Catholic practices – and thus also the electoral power base of the monarchists and conservatives – except in Brittany, where voters were exhorted from the pulpit so often and vociferously that the conservative *Breton* priests became the subject of a Senate investigation in the 1880s, when their exhortations began to affect the Opportunists national preeminence. The Republican Party,[11] Orwicz contends, saw the disappearance of a regional culture, like conservative, patriarchal, Catholic Brittany, as a chance to increase its own national consequence. Thus the *Bretons* were described by Republicans as rude, barbaric, superstitious, isolationist, and who practiced Catholicism for diversion rather than from conviction (Orwicz, 1987, p. 295-296). Ironically:

> To the consternation of Brittany's ultraconservatives, the religious issue was unexpectedly removed from Breton politics in the early 1890s by none other than Pope Leo XIII himself. Advising the faithful that there was no necessary contradiction between Catholicism and republicanism, he specifically urged French Catholics to rally to the Third Republic in order to counteract the growing strength of the socialists. (Reece, 1977, p. 51)

Nonetheless, priests were effectively barred from preaching in *Breton* following the uprising of August, 1902. Parish priests had to submit quarterly performance reports to the state that included verified residence certificate in order to be paid. Beginning on September 29, 1902 the local mayor had to confirm that the priest was a French national who had preached to his congregation in the French language, not in *Breton*, with potential income consequences. The salaries of twenty priests were withheld and some were prosecuted. 'The peasantry of Finistere, twenty years after the introduction of a universal, free educational system in the 1880s, remained ignorant of the French language, as interpreters were needed in the trials of those arrested during the resistance of 1902' (Ford, 1990, p. 25-26).

---

11. Outside of the United States of America, 'Republican' often refers to 'liberal' or 'radical', rather than 'conservative', and that is how it is used in Orwicz' context, i.e. non-conservative.

This rapprochement between religion and cultural identity is evident in Hélias' use of religious terminology to describe secular *Breton* culture: for Hélias the *Breton* 'Old Testament' began to die on August 22, 1937 when a bronze monument was erected to traditional Breton musicians: bagpipers and oboists (1978, p. 315). There was no need to erect a monument to that which still was alive.

Hudson Meadwell argues in *Forms of Cultural Mobilization in Québec and Brittany, 1870-1914* (1983), that the *Breton* elite depended on the maintenance and control of traditional social structures and local resources for its power. The July Revolution and the Third Republic returned the nobility and the monarchists to the countryside from Paris, leading the rural gentry to clash with the Republic. Fears for their social positions led the upper class to cultural mobilization on the peninsula. They formed agricultural cooperatives and cultural and language organizations in self defense against the government's attempts at cultural hegemony:

'Local elites played a leading role in the formation of the Union Regionaliste Bretonne in 1898… [in] a strategy of mobilization that emphasized the unitary but hierarchical nature of Breton rural society and the natural links between the Breton elite and the peasantry against the incursions of the French state. (Meadwell, 1983, p. 405-406].

The elite soon lost control of *Breton* cultural mobilization which began to fragment in the 1920s with the formation of the *Parti Autonomiste Breton*, when control of the cultural movement shifted away from the elite and into the hands of cultural special interest groups, especially after the war (Meadwell, 1983, p. 10).

In the mid twentieth century Brittany was devastated and reconstructed. The causes were multiple, but essentially Brittany's strategic location and excellent harbors led the Germans during the Second World War occupation to construct large submarine bases that the allies, in turn, bombed – including the surrounding towns. After a series of conflicting orders and tanks moving west, then east, then west again, Allied forces headed west into the heart of Brittany in 1944, only to be stunned by the unexpectedly heavy German defenses that they found, including mined harbors that protected important U-boat bases with 25,000 troops at L'Orient and 30,000 troops at Brest. It was decided that the bases' formidability required not tanks, which were left to seal off the port cities, but air strikes (Ganz, 1995, p. 88-95). After the war the devastated towns were cleared and planned reconstruction began under the Ministry of Re-construction and Urbanism. Brest, L'Orient and Saint-Nazaire, were reconstructed in modern architectural styles, but Saint-Malo was restored to a prewar architectural style (Clout, 2000).

The Nazi occupation was seen by some *Breton* nationalists as their opportunity to strike for independence from France just as Ireland had used the

English preoccupation in Europe as its chance for independence from England (also with German assistance) in the previous world war. Thus Kristian Hamon writes: "'England's difficulty is Ireland's opportunity": *cette célèbre maxime irlandais va tout naturellement inspirer une certain vision nationaliste de l'histoire du Mouvement Breton pendant la deuxième guerre mondiale'* (2001, p. 13-14).[12] Thus a circumstance of history was seen as a way for the *Mouvement Breton* to ally with the enemies of their oppressors without compromising either their politics or their ideology.

Hamon points out that modern cultural identity groups, such as *emsav* (see below), are only the most recent links in a chain of groups in '*le Mouvement breton*'; prior to *emsav* there were such twentieth century groups as *l'Union régionaliste bretonne* (URB), the *Groupe régionaliste Breton* (GRB), the *Unvaniez Yaouankiz Vreiz* (*Union de la jeunesse de Bretagne*) (UYV), which transformed into the *Parti autonomiste breton*, (PAB) (although the PAB rejected separatism, opting instead for autonomy within France), as well as others (2001, p. 21-22). Unfortunately, '*Bretons, nationalists intégraux, les militants n'hésitent pas à se réclaimer du national-socialisme d'Adolf Hitler. Heuresment, leur influence se limite à quelques bistrots de la rue Saint-Malo à Rennes*' (2001, p. 24).[13] The *Parti National de Breton* (PNB), which was modeled after the Irish liberation movement (see above), was dissolved by degree in 1939 because of the perceived menace of its ties to Germany (Hamon, 2001, p. 31).

Under German occupation, PNB was revived, but, although it was based in Celticism, the stigma of its alliance with the Nazis led to its disbandonment after the war. As Jean-Jacques Monnier argues in the preface to Hamon's *Les Nationalistes Bretons Sous L'Occupation*, the Breton nationalists only were playing the hand that they had been dealt by circumstance; the separatists played the German card, and the majority continued to play the autonomy card within the French state (2001, p. 8). Nonetheless, their association with the German occupation left *Breton* nationalism with an embarrassing post-war black-eye. Ironically, a large percentage of the French Resistance to Nazi Germany was composed of *Bretons* (Kuter, 1985, p. 21).

Ironically, the deprivations experienced during the German occupation in the following decade led to a temporary resurgence of peasant solidarity and communalism (Hélias, 1978, p. 316). Stephen L. Harp, in a review of Sharif Gemie's 2007 book, *Brittany, 1750–1950: The Invisible Nation*, argues that the Vichy period was particularly important as a catalyst to internecine coopera-

---

12. That celebrated Irish maxim completely naturally went on to inspire a certain nationalist vision of the history of the Breton Movement following the Second World War [our translation].

13. Breton nationalists, integrated with militants, did not hesitate to require Adolf Hitler's National Socialism. Fortunately, their influence was limited to a few bistros on the Rue Saint-Malo at Rennes [our translation].

tion among the *Breton* factions, despite their collaboration with the occupational forces:

> ...the extensive cooperation of Catholics, Protestants, anticlericals, and communists in the Resistance tended to break down long-standing social barriers impeding a sense of Breton cultural identity that went beyond the traditional nineteenth-century religious and secular divides. Thus after the war, a cultural construction of a distinct Breton identity thrived, while notions of Breton political independence had been discredited by the association of Breton nationalists with collaboration. (Harp, 2008, p. 928)

This perspective reiterates James view that the Atlantic Celts only saw themselves as a cultural group by way of their opposition to outside pressures (1999).

In *'We Are Not French!': Language, Culture and Identity in Brittany* (1989), Maryon McDonald argues that in the elate twentieth century the *Breton* language was militantly defended as a major point of cultural identity by (often) non *Breton* speaking urbanites in the *Breton* movement, or *emsav*,[14] who are astute in the uses of the media: 'As a *self-ascription*, however, it tends to be limited to those fighting for a specifically 'Breton' world in which the Breton language figures prominently', as well as folk music, folk dances, and sometimes political organizations (1989, p. 73-74, emphasis in original). Militants sometimes compare their situation to the contemporary Northern Irish situation and even have consulted with *Sinn Fein*[15] on visits to Northern Ireland, although McDonald finds this to be a political and economic mismatch (1989, p. 147-48).

Nonetheless, Al Jazeera reported on Nov 04, 2003 that five people were arrested on suspicion of providing support for a Northern Irish IRA breakaway faction, 'The Real IRA'. The arrests were made in the *département* Seine-Maritime of Normandy, and in the *département* Côte d 'Armor of Brittany. The *Armée Breton Révolutionnaire* (ARB) which is believed to have supported a Basque separatist group, ETA, in Spain also may have been behind the bombing of a McDonald's restaurant in Brittany that killed a female employee in 2000 (also in Cunliffe, 2003, p. 131).

McDonald contrasts *emsav* with her research in the rural milieu, which she found beyond 'a symbolic boundary, marking off 'real anthropology' country' (1989, p. 222) from the eastern part of the peninsula. In the 'real anthropol-

---

14. Proponents are known as an *emsaverien or ar stourmerien* in Breton, and as *les militants* in French (McDonald 1989, p. 74).

15. *Sinn Fein* (Irish *Gaeilge* for 'Ourselves Alone' or 'We, Ourselves') is a nationalist Republican party in Northern Ireland that now is legal in the Republic of Ireland, as well, although it was not at the time of McDonald's research.

ogy' country, the *commune of Plounéour-Ménez*, she found native speakers of *Breton* attempting to live up to the ideals of the French Revolution and Republicanism, glad that they had learned French, and who had viewed the more recent establishment of *Breton*-medium education by *Diwan*[16] to be nonsensical (1989, p. 237-242).

In a review of McDonald's book, Nancy C. Dorian finds a disjuncture between the real heirs of the old tradition, the rural people, and the romantic expectations of them by zealous outsiders who have come lately to the region. Dorian expects that the new comers must appear inauthentic and foolish, but she opines that their 'intrusive presence is a necessary irritant, essential to halting or slowing the steady erosion of a minority language' (1991, p. 509). We concur and compare this to John Messenger's definition of a nativistic movement as a 'conscious, organized attempt by members of a society to revive or perpetuate selected elements of its Indigenous culture under conditions of acculturation with dominance' to provide psychological compensation for cultural coordination (1983, p. 3). It is within this context of Irish nativism that Arthur Griffith founded the successful Gaelic League in Ireland in the late nineteenth century and was able to preserve and to pass on a moribund culture to future generations, who may have lost it, had it not been for Griffith's revitalization movement.[17] We see this recurring in Brittany with McDonald's emsav militants, and we suggest that critics may be considering them too harshly.

The according to the website http://www.skolanemsav.bzh/ , June 19, 2016 was the starting point for the nineteenth *Skol an Emsav* in Rennes, in which adults can learn and practice Breton and chat online about it. *Skol an Emsav* had an open house on September 03, 2016, in which interested parties could come and participate in what it means to be Breton in the twenty first century. For those wanting an English language experience of Brittany and an understanding of the Diwan programs, they may wish to visit the International Committee for the Defense of the Breton Language - U.S. Branch at http://icdbl.org/index.php, which provides a newsletter, histories, maps, information on music, language lessons, including how to learn Breton for non-speakers of French, linguist family charts, and links to Breton organizations.

Ellen Badone has observed rapid changes in Brittany during the second half of the twentieth century: agricultural *remembrement* has reorganized the small, scattered holdings of individual owners into larger, geographically

---

16. *Diwan* is *Breton* for 'seed' or 'germination' and is the name of a militant *Breton*-medium education organization (McDonald 1989, p. 175).

17. Revitalization movements were described by Anthony F. C. Wallace (1956) to explain how societies threatened by acculturation attempted to, or were able to, preserve their heritage syncretistically within their new context.

consolidated units and destroyed hedgerows and stone walls to facilitate the larger fields and access to them by modern machinery – destroying old *Breton* landmark names and their links to the past. The paleotechnic *Breton* peasant has become the neotechnic agriculturalist[18] specializing in cash crops and live-stock production. The push/pull of urban jobs has resulted in rural depopula-tion and the growth of urban estate housing (Badone, 1991, p. 532-533). Paved highways, electricity, piped water, telephones, and television have transformed *Breton* life parallel to George Foster's description of the changes that took place in Tzintzuntzan, Mexico under the same influences (Foster, 1988, p. np), and which we have observed in western Ireland between the late 1970s and the present.

Badone argues that:

> These changes have altered the very sounds, tastes, and textures of ex-perience for people…, divorcing them from the peasant world in which they grew up. The…creation of history stems from a need to come to terms with this past world and to integrate it in a coherent fashion with the ever-changing, future-oriented present. While such a need may exist to some extent in all cultural contexts at all times, it is intensified by the radical disjuncture with the past in places like contemporary Brittany, where the majority of adults have experienced massive social change in their own lifetime. This need to integrate the past with the present has motivated people throughout Brittany to join archaeology societies that run excavations and carry out archival research about local history. (1991, p. 533).

Outlook for the Future

A *Breton* historian of our acquaintance has related to us that, although his grandmother was a fluent speaker of *Breton*, she refused to speak it to her grandchildren because of the harsh punishments with which the children were dealt for speaking *Breton* at school when she was a girl. He believed that she almost was embarrassed to know the language because of the severe local ef-fects of the French policy of homogenization on the ethnic regions (personal communication). For this reason, he, his siblings, and his parents know only a very few words of their own language. Hélias wrote more than 35 years ago that one of his militant friends estimated that *Breton* would be spoken by only 25,000 people by the year 2000 (1978, p. 344), yet today *Breton* is spoken by about 200,000 people. However, that is only one fifth of the estimated million people who spoke it prior to the Second World War, according to *Al Jazeera's*

---

18. Neotechnic and paleotechnic are rural ecotypes described by Eric Wolf in his book, *Peasants* (1966), to analyze complexity levels of farming technologies.

English language broadcast on Saturday, May 15, 2010, which reported that the region is endeavoring to save the *Breton* language from dying. *Al Jazeera's* Estelle Youssouffa reports that campaigners believe the language can make a comeback. We agree that this will be the case, thanks to groups like *emsav* and *Diwan* that are working to preserve it, despite the efforts at homogenization:

> No one ever really knew enough about country people. Never did the members of the government bother to find out what stuff they were made of... the main reason was that they were taken for simple people; thus everyone had the impression that they understood the peasants' needs better than the peasants themselves did... They were in fact what is called "le peuple," the common people. *Plebs* in Latin, *plou* in Breton. That probably accounts for their having been called *ploucs*, implying "dumb hicks." Yet they were the people who came closest to being the nobility of the land, the true gentry, who had struck roots in our country and had shaped its face. (Hélias, 1978, p. 319)

> 'For too long the cultural and political importance of minority identities have been of secondary concern to EU elites in their efforts ... to be homogenized into a national culture... The perceived rights and needs of EU minorities (i.e. races, classes, women, workers, interest groups, and *nations striving for self-determination*, among others) are powerful forces that the legislators of the EU must address'. [emphasis added] (Wilson, 2000, p. 140)

Currently, the EU requires that Indigenous languages must be used, at least in translations, if requested by Members of the European Parliament. The effect of this on minority populations is problematic, but positive in terms of engendering ethnic pride (although it does not always support indigenous fishing and farming practices). Now that the peasant era, with its poverty and privations is safely in the past, symbols of that cultural past now are taking on the cache of a proud ethnic identity. An example of proud ethnic identity was evident on July 5, 2011, when *France 2* television's 8:00 AM News (http://jt.france2.fr/8h/) showed scenes from the *Breton* leg of the *Tour* holding pro-*Breton* signs and waving Breton, not French, flags. We would argue that *Breton* cultural resurgence is a healthy and thriving phenomenon, especially within the context of the Celtic sea.

References

Arensberg, Conrad M.
1988 (1937). *The Irish Countryman: An Anthropological Study*. Prospect Heights, Ill.: Waveland Press, Inc.

Arensberg, Conrad and Solon T. Kimball.
1974 (1940). *Family and Community in Ireland*. Cambridge: Harvard University Press.

Badone, Ellen.
1987. Ethnicity, Folklore, and Local Identity in Rural Brittany. *The Journal of American Folklore* Vol. 100, No. 396 (Apr. - Jun., 1987), 161-190.

Badone, Ellen.
1989. *The Appointed Hour: Death, World View, and Social Change in Brittany*. Berkeley: University of California Press.

Badone, Ellen.
1991. Ethnography, Fiction, and the Meanings of the Past in Brittany. *American Ethnologist Representations of Europe: Transforming State, Society, and Identity*. Vol. 18, No. 3, (Aug., 1991), 518-545.

Caesar, Caius Julius.
1896. First Eight Books of Caesar's Commentaries on the Gallic War: Literally Translated with Explanatory Notes, Edward Brooks, Jr., translator. New York: David McKay, Inc.

Chadwick, Nora.
1971. *The Celts: A Lucid and Fascinating History*. London: Penguin Books.

Clout, Hugh.
2000. Place Annihilation and Urban Reconstruction: The Experience of Four Towns in Brittany, 1940 to 1960. *Geografiska Annaler. Series B, Human Geography*, Vol. 82, No. 3 (2000), 165-180.

Cox, John K.
1998. *Nationalism. In Introducing Global Issues*, Michael T. Snarr and D Neil Snarr, eds. Boulder: Lynne Rienner Publishers. pp 29-44.

Cunliffe, Barry
2002 (2001). *The Extraordinary Voyage of Pytheas The Greek*. New York: Walker and Company.

Cunliffe, Barry.
2003. *The Celts: A Very Short Introduction*. Oxford: Oxford University Press.

Dorian, Nancy C.
1991. Review of Language and Hierarchy in Britain and France, by R. D. Grillo and "We Are Not French!": Language, Culture and Identity in Brittany, by Maryon McDonald. *American Anthropologist, New Series*, Vol. 93, No. 2 (Jun., 1991), 507-509.

Ford, Caroline.
1990. Religion and the Politics of Cultural Change in Provincial France: The Resistance of 1902 in Lower Brittany. *The Journal of Modern History*, Vol. 62, No. 1 (Mar., 1990), 1-33.

Foster, George.
1988 (1967). Preface, 1979. In *Tzintzuntzan: Mexican Peasants in a Changing World*. Prospect Heights, Illinois: Waveland Press.

Galliou, Patrick.
1995. Brittany and the Celtic World. *Archaeology Ireland*, Vol. 9, No. 2 (Summer, 1995), 13-14.

Ganz, A. Harding.
1995 Questionable Objective: The Brittany Ports, 1944. *The Journal of Military History*, Vol. 59, No. 1 (Jan., 1995), 77-95.

Green, Miranda Jane.
1993. *Celtic Myths*. Austin: University of Texas Press, Published in cooperation with The Trustees of the British Museum.

Hamon, Kristian.
2001. *Les Nationalistes Bretons Sous L'Occupation*. Kergleuz: An Here.

Harp, Stephen L.
2008. Review of Brittany, 1750–1950: The Invisible Nation, by Sharif Gemie. *The American Historical Review*, Vol. 113, No. 3 (June 2008), 927-928.

Hélias, Pierre-Jakez.
1978 (1975). The Horse of Pride (*Le Cheval d'Orgueil*), June Guicharnaud, translater. New Haven: Yale University Press.

James, Simon.
1999. *The Atlantic Celts: Ancient People or Modern Invention?* Madison: The University of Wisconsin Press.

Jenner, Henry.
1909. Who Is the Heir of the Duchy of Brittany? *The Celtic Review*, Vol. 6, No. 21 (Jul., 1909), 47-55.

Kuter, Lois.
1985. Labeling People: Who Are the Bretons? *Anthropological Quarterly*, Vol. 58, No. 1 (Jan., 1985), 13-29.

Llobera, Josep R.
1994. Anthropological Approaches to the study of Nationalism in Europe: The Work of Van Gennep and Mauss. In *The Anthropology of Europe: Identities and Boundaries in Conflict*, Victoria A. Goddard, Josep R. Llobera, and Cris Shore, eds. Oxford: Berg, pp. 93-111.

Malinowski, Bronislaw.
1992 (1916). Baloma; The Spirits of the Dead. In *Magic, Science and Religion: And Other Essays*. Prospect Heights, Illinois: Waveland Press.

McDonald, Maryon.
1989. *'We are not French!': Language, culture and identity in Brittany*. Routledge: London.

Meadwell, Hudson.
1983. Forms of Cultural Mobilization in Québec and Brittany, 1870-1914. *Comparative Politics*, Vol. 15, No. 4 (Jul., 1983), 401-417.

Messenger, John C.
1983 (1969). *Inis Beag: Isle of Ireland*. Prospect Heights, Illinois: Waveland Press.

Monnier, Jean-Jacques.
2001. Préface. In *Les Nationalistes Bretons Sous L'Occupation*, Kristian Hamon, author. Kergleuz: An Here.

Orwicz, Michael.
1987. Criticism and Representations of Brittany in the Early Third Republic. *Art Journal*, Vol. 46, No. 4, The Political Unconscious in Nineteenth-Century Art (Winter, 1987), 291-298

Parman, Susan.
1998 The Meaning of "Europe" in the American Anthropologist (Part I). In *Europe in the Anthropological Imagination*, Susan Parman, ed. Upper Saddle River, NJ: Prentice Hall, pp169-196.

Picard, Jeanine.
1999. *Le Cheval d'Orgueil*. Glasgow: University of Glasgow French and German Publications.

Redfield, Robert.
1960. *The Little Community and Peasant Society and Culture*. Chicago: University of Chicago Press.

Reece, Jack E.
1977. *The Bretons against France: Ethnic Minority Nationalism in Twentieth-Century Brittany*. Chapel Hill, NC: University of North Carolina Press.

Shutes, Mark T.
1998. The Place of Europe in George P. Murdock's Anthropological Theory. In *Europe in the Anthropological Imagination*, Susan Parman, ed. Upper Saddle River, NJ: Prentice Hall, pp157-168.

Simonton, Michael.
2010. Europe: Past and Present. In *Twenty-first Century Anthropology*, H. James Birx, ed. Thousand Oaks, CA: Sage Publications, Vol. 2, 716-724.

Smith, Julia M.H.
1992. *Province and Empire: Brittany and the Carolingians*. Cambridge: Cambridge University Press.

Timm, L.A.
1973. Modernization and Language Shift: The Case of Brittany. *Anthropological Linguistics* Vol. 15, No. 6 (Sep., 1973), 281-298.

Tönnies, Ferdinand.
1957 (1887). *Community and Society: Gemeinschaft und Gesellschaft*. Charles P. Loomis trans., ed. East Lansing: The Michigan State University Press. pp. 223-231.

Topinard, Paul.
1898. On the Anthropology of Brittany. *The Journal of the Anthropological Institute of Great Britain and Ireland*, Vol. 27(1898), 96-103.

Van Gennep, Arnold.
1988 (1909). *The Rites of Passage*. Chicago: The University of Chicago Press.

Wallace, Anthony F.C.
1956. Revitalization Movements. *American Anthropologist, New Series*, Vol. 58, No. 2 (Apr., 1956), 264-281.

Wilson, Thomas M.
2000. Agendas in Conflict: Nation, State and Europe in the Northern Ireland Borderlands. In *An Anthropology of the European Union: Building, Imagining and Experiencing the New Europe*, Irène Bellier and Thomas M. Wilson, eds. Oxford: Berg. pp 137-158.

Wolf, Eric.
1966. Peasants. Englewood Cliffs, NJ: Prentice-Hall, Inc.

Wolf, Eric
1982. *Europe and the People without History*. Berkeley: University of California Press.

Wylie, Laurence.
1974 (1957). *Village in the Vaucluse*. Cambridge, Mass.: Harvard University Press.

Wylie, Laurence.
1978. Forword. In Pierre-Jakez Hélias, *The Horse of Pride*. New Haven: Yale University Press. pp xi-xvii.

PART III

Indigenous Peoples in the Less
Developed Second and Third Worlds

Yanomami of Venezuela

Douglas W. Hume

Northern Kentucky University

If my people are wiped out you must destroy all photographs of us, because future generations will look at our photographs and be too ashamed at such a crime against humanity. - Davi Kopenawa Yanomami

The Yanomami[1] are an Indigenous tribe inhabiting the Alto Orinoco River region, which borders Brazil and Venezuela. The Yanomami have endured many assaults on and barriers to their survival from external and internal sources including: endemic warfare between groups, introduced diseases, invasive gold mining, and unethical misconduct of medical and anthropological researchers. Due to the remoteness of their territory, a reliable census of the Yanomami cannot be obtained, however, there is a general consensus amongst anthropologists that the Yanomami's population has decreased significantly over the past century, even though the degree of the reduction cannot be assessed. Currently, it is estimated that of the approximately 35,000 Yanomami, 15,000 of which are in Brazil and 20,000 in Venezuela. The Yanomami's language, Yanoama, has four major dialectical groups: Sanema (15%), Yanam (4%), Yanomam (25%), and Yanoama (56%) (Hames & Bierle, 1995).

The Yanomami are one of the most widely known tribes of South America, largely due to Napoleon Chagnon's seminal ethnography *Yanomamö: The Fierce People* (1968) Kenneth Good and David Chanoff's *Into the Heart: One Man's Pursuit of Love and Knowledge Among the Yanomami* (1997); and Peter Rose and Anne Conlon's *Yanomamo* (1983), a choral work famously narrated by Sir David Attenborough (in the British Broadcast version) and Sting (in the American Broadcast version). Chagnon's ethnography was and continues to be widely used in introductory anthropology courses and has sold more than a million copies (Eakin, 2013). Good and Chanoff's book became a media sensation due to Good's marriage to a young Yanomami woman, bringing her and their children to live the United States. Rose and Conlon's choral work was broadcast widely in Great Britain and the United States, resulting in many people in both countries becoming familiar with the Yanomami. The attention that the Yanomami have received from academic and popular media has brought their fight for cultural survival into public view.

Due to the remoteness of their territory, the Yanomami had limited and intermittent contact with outsiders until the early twentieth century. Beginning in the 1940s, the Serviço de Proteção ao Índio (Brazil's protection agency for its Indigenous people, now called Fundação Nacional do Índio, FUNAI) as well as several evangelical and Catholic missionaries entered Yanomami territory (Albert, 1999a). In the years following this contact, the Yanomami

---

1. The most common current spelling is Yanomami, but may also be spelled Yanomama, Yanomamo, and Yanomamö. For an explanation of the Yanomami ethnonym, see Albert, 1999b).

were encouraged by missionaries to become more sedentary as well as take advantage of newly introduced goods (i.e., steel tools and other manufactured objects) and services (i.e., healthcare and minimal educational services). This contact and enticements that caused the changes in behavior brought societal change as well as serious epidemical outbreaks (i.e., measles, influenza and whooping cough due to interaction with outsiders) (Albert, 1999a). In the late 1960s, anthropologists began to visit and study the Yanomami. The most notably of these early contacts with anthropologists was with Napoleon Chagnon in 1964, which lead to Chagnon writing extensively about the Yanomami as well as assisting in the production of anthropological documentaries about the Yanomami's culture. In the following decades, the influence of government officials, miners, missionaries, and researchers had a profound effect on the Yanomami.

Yanomami Culture Sketch

While the prehistory of the Yanomami is unknown, it is believed that the Yanomami migrated from the "Parima highlands of the Venezuelan-Brazilian border and that they have recently expanded from there as a result of the decimation of Carib speakers who occupied the upper Orinoco and its major tributaries" (Hames & Bierle, 1995) The Carib speakers were a target for capture as slaves and suffered immensely from newly introduced diseases. After having established their territory, the Yanomami had contact and traded with a variety of other Indigenous groups at the edges of the Yanomami's territory (Fergusion, 2015, p. 383-385). The Yanomami may have also been affected by Spanish, Portuguese, and Dutch attempts to trade steel tools as well as capture the Yanomami as slaves between the seventieth and twentieth centuries (Ferguson, 2015, p. 382-3). Although the Yanomami probably did not have long-term direct contact with Westerners until the mid-eighteenth century, beginning in the mid-twentieth century, there was continuous contact. Currently the Venezuelan and Brazilian Yanomami are in contact with anthropologists, missionaries, and both non-governmental and governmental aid organizations.

Each Yanomami village is autonomous, but may form one or more temporary alliances with other Yanomami villages. The village contains a singular *yano* or *shabono* (circular communal lean-to constructed of poles and palm thatching with a central open plaza) where there are no internal walls. Many anthropologists characterize the Yanomami as egalitarian, but there are achieved status differences among men, such as honor gained through combat, ability to make speeches, and shamanic skill. Older Yanomami men "dominate positions of political authority and religious practice" (Hames & Bierle, 1995). Village headmen come from one or more patrilines and must demonstrate skill in settling disputes, representing interests of the lineage, and successfully manage relationships with allies and enemies (Hames & Bierle, 1995).

The Yanomami economy is a mix between foraging, horticulture, trade, and wage labor, depending upon their proximity to resources and available trading partners and labor opportunities. Foraging involves gathering, hunting, and fishing. The *yano* or *shabono* is surrounded by individually managed swidden gardens that includes such crops as plantains, bananas, tobacco, and peach palm. While trade within and between Yanomami communities is central to forming alliances, outside trade is limited to missions and Ye'kwana communities, a nearby Indigenous group (Hames & Bierle, 1995). By the 1990s, most Yanomami had become "dependent on outside sources of axes, machetes, aluminum pots, and fish hooks and line" (Hames & Bierle, 1995).

Yanomami divide their labor between the sexes, even when working cooperatively. Only males participate in "weapon making, tree felling (in preparation of gardens), and hunting" while women exclusively "spin cotton threat and plait baskets" (Hames & Bierle, 1995). In other activities, both men and women may participate, but the activity typically is predominantly the responsibility of one sex over the other, as exemplified by the activities of "weeding and harvesting, food processing, and in fuel and water collection" which are usually done by women. (Hames & Bierle, 1995).

Yanomami kinship is organized by patrilineal descent where "members of the same patrilineage refer to themselves as *mashi*" with Iroquoian kinship terminology (Hames & Bierle, 1995). Marriages are ideally between double cross-cousins, but must be at least cross-cousins. Sister exchange is common and when polygyny occurs, it is sororal. Before marriage, males provide bride service to the future bride's father's household. This service can be for various lengths of time and can last several years. Approximately 75% of marriages end in divorce with the remaining cause being death of a partner where both the levirate and sororate are practiced (Hames & Bierle, 1995).

Shamans play a central role in the Yanomami's religious beliefs and ceremonial life. The Yanomami believe that there are four spiritual planes: (1) upper-most layer "once occupied by ancient beings who descended to lower layers"; (2) the sky that is "home of spirits of dead men and women and it resembles the earth except that the hunting is better, the food tastier, and the spirits of the people are young and beautiful"; (3) the earth that contains humans, plants, and animals; and (4) the underworld that contains "*amahi-teri*, ancient spirits who bring harm to humans" (Hames & Bierle, 1995). Many of the illnesses that afflict the Yanomami are attributed to shamans using spirits to attack one or more of an individual's souls. Shamans control *hekira* spirits, which they use to cure or cause illnesses (Hames & Bierle, 1995). To remove the attacking spirit from a person, shamans decorate themselves and inhale a hallucinogenic snuff (made from the seeds of the *yopo* tree, *Anadenanthera peregrina*), which enables them to interact with the spirit world. Shamans also concoct herbal remedies to cure people's illnesses not caused by attacking spirits. While many of the shamans' activities are focus on the living, shamans are also an integral part of funerary services. Shamans preside over mortuary ceremonies, where the cremated ash of the "deceased is mixed in a plantain puree and consumed by the mourners in a demonstration of respect for the deceased and in consolation to his or her close relative" (Hames & Bierle, 1995).

Endemic Yanomami Conflict/Violence

Interpersonal violence and feuding is endemic among the Yanomami. It is estimated that, in the 1980s, thirty percent of male deaths was due to violence (Chagnon, 1988, p. 239). While most early research argued that intra-village violence was caused by reproductive access to women, later research argued that violence was linked with outside contact and natural resource use (see Fergusson, 2015). As with other Indigenous Peoples caught in the cycle of endemic feuding (i.e., the Dani of Papua New Guinea), the informants often do not know the cause for the initial conflict while the explanation for the current conflict is one of vengeance.

In a feud, the patrilineal kin of one village forms a unit of vengeance against patrilineal kin of another village. The aim of a feuding raid is to kill a mature member of the opposing patriline, but either another male will be killed or a woman captured if the primary target is not found. Alliances are made with at least one other village and the feuding patriline relies upon village co-residents for protection against attacks. Elaborate ceremonial rituals bind intervillage allies as well as cement internal village ties. Some villages are more peaceful than others, but there is a constant threat of raids from other villages and a need to reinforce alliances.

There have been three main anthropological explanations for feuding among the Yanomami: cultural materialist – conflict caused by lack of animal protein (Harris, 1984a, 1984b), sociobiologist – conflict caused by access to reproductive rights of women (Chagnon, 1988, 1990), and political economist – conflict caused by access to introduced steel tools (Ferguson, 1992, 1995, 2015) (Sponsel, 1998, p. 100). As of yet, there is not consensus among anthropologists as to which theory and explanation best fits Yanomami feuding. Instead, anthropologists are most concern with the characterization of Yanomami violence (Ramos, 2008, p. 469). For example, the past president of the Brazilian Anthropological Association claimed that Chagnon's characterization of Yanomami violence was publicized by the Brazil conservative press and used as to justify the pacification and assimilation of the Yanomami (Carneiro da Cuna, 1989, and see Chagnon's [1989] response).

Gold Mining

While natural resource extraction (e.g., rubber and hunting) occurred in the Yanomami's territory throughout the 1900s, during the 1980s nearly 40,000 Brazilian gold-miners entered Yanomami's territory in search of gold. In the ensuing violent conflict several Yanomami were killed, villages were destroyed, and exotic diseases were introduced to the Yanomami populations. These diseases were especially devastating to the population as the Yanomami had no prior experience in treating the diseases and its symptoms or immunity built up to resist these diseases. This exposure resulted in approximately twenty percent of the Yanomami dying in a seven-year time span (Survival International, n.d.a). In the 1970s, the *Comissão Pró-Yanomami* (CCPY), a Brazilian nongovernmental organization was established. CCPY, Survival International and Davi Kopenawa, a member of the Yanomami, lobbied the Brazilian government to demark the Yanomami's territory, which would provide protection to the Yanomami and grants the Yanomami land rights to the territory they inhabited (Survival International, n.d.a). In 1991, the president of Brazil signed into law the establishment of the Yanomami Park and in 1992 most of the miners were expelled from the Yanomami's territory. Miners later returned to the area in which tensions between the Yanomami and miners sometimes led to violent conflict, such as in 1993 when miners killed 16 Yanomami in Haximú village (Survival International, n.d.a). Five of the miners were later caught, tried and found guilty of genocide (Survival International, n.d.a). Although the number of gold miners within the Yanomami's territory has diminished, conflicts still occur. Gold miners attacked a Yanomami community in 2012 killing up to 80 people (British Broadcasting Corporation, 2012).

In addition to violent conflict between miners and the Yanomami, the process of mining gold from Yanomami territory is having negative impacts upon the Yanomami's environment and health. During the process of mining, mercury is used to extract the gold from substrate materials and the usually released in the wastewater from the mine. The mercury can than easily enter groundwater and streams traveling hundreds of kilometers. Mercury is not degradable in the environment, nor can an organism excrete it once it is ingested by an organism. It is stored in an organism's tissues. Therefore, an organism will accumulate mercury in a body over time. Through bioaccumulation of mercury, organisms at higher levels of the food chain will have greater exposure to mercury. Humans in a mercury contaminated area can accumulate mercury through direct exposure to mercury such as drinking or swimming in the polluted water or through eating contaminated organisms. High levels of mercury in humans can lead to long term illnesses and death. In a recent study, the inhabitants of Aracaçá, one of the Yanomami communities closest to illegal mining sites, had elevated levels of mercury with 92 percent of the sampled population were contaminated with unsafe levels of mercury (Basta et al., 2016).

Yanomami Disease and Health

The Yanomami are not dissimilar to other equatorial peoples in either the diseases that they suffer or their general ill health. However, the most pressing threats to Yanomami health are infectious diseases that were only recently introduced from Europe and Africa. In regions with the most direct contact between the Yanomami and gold miners, there have been unprecedented increases in malaria, anemia, splenomegaly, respiratory infections, and tuberculosis (Ramos, 1995, p. 278–279). Of these introduced diseases, the most virulent are "mycobacterial infection tuberculosis, the hepatitis viruses (both B and delta), other viral infections such as measles, and parasitic infections such as onchocerciasis [river blindness] and a variety of intestinal helminths [parasitic worms]" as well as new strains of malaria (Kuzara & Hames 2004, p. 1017).

While several of the diseases and parasites affecting the Yanomami probably have pre-contact origins, some are more recent introductions. Tuberculosis is thought to have not existed within the Yanomami before contact, but now is prevalent within Yanomami territory (Kuzara & Hames 2004, p. 1018). While some disease origins are not well known, others have a well-documented epidemiology. Hepatitis delta was first introduced in 1968 by an American missionary who had reused needles in administering multivitamin complexes to himself and to the Yanomamö in the village (Torres & Mondolfi, 1991)" (Kuzara & Hames, 2004, p. 1017).

As with other New World peoples, measles epidemics have caused many deaths among the Yanomami. The first records of measles among the Yanomami are thought to have been introduced by a Brazilian missionary in the late 1960s (Kuzara & Hames 2004, p. 1019). In a 1968 epidemic, medical researchers, government teams, and missionaries supplied vaccinations and antibiotics to prevent secondary infections, but still nearly 20% of those infected still perished (Kuzara & Hames, 2004, p. 1019).

Parasitic infections usually are not fatal, but will have a negative impact on the infected individual to thrive. One such parasite affecting the Yanomami is *Onchocerca volvulus* which causes onchocerciasis (river blindness). *Onchocerca volvulus* was introduced from Africa to South America during the slave trade, but did not reach the territory of the Yanomami until the early 1970s and is currently common among highland communities (Kuzara & Hames, 2004, p. 1019). Onchocerciasis can result in blindness and debilitate the lymphatic system (Kuzara & Hames, 2004, p. 1019). Several other parasites infect the Yanomami, including "intestinal helminth, such as *Ancylostoma duodenale* and *Ascaris lumbricoides*, as well as a variety of roundworms, flatworms, tapeworms, and filarial worms and protozoans" (Kuzara & Hames, 2004, p. 1019). These intestinal parasites may cause a variety of serious health problems, but more often affect the host's ability to absorb nutrients.

As with other New World peoples living in humid tropical environments, malaria is present among the Yanomami and greatly affects their health. The most common species of malaria impacting the Yanomami is *Plasmodium falciparum* and *Plasmodium vivax*. *P. falciparum* can cause an acute infection which can be fatal if not treated quickly. Though less acute, *P. vivax* can relapse as the parasite can stay dormant in cells and have episodic outbreaks (Kuzara & Hames, 2004, p. 1020). The lack of mosquito nets, prophylactic medicine and treatment medications results in high infection rates of malaria among the Yanomami.

Over the past few decades, several governmental and nongovernmental organizations have provided health care assistance to the Yanomami. Since 1967, *CCPY* has advocated for rights, education, and health care. FUNAI, the Brazilian Indigenous protection agency, has worked with Brazilian Government's National Health Foundation (FUNASA) to provide health care for the Yanomami, but are plagued by corruption and disorganization. Since 2004, the Brazilian Yanomami's own NGO, Hutukara (the part of the sky from which the earth was born), has been advocating for the Yanomami and working towards improving education and health care. In the same vein, Venezuelan Yanomami organized their own NGO, Horonami, was created in 2011. In addition, another NGO called Urihi, has been working with the Yanomami specifically on Malaria since 2000. At times these governmental and non-governmental organizations work together, but more often political differences between members of the leadership of each group lead to dysfunctional collaboration.

Research Misconduct by Anthropologists[2]

The Yanomami have been the subject of research by anthropologists and medical researchers since the 1960s in part due to their minimal contact with outsiders and strong sense of cultural identity. While reports of ethics violations were dotted throughout the four decades since research began with the Yanomami, it was not until 2001 that these alleged violations became widely known outside of the small community of researchers and advocates of the Yanomami. A memo by Terrance Turner and Leslie Sponsel marked the beginning of a scandal in anthropology in a viral email to the American Anthropological Association:

> We write to inform you of an impending scandal that will affect the American Anthropological profession as a whole in the eyes of the public, and arouse intense indignation and calls for action among members of the Association. In its scale, ramifications, and sheer criminality and corruption it is unparalleled in the history of Anthropology... (Turner & Sponsel, 2000)

The prediction by Turner and Sponsel in their email to the AAA leadership has largely come true, "this nightmarish story... will be seen (rightly in our view) by the public, as well as most anthropologists, as putting the whole discipline on trial" (Turner & Sponsel, 2000). The story to which Turner and Sponsel were referring was Patrick Tierney's *Darkness in El Dorado: How*

---

2. For much more information, including biographies, blog posts, book reviews, email threads, film reviews, journal and news articles, position statements, and bibliography of materials related to the Darkness in El Dorado controversy, see the author's web site http://anthroniche.com/darkness-in-el-dorado-controversy/.

Scientists and Journalists Devastated the Amazon (2002), which detailed accounts from missionaries, researchers, advocates, and anthropologists about research misconduct by anthropologists and medical researchers. The main accusations of misconduct in Tierney's book included: (1) Timothy Asch (anthropologist and filmmaker) and Napoleon Chagnon (anthropologist) staging documentary footage, (2) Napoleon Chagnon and James Neel (medical epidemiologist) committing genocide by introducing measles, and (3) both Jacques Lizot (anthropologist) and Kenneth Good (anthropologist) committing pedophilia. In the months after Turner and Sponsel's viral email, hundreds of news agencies wrote articles, thousands of listserv emails were sent, journal articles were published, professional research associations made official statements and held public meetings, and the American Anthropological Association created the El Dorado Task Force to investigate the claims made in Tierney's book. Historical accounts of the controversy and ensuring investigation were written by Borofsky (2005) and Hume (2016) as well as being made into a documentary film, *Secrets of the Tribe* (Padilha, 2010).

The effect that Asch and Chagnon's films had on the Yanomami are complicated by notions of the noble savage myth and ethnocentric perceptions of viewers. The noble savage myth is the romanticization of Indigenous Peoples as intrinsically good and close to nature, often attributed to eighteenth-century French philosopher Jean-Jacques Rousseau—still accepted by some anthropologists, many environmentalists, and the majority of the general public. Asch and Chagnon's films, most famously *The Ax Fight* (1975), *The Feast* (1970), and *Man Called Bee: Studying the Yanomamo* (1974), showed the Yanomami behaving in ways that portrayed them as anything but noble. In *The Ax Fight*, the Yanomami are shown participating in violent club and ax fights as well as verbally insulting one another. In *The Feast*, the Yanomami are shown in ceremonial displays of warfare and chewing *Pe* (green tobacco). Finally, in *Man Called Bee*, the Yanomami are shown interacting with spirits after taking hallucinogenic snuff – an activity that makes them appear to be acting as monkeys eating dirt. While the Yanomami behavior in the films is not strange to the Yanomami, to outsiders their behavior appears strange, animal-like, primitive, and violent, to name a few. The portrayal of the Yanomami in Asch and Chagnon's films directly confronts the myth of the noble savage, but also results in the perception of them as needing outside intervention to civilize their savage nature, be it education, pacification, or missionization.

A team of researchers in a 1968 expedition to Yanomami territory lead by Napoleon Chagnon and James Neel are accused of committing genocide by introducing measles and other contagious diseases in *Darkness in El Dorado*. While the claim that the expedition caused the epidemic leading to many Yanomami deaths has been discredited (American Anthropological Association, 2002), hundreds of Yanomami still fell ill and many died. From the expedition lead researcher's perspective (i.e., Chagnon and Neel), they came prepared to collect biological and cultural data on Yanomami diseases as well as bringing various medication, including measles vaccines, to treat the Yanomami. Early in the expedition, Chagnon and Neel realized that a measles epidemic was spreading through Yanomami communities and they endeavored to administer the vaccine to as many Yanomami as possible. However, although many attempts were made to acquire more vaccines from various sources while they were in the field, Chagnon and Neel did not have enough of the vaccine to vaccinate all of the population with whom they came into contact. In addition, many of the communities where they administered the vaccine already had prior exposure to measles. From the Yanomami's perspective, the expedition arrived, gave them medication, and soon afterwards their friends and family members acquired measles, many dying from the disease or secondary infections. Given the order of events and the perspective of the Yanomami, the researchers are to blame for the numerous deaths in their communities.

In Tierney's *Darkness in El Dorado*, two anthropologists, Jacques Lizot and Kenneth Good, are accused of pedophilia while they were conducting long-term ethnographic research in Yanomami communities. While the American Anthropology Association's (AAA) El Dorado Task Force did not investigate claims against anthropologists other than Chagnon, the later documentary film *Secrets of the Tribe* (2010) takes the accusations of Lizot and Good's behavior as one of the major points it investigates. Lizot, a student of Claude Levi-Strauss, spent three decades living with and studying the Yanomami. His written ethnographies (Lizot, 1977, 1985) have been celebrated, while his sexual relationships with young male Yanomami, often in exchange for trade goods, either went unnoticed or were ignored. While the Yanomami still remember his sexual behavior (Padilha, 2010), he returned to France and has not been charged or censured. Kenneth Good in David Chanoff's ethnography on the Yanomami, *Into the Heart: One Man's Pursuit of Love and Knowledge Among the Yanomami* (1997), describes how Good was betrothed to a Yanomami girl when she was approximately nine years old. Good consummated the marriage when she was approximately 14 years old and Good was in his thirties. While among Yanomami, the ages for Good's wife to marry and consummate her marriages is customary, Good was heavily criticized for following Yanomami, rather than his own, cultural norms for the minimum age of consent for marriage and sex.

One of the recently resolved controversies surrounding research ethics is the issue of blood samples collected from the Yanomami from the 1960s to 1990s. In addition to the Yanomami not understanding why the blood samples were initially taken (informed consent requirements in the 1960s to 1980s were not as regulated as they are today), the Yanomami do not keep physical remains or possessions of the deceased. At death, a Yanomami's body is cremated and their possessions destroyed, separating the dead from the living. After nearly a decade of requesting that the blood samples be returned to the Yanomami, in 2006, the laboratories holding the samples agreed to return them to the Yanomami (Adams, 2010). It was not until 2015 that 2,693 blood samples were returned to the Yanomami and buried "during a special funerary ceremony presided over by shamans in the Yanomami community where many of the samples were collected" (Survival International, 2015a). The return of the Yanomami's blood samples is the only research ethics controversy that has been resolved.

Missionaries Among the Yanomami

The primary aim of missionary groups that work with the Yanomami is to convert the Yanomami to the missionaries' system of religious beliefs, which attempts to replace an Indigenous worldview (i.e., religious beliefs, knowledge, values, morals, and ethics) with a Western worldview. The Indigenous worldview is never wholly replaced, rather, results in a syncretism—a combination of both world views. In addition to religious conversion, missionary groups purport to have more secular and humanitarian goals related to health, economic, and education to achieve. Depending upon the missionary organization's objectives secular and non-secular goals are given varied in importance in both the public and implicit agendas.

The three largest and longest-term missionary groups working in Yanomami territory are: Salesian Missions (http://www.salesianmissions.org/), a Catholic missionary organization that has been among the Yanomami since the 1950s; Mission Padamo Aviation (http://www.mpaviation.org), an evangelical Christian missionary organization that focuses their efforts on the Yanomami; and New Tribes Mission (https://usa.ntm.org) an evangelical Christian missionary organization that operates worldwide. In October 2005, Venezuelan President Hugo Chavez expelled New Tribes missionaries, a Florida based evangelical Christian mission, from the Yanomami territory in Venezuela (British Broadcasting Corporation, 2005b). Chavez cited concerns that they were collecting information for the United States Central Intelligence Agency as well as using luxury planes and dwellings, thus bringing capitalism to Venezuela, charges that New Tribes denies (British Broadcasting Corporation, 2005b).

While there are some anthropologists who support the work of missionaries in the same communities in which the anthropologists are working, many more researchers view missionary work as being destructive to Indigenous cultures because the missionary work are agents of culture change. One such anthropologist who views missionary work as having a negative effect upon the people he studies is Napoleon Chagnon. Chagnon has a long history of conflict with Salesian missionaries, whom he viewed as not only changing Yanomami culture, but also for increasing violence and disease among the Yanomami (Chagnon, 2013, p. 405-422). Chagnon interviewed one missionary to investigate why the missionaries were giving Yanomami shotguns and ammunition when the Yanomami had previously only had clubs, bows, and arrows. He was informed that as the Yanomami became more reliant on non-renewable materials such as ammunition for hunting, the Yanomami would have be more dependent upon source (i.e. the mission) of these difficult to obtain materials. Thus the Yanomami would be forced to return to the mission with increasing regularity. Therefore, the missionaries had more access and time to convert them to Christianity. When Chagnon informed the missionary that a shotgun had been used by a Yanomami to kill another Yanomami, the missionary reported that it probably was not one of the shotguns that they had given to the Yanomami.

The Yanomami Fight for Cultural Survival and Self-Determination
At the forefront of the Yanomami's fight for cultural survival and self-determination is Davi Kopenawa Yanomami. He is instrumental in the Yanomami's struggle for self-determination as he is the face and voice of the Yanomami to the outside world. Kopenawa was born around 1956 in *Marakana*, a Brazilian Yanomami village near the Venezuelan border (Kopenawa & Albert, 2013, p. 3). When he was a child, his parents died from introduced diseases brought to his community by missionaries, road workers, and gold miners. Later in the *Watoriki* village, he apprenticed to be a shaman under his father-in-law. As a shaman he was attributed high status in his community. Along with having achieved high status as a shaman, Kopenawa also acquired essential communication skills. Unlike most Yanomami, he is fluent in Portuguese which he learned from a nearby mission. This skill enables him to be a voice for the Yanomami and communicate directly with the outside world.

Kopenawa began working with FUNAI in the 1976 as an interpreter and traveled to many uncontacted Yanomami communities (Kopenawa & Albert, 2013, p. 3). He assisted in bringing medical aid to the Yanomami. This began his lifelong career as a spokesperson for the Yanomami and an advocate for their human rights. In the late 1980s, Kopenawa left Brazil at the invitation of Survival International and spoke to the Swedish Parliament about the plight of the Yanomami people. He has since visited, spoken, and advocated for Indigenous rights in the United States, Japan, Venezuela, and several European counties. Kopenawa has also addressed the United Nations in Geneva and New York where he was presented the United Nations Global 500 award in 1988 for his contribution for environmental preservation (Survival International, n.d.b). In the years following, Kopenawa founded and became the president of *Hitukara* (Yanomami Association) in 2004, honored by the Bartolome de las Casas award in Spain in 2008 and awarded Brazil's Order of Cultural Merit in 2009 (Kopenawa & Albert, 2013, p. 4-5). Kopenawa, with his close friend the anthropologist Bruce Albert, wrote an autoethnography of his life, *The Falling Sky: Words of a Yanomami Shaman*, published in 2013.

In addition to Kapenawa's advocacy for Yanomami cultural survival, governmental (i.e., FUNAI) and non-governmental (i.e., CCPY and Hitukara) agencies have worked towards securing Yanomami rights and assisting them with health and educational development. Over the past three decades, these organizations have had several successes. In 1995, the CCPY began to work on a literacy program in a limited group of villages and, by 2004, "there were 38 schools operating in seven regions totaling nearly 1,700 people, 470 students, and 25 Yanomami teachers" (Ramos, 2008, p. 473). Although the official language of Brazil is Portuguese, the classrooms are mostly taught in the local language, which has enabled the Yanomami to communicate throughout their territory with written messages. Their ability to write in Portuguese has enabled the Yanomami to make their case to Brazil's government for rights and protection. The schools also facilitate visits to other Indigenous communities outside of the Yanomami's territory as well as visits from outside Indigenous groups.

In 2011, the Venezuelan Yanomami developed their own advocacy organization, called Horonami (Survival International n.d.a). Horonami released a statement in 2012 which detailed the negative impact (e.g. violence, disease, and environmental destruction) that illegal gold mining was having on their communities (Horonami Yanomami Organization, 2012). It is unclear whether their statement spurred the Venezuelan government to action, other than opening an investigation into the allegations (Neuman & Díaz, 2012).

The Future

While the Yanomami have suffered invasions into their territory by anthropologists, gold miners, missionaries, and others, there is hope among the Yanomami and their advocates that the Yanomami and their culture will persist into the future. As is the case with other Indigenous Peoples, advocating for land rights, health care, education, and other development opportunities communication with the outside has proven difficult largely due to language and cultural barriers. The Indigenous people are required to participate in, what amounts to, a foreign culture's political and legal system while communicating in a foreign language. Most Indigenous groups must rely upon outside organizations to advocate for them. For the Yanomami, these outside organizations include FUNAI and CCPY. However, the advocacy of Davi Kopenawa, whose skill for speaking on behalf of the Yanomami to politicians in Brazil and other leaders in the international community has brought the concerns of the Yanomami to the general public directly from an Indigenous perspective. In addition, the Brazilian Yanomami's Hitukara and Venezuelan Yanomami's Horonami organizations have begun to build cohesion within internal Yanomami advocacy work. For advocates of the Yanomami, there is reserved hope that the Yanomami people will survive and have the right to determine their own future.

References

Adams, Guy.
2010. *The Tribe that Won Its Blood Back.* The Independent. Available at http://www.independent.co.uk/news/world/americas/the-tribe-that-won-its-blood-back-1981974.html, accessed July 26, 2016.

Albert, Bruce.
1999a. *First Contacts.* Available at https://pib.socioambiental.org/en/povo/yanomami/573, accessed July 26, 2016.

Albert, Bruce.
1999b. *The Name Yanomami.* Available at https://pib.socioambiental.org/en/povo/yanomami/570, accessed July 26, 2016.

American Anthropological Association.
2002. El Dorado Task Force Papers, Volume I Submitted to the Executive Board as a Final Report, May 18, 2002. Available at http://anthroniche.com/darkness_documents/0598.pdf, accessed July 26, 2016.

Asch, Timothy and Napoleon Chagnon.
1970. *The Feast.* Watertown, Massachusetts: Documentary Educational Resources.

Asch, Timothy and Napoleon Chagnon.
1974. *Man Called Bee: Studying the Yanomamo.* Watertown, Massachusetts: Documentary Educational Resources.

Asch, Timothy and Napoleon Chagnon.
1975. *The Ax Fight.* Watertown, Massachusetts: Documentary Educational Resources.

Basta, Paulo Cesar, Sandra de Souza Hacon, Claudia Maribel Vega Ruiz, José Marcos Godoy, Rodrigo Araujo Gonçalves, Marcos Wesley de Oliveira, Ana Maria Machado, Helder Perri Ferreira, Davi Kopenawa Yanomami, Reinaldo Wadeyuna Ye'kwana, Jesem Douglas Yamall Orellana, Cristiano Lucas de Menezes Alves, and Maurício Caldart.
2016. *Avaliação da Exposição Ambiental ao Mercúrio Proveniente de Atividade Garimpeira de Ouro na Terra Indígena Yanomami, Roraima, Amazônia, Brasil.* Brazil: Escola Nacional de Saúde Pública Sérgio Arouca, Pontifícia Universidade Católica do Rio de Janeiro, Instituto Socioambienta, Hutukara Associação Yanomam, and Associação do Povo Ye'kwana do Brasi. Available at https://www.socioambiental.org/sites/blog.socioambiental.org/files/diagnostico_contaminacao_mercurio_terra_indigena_yanomami.pdf, accessed July 26, 2016.

Borofsky, Rob, (ed.)
2005. *Yanomami: The Fierce Controversy and What We Can Learn from It* (California Series in Public Anthropology). Berkeley: University of California Press.

British Broadcasting Corporation
2005a. *Chavez Moves Against us Preachers*, 12 October 2012. Available at http://news.bbc.co.uk/2/hi/americas/4336660.stm, accessed July 26, 2016.

British Broadcasting Corporation
2005b. *Venezuela Orders Missionaries Out*, 16 November 2005. Available at http://news.bbc.co.uk/2/hi/americas/4341592.stm, accessed July 26, 2016.

British Broadcasting Corporation
2012. *Miners' Attack on Yanomami Amazon Tribe 'Kills Dozens'*, 29 August 2012. Available at http://www.bbc.com/news/world-latin-america-19413107, accessed July 26, 2016.

Carneiro da Cuna, Maria Manula
1989. Letter to the Editor. *Anthropology Newsletter* 30(1), 3.

Chagnon, Napoleon A.
1968. *Yanomamö: The Fierce People*. New York: Holt, Rinehart and Winston.

Chagnon, Napoleon A.
1988. Life Histories, Blood Revenge, and Warfare in a Tribal Population. *Science* 239(4843), 985-992.

Chagnon, Napoleon A.
1989. Letter to the Editor. *Anthropology Newsletter* 30(1), 3, 24.

Chagnon, Napoleon A.
1990. Reproductive and Somatic Conflicts of Interest in the Genesis of Violence and Warfare among Tribesmen. In *The Anthropology of War*, Jonathan Haas, ed, pp. 77–104. New York: Cambridge University Press.

Chagnon, Napoleon A.
2013. *Noble Savages: My Life Among Two Dangerous Tribes—The Yanomamö and the Anthropologists*. New York: Simon & Schuster.

Eakin, Emily.
2013. How Napoleon Chagnon Became Our Most Controversial Anthropologist, February 13, 2013. *New York Times Magazine*. Available at http://www.nytimes.com/2013/02/17/magazine/napoleon-chagnon-americas-most-controversial-anthropologist.html, accessed July 26, 2016.

Ferguson, R. Brian.
1992. A Savage Encounter: Western Contact and the Yanomami War Complex. In *War in the Tribal Zone: Expanding States and Indigenous Warfare*, R. Brian Ferguson and Niel L. Whitehead, eds, pp. 199–227. Santa Fe, New Mexico: School for American Research Press.

Ferguson, R. Brian.
1995. *Yanomami Warfare: A Political History*. Santa Fe, New Mexico: School of American Research Press.

Ferguson, R. Brian.
2001. Materialist, Cultural and Biological Theories on Why Yanomami Make War. *Anthropological Theory* 1(1), 99-116.

Ferguson, R. Brian.
2015. History, Explanation, and War Among the Yanomami: A Response to Chagnon's Noble Savages. *Anthropological Theory* 15(4), 377-406.

Good, Kenneth and David Chanoff.
1997. *Into the Heart: One Man's Pursuit of Love and Knowledge Among the Yanomami*. Boston: Addison-Wesley Publishing Company.

Hames, Raymond.
1994. Yanomamö. *In Encyclopedia of World Cultures, Volume VII, South America*. Johannes Wilbert, ed, pp. 374-377. New York: G.K. Hall & Company.

Hames, Raymond and John Bierle.
1995. *Culture Summary: Yanoamo*. New Haven, Connecticut: Human Relations Area Files.

Hames, Raymond and Jennifer Kuzara.
2004. The Nexus of Yanomamo Growth, Health and Demography. In *Lost Paradises and the Ethics of Research and Publication*. Francisco M. Salzano and A. Magdalena Hurtado, eds, pp. 110-145. Oxford: Oxford University Press.

Harris, Marvin.
1984a. A Cultural Materialist Theory of Band and Village Warfare: The Yanomamo Test. In *Warfare, Culture, and Environment*, R. Brian Ferguson, ed, pp. 111-140. New York: Academic Press.

Harris, Marvin.
1984b. Animal Capture and Yanomamo Warfare: Retrospect and New Evidence. *Journal of Anthropological Research* 40(1), 183–201.

Hume, Douglas William.
2013. Anthropology: Tribal Warfare. *Nature* 494(7437), 310.

Hume, Douglas William.
2016. Darkness in Academia: Cultural Models of How Anthropologists and Journalists Write About Controversy. *World Cultures eJournal* 21(1). Available at, http://escholarship.org/uc/item/75j9q56x, accessed August 2, 2016.

Horonami Yanomami Organization.
2012. Pronouncement of Horonami Yanomami Organization on the Presence of Illegal Miners in the Upper Ocamo Region. Available at, http://assets.survivalinternational.org/documents/825/120925hoy-statement-english.pdf, accessed July 26, 2016.

Kopenawa, Davi and Bruce Albert.
2013. *The Falling Sky: Words of a Yanomami Shaman.* Cambridge, Massachusetts: The Belknap Press of Harvard University Press.

Kuzara, Jennifer and Raymond Hames.
2004. Yanomamö. In *Encyclopedia of Medical Anthropology – Health and Illness in the World's Cultures – Volume I, Tropics – Volume II – Cultures.* Carol R. Ember and Melvin Ember, eds, pp. 1017-1028. New York: Kluwer Academic/Plenum Publishers.

Lizot, Jacques.
1977. Population, Resources and Warfare among the Yanomami. *Man* 12(3/4), 497–515.

Lizot, Jacques.
1985. *Tales of the Yanomami: Daily Life in the Venezuelan Forest.* New York: Cambridge University Press.

Neuman, William and María Eugenia Díaz.
2012. Venezuela to Investigate Report That Brazilian Miners Massacred Indian Village, August 30, 2012. *New York Times*. Available at http://www.nytimes.com/2012/08/31/world/americas/venezuela-to-investigate-report-that-miners-massacred-indians.html?_r=0, accessed July 26, 2016.

Padilha, José.
2010. *Secrets of the Tribe*. Watertown, Massachusetts: Documentary Educational Resources.

Ramos, Alcida Rita.
1995. *Sanuma Memories: Yanomami Ethnography in Times of Crisis*. Madison, Wisconsin: University of Wisconsin Press.

Ramos, Alcida Rita.
2008. Disengaging Anthropology. In *A Companion to Latin American Anthropology*, Deborah Poole, ed, pp. 466-484. 2008. Malden, Massachusetts: Blackwell Publishing.

Rocha, Jan.
1999. *Murder in the Rain Forest: The Yanomami, the Gold Miners, and the Amazon*. London: Latin American Bureau.

Rose, Peter and Anne Conlon.
1983. *Yanomamo*. London: Josef Weinberger, Ltd.

Sponsel, Leslie E.
1998. Yanomami: An Arena of Conflict and Aggression in the Amazon. *Aggressive Behavior* 24(2), 97-122.

Sponsel, Leslie E.
2006a. Yanomamo. In *Encyclopedia of Anthropology*. H. James Brix, ed, pp. 2347-2351. Thousand Oaks, California: Sage Publications, Inc.

Sponsel, Leslie E.
2006b. Darkness in El Dorado Controversy. In *Encyclopedia of Anthropology*. H. James Brix, ed, pp. 667-672. Thousand Oaks, California: Sage Publications, Inc.

Survival International.
n.d.a. *The Yanomami*. Available at http://www.survivalinternational.org/tribes/Yanomami, accessed July 26, 2016.

Survival International.
n.d.b. *Davi Kopenawa Yanomami Amazonian Indian Leader and Shaman.*
Available at http://www.survivalinternational.org/davi, accessed July 26,
2016.

Survival International.
2015a. *Brazil: Blood Samples Returned to Yanomami After Nearly 50 Years.*
Available at http://www.survivalinternational.org/news/10727, accessed July
26, 2016.

Survival International.
2015b. *Brazil: Davi Yanomami Awarded Top Honour.* Available at http://www.
survivalinternational.org/news/11010, accessed July 26, 2016.

Tierney, Patrick.
2002. *Darkness in El Dorado: How Scientists and Journalists Devastated the
Amazon.* New York: W. W. Norton & Company.

Torres, Jaime R., and Alejandro Mondolfi.
1991. Protracted Outbreak of Severe Delta Hepatitis Experience in an Isolated Amerindian Population of the Upper Orinoco Basin, Venezuela. *Reviews
of Infectious Diseases* 13(1), 52-55.

Turner, Terrance.
2001. *The Yanomami and the Ethics of Anthropological Practice* (Latin American Studies Program Occasional Paper Series, Vol. 6). Ithaca, New York:
Cornell University Press.

Turner, Terrance and Leslie Sponsel.
2000. *Imminent Anthropological Scandal.* Available at http://anthroniche.
com/darkness_documents/0055.htm, accessed July 26, 2016.

San of Botswana, Namibia, South Africa, and Zimbabwe

Robert Hitchcock
Michigan State University

and

Maria Sapignoli
Max Planck Institute for Social Anthropology

The San (Bushmen) of southern Africa are among the most heavily documented and best known of Africa's Indigenous Peoples (Barnard, 1992, 2007; Lee & DeVore, 1976; Takada, 2016; Tobias, 1978). San peoples, all of whom were originally hunter-gatherers, experienced massive environmental, social, economic, and political changes, especially in the past two millennia (Gordon & Douglas, 2000; Suzman, 2001; Wilmsen, 1989). In part as a response to incursions of other groups with different livelihoods and sociopolitical systems, combined with colonization and the formation of modern African nation-states, San have engaged in a variety of efforts to promote their human rights and well-being in the face of dispossession, exploitation, subjugation, and discrimination.

The current San population estimates are 120,000 in seven southern African countries: Angola (3,500), Botswana (62,500), Lesotho (400), Namibia (38,000), South Africa (7,800), Zambia (1,300), and Zimbabwe (2,600) (Hitchcock, Begbie-Clench, & Murwira 2016, p. 13). Their population size at the time of contact was about two to three times what it is now. One estimate of the numbers of San in the southern African region is that by anthropologist Richard Lee (1976, p. 5) who says that their numbers in 1650 could be roughly estimated to be 150-300,000 people.

The majority of the San reside in the Kalahari Desert region which covers portions of Angola, Botswana, Namibia, South Africa, Zambia, and Zimbabwe (Passarge, 1904; Thomas & Shaw, 2010). The Kalahari is a vast sandy basin that is both environmentally and topographically diverse stretching from Angola to the Cape region of South Africa. While characterized as a desert or thirstland, the Kalahari is in fact a largely semi-arid tree-bush savanna ecosystem which shows evidence of pronounced climatic change over time. Like many savannas, there is significant season variability in rainfall; the rains, which generally come between November and March, average between 250-700 mm per annum. There are times when there is significantly more or less rainfall, and droughts and floods in the Kalahari are not uncommon.

The San, who have occupied the Kalahari for over 40,000 years, have adapted to diverse habitats ranging from the Maluti-Drakensberg Mountains in the southeastern portion of southern Africa to the dry central Kalahari in Botswana and riverine forest areas and wetlands in southern Angola, western Zambia, and northern Namibia (LeRoux & White, 2004). In some areas, such as southeastern Africa, San have largely been assimilated into other groups or incorporated as laborers on the farms of other people. In recent years, however, some Sam descendants have begun a cultural resurgence, identifying themselves distinctly as San whose ancestors occupied the highlands and uplands plains of the Maluti-Drakensberg (Challis, 2012; Francis, 2009; Prins, 2009). Other San groups, such as those in the central and northwestern Kalahari, have attempted to retain some of their traditional social systems and have continued to depend, at least to a limited extent, on foraging for part of their subsistence. While most San in the past were hunter-gatherers, today the vast majority of

San are small-scale agro-pastoralists, cattle post and agricultural workers, and people with mixed economies who reside both in rural and urban areas.

Who Are the San?

The San are sub-divided into a large number of named groups, many of whom speak their own mother tongue click languages in addition to other languages. These groups include the Ju/'hoansi, !Xun, Khwe, Khwe-‖Ani, Ts'ixa, ǂX'ao-ǁ'aen, !Xóõ, ǂHoan, ǂKhomani, Naro, G/ui, G//ana, Tsasi, Tsila, Deti, Shua, Tshwa, Danisi and /Xaise. San prefer to use their own names to refer to themselves. Collectively, they have been called Bushmen (Passarge, 1907; Tanaka, 2014; Tobias, 1978), San (Dieckmann et al., 2014; Hitchcock et al., 2006; Lee 1979; Lee & DeVore, 1976), Kua (Kiema, 2010; Valiente-Noailles, 1993), Khoisan, a term that includes Khoekhoe, or Nama-speaking people (Barnard, 1992; Schapera, 1930), Basarwa, a term used by Tswana-speakers and the government of Botswana (Mogwe, 1992), Amasili, an Ndebele term used in Zimbabwe (Hitchcock, Begbie-Clench, & Murwira 2016). Batwa, a term also used to describe Central African forest peoples known pejoratively as 'Pygmies' (Hewlett, 2014), and 'First People of the Kalahari' (Barnard & Kenrick, 2001; Saugestad, 2001; Sapignoli, 2015). The San are minorities in all of the countries where they reside today. In Botswana, for example, San made up less than 3% of the 2016 population of 2,209,208, while in Namibia, if one uses and estimate of 38,000 San, the percentage of the country's population of 2,212,307 was 1.7% in 2016.

One of the questions asked by other Indigenous people is whether the San consider themselves a 'Native nation.' Some San yes, definitely, they are a 'Native nation.' Other San say that the term 'Native' has a problematic connotation in Africa, as it has often used by racially based colonialist systems in the past. They suggest that a better term to describe them is 'first nations' and 'Indigenous' people. Some San see themselves as Fourth World Peoples in Third World states. Southern African governments, on the other hand, tend to argue that all of the people in their countries are Indigenous (Sapignoli, 2015). Most San today prefer to be called by their individual group names and say that they want to be treated like other people in the countries where they reside.

A characteristic feature of San and Khoekhoe peoples in southern Africa is that they speak languages that contain click consonants. These languages have the largest number of sounds of all the world's languages (Güldemann & Stoneking, 2008). This is particularly true for what is known as the Taa languages in the southern Kalahari, one of which is !Xoon (!Xóõ), which contains five clicks, including the rare kiss or bilabial click (Ⓞ) (Traill, 1985). The Khoesan languages consist of three language families: the Khoe-Kwadi, the Ju/'hoan, and the Tuu (Güldemann, 2014; Vossen, 2013). Other southern African groups, including the Xhosa, Zulu, and Swazi, also speak languages with clicks. A long-standing question regarding click languages has been the relationships between groups in east Africa that speak click languages, such as the

Hadza and Sandawe of Tanzania, and the Khoisan languages of southern Africa (Sands, 1998). It is interesting to note that Hadza and San have worked together at the international level, attending, for example, meetings of the United Nations Permanent Forum on Indigenous Issues and global discussions on human rights, climate change, and biodiversity protection.

San societies traditionally were mobile kinship-based small-scale social systems, moving from place to place in response to seasonal changes in the availability of wild plant and animal foods, surface water and the presence of other groups (Lee, 1979; Marshall, 1976; Silberbauer, 1981; Tanaka, 2014; Takada, 2015; Valiente-Noailles, 1993). Like some other hunter-gatherers such as the Aboriginals of Australia, San were largely egalitarian, sharing food, goods and labor among group members. Division of labor was along age and gender lines although there were individuals who had particular skills who played important roles such as healing (Katz, Biesele, & St. Denis, 1997).

It has been argued that the Ju/'hoan San were among the most gender equitable societies in existence, and women played significant roles in decision-making (Draper, 1975). Not only did San women provide much of the subsistence of San groups, they also did much of the care-giving of children. In some groups, women maintained much of the traditional environmental knowledge about plant foods and medicines, and they passed this information down from one generation to the next. San women have been at the forefront of efforts to promote women's empowerment and to reduce levels of domestic violence and poverty in local communities. (Felton & Becker, 2001). While currently there are no San women in national level institutions such as Parliament in southern Africa, they do play major roles at the local level and are key figures in village development committees, Parents-Teachers Associations, and other community-level organizations.

San women have played significant roles at the local, national, and international levels; a key figure among the !Kung of the N≠a Jaqna area in northeastern Namibia is Sarah Zungu, who is a traditional councilor for the !Kung and in the past served as the chairperson of the N≠a Jaqna Conservancy Conservancy (NJC). Another important San woman leader was Mama Rampadi, a Kua from Kweneng District in Botswana who served as the chairperson and director of First People of the Kalahari (FPK), one of the earliest San non-government organizations. A third example of a San woman in a position of significance is Masego Nkelekang Mogodu, a Tshwa from Man/otai on the Nata River in northeastern Botswana who is in charge of the national planning process in the Ministry of Finance and Development Planning in Botswana.

Maintenance of social order has been seen as key to long-term survival, and the San developed sophisticated conflict management systems that provide lessons for contemporary negotiation (Ury, 1995). One of the ways that San deal with disputes is that they use social pressure of the group that is brought to bear on the individual who is causing difficulties. This is often done through joking and criticism rather than imposing social sanctions on the individual such as corporal or capital punishment. There were cases, however, where violence occurred and people did lose their lives in local disputes, as noted by Marshall (1976, p. 285-289) and Lee (1979, p. 370-400) among the Ju/'hoansi. Characterized by Elizabeth Marshall Thomas (1958) as "the harmless people," it has been assumed that the San tend to have lower levels of conflict and violence than other people. A major issue debate in the past decade has revolved around the degree to which the Ju/'hoansi and other San engaged in violent acts (Guenther, 2014). Like other Indigenous Peoples confronted with invasions of their lands by colonial forces, they did engage in resistance efforts, as was seen, for example, among the Khwe and other San of northern Namibia in the latter part of the 19th century (Guenther, 2005). In general, however, the San tended to avoid hostility and conflict if at all possible, as noted by Lorna Marshall (1976, p. 288).

On an organizational level, San societies can be described as 'three-tiered,' with one tier consisting of the family (or the 'domestic group', see Barnard, 1992, p. 226); a second tier consisting of a band (Silberbauer, 1981, p. 138), and the third consisting of a 'band cluster' (Guenther, 2000, p. 23). These units are tied together in a variety of ways. Alliance formation is a key feature of San societies. This is done through paying visits to other groups, arranging marriages, working cooperatively with other people, and engaging in reciprocal exchange systems. The Ju/'hoansi, for example, have a system known as hxaro (haro), a delayed exchange system that serves to link individuals and groups over wide areas. This system gave individuals the option of moving to other places to join *hxaro* partners during stress periods and thus to reduce risk (Barnard, 1992, p. 141-142; Wiessner, 2005). The Ju/'hoansi also have a 'name relationship,' a kind of fictive kinship system in which individuals who share the same name have mutual rights and obligations; this system allow allows individuals to call on their namesakes in time of need (Draper & Haney, 2005; Marshall, 1976, p. 238-242).

The San today are not organized into large socio-political units like chiefdoms or states but instead are divided into small dispersed groups that differ socially, culturally, and linguistically. Much of the daily decision-making among San is done on the basis of consensus (Silberbauer, 1982). In some localities, decision-making is in the hands of local leaders appointed by the government under government legislation such as the *Traditional Authorities Act* (Republic of Namibia, 2000). Traditional authorities in Namibia do not have the right to allocate land; instead, communal land is in the hands of Regional Land Boards in Namibia (Kuelder, 2000; Republic of Namibia, 2000). There are five San Traditional Authorities in Namibia at the present time (2016), and two others, who would represent the Khwe in Zambezi Region and the ‡Khomani in the Khomas Region whose appointments are awaiting Namibian government ratification.

Both San and non-government organizations working with San and other minorities point out that it is difficult for San to feel comfortable with government-appointed leaders. The San have individuals who do play important roles in issues such as land management, such as the n!ore kxausi of the Ju/'hoansi and the //aiha of the Tshwa. Admittedly, San sometimes have difficulties making decisions as a large group (Biesele & Hitchcock, 2013; Lee, 2013). They also note that the notion of pan-San decision-making is something that relatively few San have thought seriously about until recently. The San nearly all say that they 'wish to speak for themselves' rather than to have other people speak for them. San also believe that they should have the right to political representation chosen by themselves at the local, district, and national levels in southern African nation-states.

One of the prevailing myths about the San is that they are 'disappearing.' In fact, San fertility rates are on the increase and populations are growing (Howell, 2010; Leon Tsamkxao, Jumanda Gakelebone, Job Morris, Laura Martindale, personal communications, 2016). Some of the reasons for this increase are greater access to medical services in remote areas, sedentarization, changes in the types of foods consumed, with an increase in carbohydrates and milk, provision of food and other goods through commodity support programs, drought relief feeding, and assistance to pregnant and lactating mothers (Dieckmann et al., 2014; Howell, 2010; Seleka et al., 2007; World Bank, 2015). Morbidity (illness) rates are moderate, with HIV/AIDS and other sexually transmitted disease rates among San falling well below national averages. Antiretroviral drugs (ARVs) and drugs for tuberculosis and other illnesses are more available today than they were in the past in southern Africa. San have pushed for greater efforts on the part of the governments in the countries where they live to provide health facilities, doctors, nurses, medicines, and preventative health care.

The Kalahari Debate and Contact History
Over the past several decades, a major intellectual dispute called the Kalahari Debate has been on-going among Southern African archaeologists, anthropologists, historians, and development workers (Barnard, 2007, p. 97-111; Kuper, 2003; Lee, 2013, p. 203-226; Solway & Lee, 1990; Wilmsen, 1989). This debate relates in part to the issues of whether the San were isolated historically, the kinds of interactions San had with other groups (e.g. Herero, Ovambo, Mbukushu, Tswana), and the degree to which San were oppressed or exploited or maintained symbiotic relations with other groups over the past two millennia.

Questions raised in the Kalahari Debate include the ways in which the immigrant Bantu-speaking groups affected the Ju/'hoansi and other San beginning approximately 2000 years ago, and whether San attempted to maintain their autonomy by moving further into the bush or engaging in resistance strategies including resorting to violence (Guenther, 2014; Penn, 2006). Wilmsen (1989), for example, argues that Iron Age populations Bantu-speaking incorporated the San into larger sociopolitical structures, utilized their services to their own advantage (for example in hunting, livestock management, agricultural work, and domestic service). Iron Age and contemporary agropastoral populations did assist San in some cases, enabling them to become independent livestock producers through providing them with cattle and small stock through long-term loans (*mafisa*), and engaging in exchanges of goods such as ceramics, metal tools, tobacco, beads, and domestic food items.

In the Cape region of South Africa, after contacts were established with Dutch, British, Portuguese, and other Europeans whose ships landed at the Cape of Good Hope in the mid-17th century, San and Khoikhoi traded with them for goods, supplying the Europeans with livestock and wild meat. European and Cape Malay demand for these products expanded over time, resulting in pressure on Indigenous groups and conflicts over cattle raiding by members of the Dutch East India Company and others after 1652. Movement of White settlers into the hunting and grazing lands of Khoikhoi and San peoples in the Cape interior in the latter part of the 17th and 18th centuries saw competition over resources (Elphick, 1977). Claiming that the land was 'empty' or that the land use activities of Khoisan peoples such as hunting and gathering were 'uncivilized' and 'unproductive,' White settlers and pastoralists began engaging in violent conflicts with resident Indigenous populations who they all too frequently characterized as 'savages' (Brantlinger, 2003). The Indigenous populations thus were not only exposed to what some scholars have described as genocide (e.g. Adhikari, 2010; Penn, 2006), they were also affected by communicable diseases and by the taking of men, women, and children from Indigenous groups for use as labor on settler farms. Both hunter-gatherer and pastoral societies were affected badly by these processes, which saw the dispossession and near-extinction of the Cape San by the latter part of the 19th century.

In what are now Botswana and Namibia, the situations for San were somewhat different. In both countries San were incorporated into the colonial economies as laborers in the mines and on the ranches of settlers, as seen, for example, on the Ghanzi Farms of Botswana and the freehold commercial farms of Namibia (Dieckmann et al., 2014; Guenther, 2015). There were cases where San were targeted for genocide, as occurred, for example, in the 1912-1915 period toward the end of German colonial control of what was then South West Africa (Gordon, 2009). There were also cases of human rights violations including torture and murder of San in all of the southern African countries in the 19th and early 20th centuries (Hitchcock & Babchuk, 2009; Mogwe, 1992). This complex history is a major reason why San have put so much emphasis on human rights in their recent advocacy efforts.

There is a small population of 'Batwa', 'Duma' and AmaTole in Lesotho who claim to be the descendants of San who were largely assimilated or who were destroyed as a result of settler-hunter-gatherer conflicts by the latter part of the 19th century (Wright, 1971). Some of these peoples, who number about 400 today, live in the highlands of the Maluti-Drakensberg Mountains on the border of Lesotho and South Africa. They have been described as 'creolized San' or 'secret San' (Francis, 2009; Prins, 2009). A number of them now claim San identity. One driving factor is the increased awareness of what is happening among San in other countries in the region who are claiming San identity (Sapignoli, 2015). Another factor, apparently, is the desire to claim rights over rock shelters and other culturally significant sites that have rock art and archaeological materials in order to take advantage of tourism opportunities, as seen, for example, in the Ukhahlamba Drakensberg Park in South Africa which is part of the Maluti-Drakensberg Transfrontier Park which became a World Heritage Site on 30 November, 2000.

It should be noted that the establishment of protected areas in many parts of southern Africa have played an important role in the history of dispossession of San and other people in the region.

Contemporary Challenges Facing the San

Contemporary challenges facing San in southern Africa include the expansion of livestock, agricultural, and extractive industries including mining, timber exploitation, and the commercialization of high value wild natural resources such as Devil's Claw (*Harpagophytum procumbens*) and *Hoodia gordonii*. Changes in land policies such as those in Botswana (see Republic of Botswana, 2015) have led to a privatization of land in communal (tribal) areas, which have had the effect of either displacing or reducing access to land and natural resources of San communities. There have also been several cases of involuntary relocation out of protected areas, for example, in Tsodilo Hills National Monument (now a World Heritage Site) in 1995 and the Central Kalahari Game Reserve, Botswana's largest protected area, in 1997 and 2002. San and their neighbors who have occupied these areas have resisted government's efforts to resettle them. In the case of the Central Kalahari, San and Bakgalagadi took the Botswana government to court over the right to return and use resources in the Central Kalahari Game Reserve in a High Court Case that was the longest in Botswana's History (July, 2004-December, 2006) (see Sapignoli, 2015). There have been other cases where groups have sought to return to their ancestral homelands and have used the courts as a means of accomplishing that objective.

San and Nama have also gone to court in South Africa in the cases of the Nama-Richtersveld Park and the Kgalagadi Transfrontier Park (Ellis, 2013; Hitchcock & Vinding, 2004). In the process, they have obtained legal settlements that include rights of access to the parks, shares of the benefits, and in the case of the Richtersveld case in South Africa, sub-surface rights. San and Bakgalagadi won the right to return to the Central Kalahari in December, 2006, and they later won the right to water in the reserve in the Botswana Court of Appeal in 2011 in a case that may well set a precedent not only for the people of the Central Kalahari but for the rest of the world (Sapignoli, 2015). The Hai//om of Namibia filed a collective action lawsuit against the government of Namibia in August, 2015 for the return of Hai//om land and access to benefits from the Etosha National Park, and the people of the N≠a Jaqna Conservancy in northeastern Namibia won a case against 35 illegal grazers and fencers in N≠a Jaqna in September, 2016 which requires the illegal immigrants to vacate the conservancy (Hitchcock & Babchuk, 2016). Through seeking support from such organizations as the International Labour Organization and the Open Society Initiative for Southern Africa (OSISA), San have begun to make substantial progress on dealing with land rights and resource issues; they have sought to reduce the impacts of hydraulic fracturing (fracking) and its effects on the environment in the Kalahari, and they are attempting to cope more effectively with global and local climate change through participating in global and regional meetings and engaging in their own conservation and natural resource management efforts.

Strategies employed in social activism by the San have included the following: forming conservancies community trusts, associations, community-based organizations, and non-government organizations; taking part in direct action (demonstrations), as occurred, for example, at the gates of Etosha National Park in Namibia in August, 1997 and at New Xade near the Central Kalahari Game Reserve in September 2005; getting involved in the political process, as occurred in October 2014 with the election of Jumanda Gakelebone, a G//ana from New Xade to the Ghanzi District Council in Botswana; seeking international attention on issues facing the San by attending international meetings such as the Permanent Forum on Indigenous issues (UNPFII) in New York and the African Working Group on Indigenous Populations/Communities of the African Union in Gabon and Ethiopia; and forming alliances with other Indigenous and minority groups and organizations such as the Indigenous Peoples of Africa Coordinating Committee (IPACC) (Crawhall, 2011; Sapignoli, 2015, 2016) and the National Khoe and San Council (NKC) in South Africa. Negotiations with transnational corporations and research institutions have resulted in benefit-sharing agreements with San and Khoekhoe in southern Africa (Chennels, 2013; Wynberg, Schroeder, & Chennells 2009). Many San say that they prefer to engage in negotiations with governments rather than having to resort to legal action, which they feel is both expensive and risky.

The Future

The San are making significant progress in promoting their rights as citizens of the countries in which they reside and as members of the international community. As Fourth World Peoples, they still face many of the same problems as do other Indigenous groups, including discrimination and lack of fair and equal treatment in courts at the local and state levels. San have opposed the death penalty in cases in Botswana, and they have pushed hard for sentences that are fair and just in the courts.

San have organized nearly two dozen non-government and community-based organizations, some of which are transboundary in nature, such as the Working Group of Indigenous Minorities in Southern Africa (WIMSA). They have also formed alliances with minority rights groups and legal organizations such as the legal Assistance Center in Botswana, Ditshwanelo, the Botswana Center for Human Rights, and the Legal Resources Foundation in South Africa. As a result of these efforts, some San groups have been able to get *de jure* (legal) tenure over land, as seen in the cases of Dqae Qare in Botswana and the Hai//om resettlement farms in Namibia (Dieckmann, 2014; Sapignoli, 2015, 2016). There has also been some progress on the preservation of cultural traditions, including traditional dances, healing ceremonies that involve going into trance, and the protection of biological and intellectual property rights (Biesele & Hitchcock, 2013; Chennels 2016; Marshall, 1999). San continue to seek the right of Free, Prior, and Informed Consent (FPIC), the right to make decisions about development projects in their areas, and the right to practice their own cultures, traditions, and rituals, much as other Indigenous Peoples do in countries such as the United States, Canada, Australia, New Zealand, India, the Philippines, and Bolivia.

Some San children are now becoming literate in their own mother tongue languages (e.g. the Ju/'hoansi, the Khwe, and the Naro) as a result of language and educational activities, some of which have drawn on lessons and insights generated by local people themselves (Biesele & Hitchcock, 2013; LeRoux & White, 2004; Hays, 2016). It is anticipated that with greater numbers of San children and adults having the opportunity to get formal and non-formal education, the expansion in the support for post-secondary and post-graduate education and the availability of funds to support San teachers and learners, progress will be made in this important area. In the future one can anticipate that San will engage in concerted efforts to organize themselves and to seek greater recognition of their languages, cultures, and identities. They will build on San customs and traditions as part of their efforts to obtain what they see as 'value-driven development' (Morris, 2011). They will continue to press for recognition as Indigenous Peoples and as citizens of the countries where they live. With support from each other, the nation-states of southern Africa, and the international community, San will be able to achieve their goals of human rights, social and environmental justice, equal treatment before the law, and culturally sensitive sustainable development.

References

Adhikari, Mohamed.
2010. *The Anatomy of a South African Genocide: The Extermination of the Cape San Peoples*. Cape Town: University of Cape Town Press and Athens: Ohio University Press.

Barnard, Alan.
1992. *Hunters and Herders of Southern Africa: A Comparative Ethnography of the Khoisan Peoples*. Cambridge: Cambridge University Press.

Barnard, Alan
2007. *Anthropology and the Bushmen*. Oxford and New York: Berg.

Barnard, Alan and Justin Kenrick, (eds.).
2001. *Africa's Indigenous Peoples: 'First Peoples' or 'Marginalized Minorities'?* Edinburgh: Center of African Studies, University of Edinburgh.

Biesele, Megan.
1993. *"Women Like Meat": Ju/'hoan Bushman Folklore and Foraging Ideology*. Johannesburg: Witwatersrand University Press.

Biesele, Megan and Robert K. Hitchcock.
2013. *The Ju/'hoan San of Nyae Nyae and Namibian Independence: Development, Democracy, and Indigenous Voices in Southern Africa*. Paperback Edition. New York and Oxford: Berghahn Books.

Brantlinger, Patrick.
2003. *Dark Vanishings: Discourse on the Extinction of Primitive Races, 1800-1930*. Ithaca, New York: Cornell University Press.

Challis, Sam.
2012. Creolisation on the Nineteenth Century Frontiers of Southern Africa: A Case Study of the AmaTola 'Bushmen' in the Maloti-Drakensberg. *Journal of Southern African Studies* 38(2), 265-280.

Chennells, Roger.
2016. *Equitable Access to Human Biological Resources in Developing Countries: Benefit Sharing Without Undue Inducement*. New York: Springer.

Draper, Patricia
1975. !Kung Women: Contrasts in Sexual Egalitarianism in the Foraging and Sedentary Contexts. In *Toward An Anthropology of Women*, Rayna R. Reiter (ed.) pp. 77-112. New York: Monthly Review Press.

Draper, Patricia and Christine Haney.
2005. Patrilateral Bias among a Traditionally Egalitarian People: Ju/'hoansi Naming Practice. *Ethnology* 44(3), 243-259.

Ellis, William F.
2013. Genealogies and narratives of San Authenticities: The ≠Khomani San Land Claim in the Southern Kalahari. Ph.D. Dissertation, University of the Western Cape, South Africa.

Elphick, Richard.
1977. *Kraal and Castle: Khoikhoi and the Founding of White South Africa.* New Haven: Yale University Press.

Francis, Michael.
2009. Silencing the Past: Historical and Archaeological Colonization of the Southern San in Kwazulu-Natal, South Africa. *Anthropology Southern Africa* 32(1&4), 106-116.

Gordon, Robert J.
2009. Hiding in Full View: The "Forgotten" Bushman Genocides in Namibia. *Genocide Studies and Prevention* 4(1), 29-57.

Gordon, Robert J. and Stuart Sholto Douglas.
2000. *The Bushman Myth: The Making of a Namibian Underclass.* Second Edition. Boulder, Colorado: Westview Press.

Guenther, Mathias G.
2014. War and Peace among Kalahari San. *Journal of Aggression, Conflict and Peace Research* 6(4), 229-239.

Guenther, Mathias G.
2015. Why Racial Paternalism and not Genocide? The Case of the Ghanzi Bushmen of Bechuanaland. In Genocide on Settler Frontiers: When Hunter-Gatherers and Commercial Stock Farmers Clash, Mohamed Adhikari, ed. pp. 134-158. New York and Oxford: Berghahn books.

Guenther, Mathias. (ed.).
2005. *Kalahari and Namib Bushmen in German South West Africa: Ethno-graphic Reports by Colonial Soldiers and Settlers.* Koln: Rudiger Koppe Verlag.

Güldemann, Tom.
2014. 'Khoisan' linguistic classification today. In *Beyond 'Khoisan': Historical Relations in the Kalahari Basin*, Tom Güldemann & Anne-Maria Fehn, eds. pp. 1-44. Amsterdam: John Benjamins.

Güldemann, Thomas and Mark Stoneking.
2008. A Historical Appraisal of Clicks: A Linguistic and Genetic Population Perspective. *Annual Review of Anthropology* 37, 93–109.

Hays, Jennifer.
2016. *Owners of Learning: The Nyae Nyae Village Schools Over Twenty-Five Years*. Basel, Switzerland: Basler Afrika Bibliographien.

Hewlett, Barry S. (ed.).
2014. *Hunter-Gatherers of the Congo Basin: Cultures, Histories, and Biology of African Pygmies*. New Brunswick and London: Transaction Publishers.

Hitchcock, Robert K. and Wayne A. Babchuk.
2011. Genocides and Ethnocides among the Khoekhoe and San of Southern Africa. In *Genocide of Indigenous Peoples*, Samuel Totten and Robert K. Hitchcock, eds. pp. 143-171. New Brunswick, New Jersey: Transaction Publishers.

Hitchcock, Robert K. and Wayne A. Babchuk.
2016. San Traditional Authorities, Communal Conservancies, Conflicts, and Leadership in Namibia Paper presented the 115th annual meetings of the American Anthropological Association (AAA), Minneapolis, Minnesota, November 16-20, 2016.

Hitchcock, Robert K., Benjamin Begbie-Clench, and Ashton Murwira.
2016. *The San of Zimbabwe: Livelihoods, Land, and Human Rights*. Copenhagen: International Work Group for Indigenous Affairs and Johannesburg: Open Society Institute for Southern Africa.

Hitchcock, Robert K., Kazunobu Ikeya, Megan Biesele, and Richard B. Lee. (eds.).
2006. *Updating the San: Image and Reality of an African People in the 21st Century*. Senri Ethnological Studies 70. Osaka, Japan: National Museum of Ethnology.

Hitchcock, Robert K. and Diana Vinding. (eds.).
2004. *Indigenous Peoples' Rights in Southern Africa*. Copenhagen: International Work Group for Indigenous Affairs.

Howell, Nancy.
2010. *Life Histories of the Dobe !Kung: Food, Fatness, and Well-being Over the Life-Span*. New York: Aldine de Gruyter.

Kiema, Kuela.
2010. *Tears For My Land: A Social History of the Kua of the Central Kalahari Game Reserve, Tc'amnqo.* Gaborone: Mmegi Publishing House.

Kuper, Adam J.
2003. The Return of the Native. *Current Anthropology* 44(3), 389-411.

Lee, Richard B.
1976. Introduction. In *Kalahari Hunter Gatherers: Studies of the !Kung San and Their Neighbors,* Richard B. Lee and Irven DeVore, eds. pp. 3 24. Cambridge: Harvard University Press.

Lee, Richard B.
1979. *The !Kung San: Men, Women, and Work in a Foraging Society.* Cambridge: Cambridge University Press.

Lee, Richard B.
2013. *The Dobe Ju/'hoansi.* Independence, Kentucky: Cencage.

Lee, Richard B. and Irven DeVore. (eds.).
1976. *Kalahari Hunter Gatherers: Studies of the !Kung San and their Neighbors.* Cambridge, Massachusetts: Harvard University Press.

LeRoux, Willemien and Alison White. (eds.).
2004. *Voices of the San: Living in Southern Africa Today.* Cape Town: Kwela Books.

Marshall, John.
2003. *A Kalahari Family.* (film). Watertown, Massachusetts: Documentary Educational Resources.

Marshall, Lorna.
1976. *The !Kung of Nyae Nyae.* Cambridge: Harvard University Press.

Marshall, Lorna.
1999. *Nyae Nyae !Kung: Beliefs and Rites.* Cambridge, Massachusetts: Peabody Museum Monographs.

Mogwe, Alice
1992. *Who Was (T)here First? An Assessment of the Human Rights Situation of Basarwa in Selected Communities in the Gantsi District, Botswana.* Gaborone: Botswana Christian Council.

Morris, Job.
2011. Indigenous leadership: Value Driven Development: A San Perspective. Paper presented at a seminar on Responsible Leadership: lessons Learned, organized by the Albert Luthuli Center for Responsible Leadership, University of Pretoria, Pretoria, South Africa, 15 September, 2011.

Passarge, Siegfried.
1904. *Die Kalahari*. Berlin: Dietrich Riemer.

Passarge, Siegfried.
1907. *Die Buschmanner der Kalahari*. Berlin: Dietrich Reimer.

Penn, Nigel.
2006. *The Forgotten Frontier: Colonist and Khoisan on the Cape's Northern Frontier in the 18th Century*. Athens: Ohio University Press.

Prins, Frans E.
2009 Secret San of the Drakensberg and their Rock Art Legacy. *Critical Arts* 23(2),190-208.

Republic of Botswana.
2015. *Botswana Land Policy*. Government Paper No. 4 of 2015. Gaborone: Botswana Government Printer.

Republic of Namibia.
2000. *Traditional Authorities Act of 2000* (No. 25 of 2000). Windhoek: Government of the Republic of Namibia.

Sands, Bonny.
1998. *Eastern and Southern African Khoisan: Evaluating Claims of Distant Linguistic Relationships*. Quellen zur Khoisan-Forschung/Research in Khoisan Studies 14. Köln: Rüdiger Köppe.

Sapignoli, Maria.
2015. Dispossession in the Age of Humanity: Human Rights, Citizenship, and Indigeneity in the Central Kalahari. *Anthropological Forum: A Journal of Social Anthropology and Comparative Sociology* 25(3), 285-305.

Sapignoli, Maria
2016. Indigenous Mobilization and Activism: The San, the Botswana State, and the International Community. In *Handbook of Indigenous Peoples' Rights*, Corinne Lennox and Damien Short, eds. pp. 268-281. London and New York: Routledge.

Saugestad, Sidsel.
2001. *The Inconvenient Indigenous: Remote Area Development in Botswana, Donor Assistance, and the First People of the Kalahari.* Uppsala: The Nordic Africa Institute.

Schapera, Isaac.
1930. *Khoisan Peoples of South Africa: Bushmen and Hottentots.* London: Routledge and Kegan Paul.

Silberbauer, George B.
1981. *Hunter and Habitat in the Central Kalahari Desert.* New York: Cambridge University Press.

Silberbauer, George B.
1982. Political Process in G/Wi Bands. In *Politics and History in Band Societies*, Eleanor Leacock and Richard Lee, eds. pp. 23 35. Cambridge: Cambridge University Press.

Seleka, T., H. Siphambe, D. Ntseana, N. Mbere, C. Kerapeletswe, and C. Sharp.
2007. *Social Safety Nets in Botswana: Administration, Targeting, and Sustainability.* Gaborone: Lightbooks.

Suzman, James.
2001. *An Introduction to the Regional Assessment of the Status of the San in Southern Africa.* Windhoek, Namibia: Legal Assistance Center.

Takada, Akira.
2015. *Narratives on San Ethnicity: The Cultural and Ecological Foundations of Lifeworld among the !Xun of North-Central Namibia.* Kyoto: Kyoto University Press and Melbourne: Trans Pacific Press.

Takada, Akira. (ed.).
2016. *Natural History of Communication among the Central Kalahari San.* African Study Monographs Supplementary Issue 52. Kyoto: African Study Monographs.

Tanaka, Jiro.
2014. *The Bushmen: A Half-Century Chronicle of Transformation in Hunter-Gatherer Life and Ecology.* Translated by Minako Sato. Kyoto: Kyoto University Press and Melbourne: Trans Pacific Press.

Thomas, Elizabeth Marshall.
1958. *The Harmless People.* New York: Random House, Vintage Books.

Thomas, David S.G. and Paul A. Shaw.
2010. *The Kalahari Environment*. Cambridge: Cambridge University Press.

Tobias, Phillip V. (ed.).
1978. *The Bushmen: San Hunters and Herders of Southern Africa*, Cape Town and Pretoria: Human and Rousseau.

Traill, Anthony.
1985. *Phonetic and Phonological Studies of !Xoo Bushmen*. Hamburg: Helmut Buske Verlag.

Ury, William.
1995. Conflict Resolution among the Bushmen: Lessons in Dispute Systems Design. *Negotiation Journal* 11, 579-589.

Valiente-Noailles, Carlos.
1993. *The Kua: Life and Soul of the Central Kalahari Bushmen*. Amsterdam: A.A. Balkema.

Vossen, Rainer. (ed.).
2013. *The Khoesan Languages*. New York: Routledge.

Wiessner, Polly.
2005. Norm Enforcement among the Ju/'hoansi Bushmen: A Case of Strong Reciprocity? *Human Nature* 16(2), 115-145.

Wiessner, Polly.
2014. Embers of Society: Firelight Talk among the Ju'hoansi Bushmen. *Proceedings of the National Academy of Sciences* 111(39), 14027-14035.

World Bank.
2015. *Botswana Poverty Assessment*. Washington, DC: The World Bank, March, 2015.

Wright, John.
1971. *Bushman Raiders of the Drakensberg, 1840-1870*. Pietermaritzburg: University of Natal Press.

Wynberg, Rachel, Doris Schroeder, and Roger Chennells. (eds.).
2009. *Indigenous Peoples, Consent, and Benefit Sharing: Lessons from the San-Hoodia Case*. Dordrecht, Heidelberg, and New York: Springer.

Yellen, John E.
1977. *Archaeological Approaches to the Present: Models for Reconstructing the Past*. New York: Academic Press.

Table 1. Numbers of San in Angola, Botswana, Lesotho, Namibia, South Africa, Zambia, and Zimbabwe

Country	Population Size (2016)	Size of country (in Km²)	Numbers of San (National)
Angola	19,625,353	1,246,700	3,500
Botswana	2,182,719	581,730	63,500
Lesotho	1,942,701	30,355	400
Namibia	2,212,307	824,292	38,000
South Africa	53,675,563	1,219,090	7,800
Zambia	15,066,266	752,618	1,500
Zimbabwe	14,229,541	390,757	2,600
TOTALS	108,939,450	2,658,955	120,900

Note: Data obtained from the following: population data from the *World Factbook*, accessed 13 August 2016; fieldwork and Nyae Nyae Development Foundation of Namibia (NNDFN), Nyae Nyae Conservancy (NNC), Namibia, Legal Assistance Centre (LAC), Namibia, Desert Research Foundation of Namibia (DFRN), Botswana Khwedom Council (BKC) (Botswana), First People of the Kalahari (FPK) (Botswana), the National KhoeSan Council (South Africa), the Tsoro-o-tso San Development Trust, Zimbabwe.

Table 2. Southern African Khoisan (Non-Bantu) Languages and Classifications

Name of Language Group	Languages or Dialects	Comments
KHOE-KWADI		
• Kwadi	Single language	
• Khoe (Central Khoisan)		
- Khoekhoe		
North	Eini†, Nama-Dama, Haiǀom ǂAakhoe	
South	ǃOra†, Cape Varieties	
- Kalahari		
East		
Shua	Deti†, Cara, ǀXaise, Danisi, Ts'ixa, etc.	Ts'ixa = Ts'ɛxakhwe
Tshwa	Kua, Cua, Tsua	
West		
Kxoe	Khwe, ǁAni, Buga, ǀGanda, etc.	
Gǁana	Gǁana, Gǀui, ǂHaba, etc.	
Naro	Naro, etc.	
JUǀ'HOAN		
• Juǀ'hoan	Single language	
• Ju (Northern Khoisan)		
- Northwest	ǃ'OǃXuun, Northern ǃ'Xuun, Ekoka ǃ'Xuun, Okongo ǃ'Xuun (North-central Namibia), Grootfontein ǃ'Xuun (Central Namibia)	Northern ǃ'Xuun (Angola)
- Southeast	Juǀ'hoan, ǂX'ao-ǁ'aen	ǂX'ao-ǁ'aen = ǂKx'aulʼen
TUU (Southern Khoisan)		
• Tsa - Lower Nossob		
- Taa		
West	Nǀuǁ'en†, West ǃXoon	ǃXoon = ǃXóõ
East	Nǁamani†, Kakia†, 'Nǀohan, East ǃXoon, Tsasi*, ǁHasi, Seroa (ǂHoan)*	
- Lower Nossob	ǀAuni†, ǁHausi†	
• ǃUi	ǀXam, ǁXegwi†, Nǀng, Nǀuu ǂKhomani, ǂUngkue†	

† = generally considered to be extinct.
* = added by Gertrud Boden.
Note: Data obtained from Guldemann (2006, 2008, p. 98, Table 4) and Gertrud Boden, Hessel Visser, Bonny Sands, and Hirosaki Nakagawa (personal communications, 2016).

Table 3. Legal Cases Involving Land and Resource Rights of San and Khoekhoe in Southern Africa

Group	Locality	Country	Issue	Workers
‡Khomani San 1998	Kgalagadi Transfrontier Park	South Africa	Land rights, co-management rights (settled out of court)	Roger Chennels (lawyer), Hugh Brody, Nigel Crawhall (anthropologists)
Nama *Richtersveld Community vs* Alexkor Ltd (Constitutional Court, October, 2003)	Nama people, Richtersveld National Park	South Africa, Constitutional Court decision 2003	Mineral rights, grazing rights	Legal Resources Foundation (Henk Smith) lawyer; Emile Boonzaier (anthropologist)
G/ui, G//ana, Bakgalagadi (High Court Case, Lobatse, (13 December, 2006)	Central Kalahari Game Reserve	Botswana (2004-2006)	Land rights, subsistence hunting rights	John Whitehead Gordon Bennett (lawyers), George Silberbauer, (anthropologist)
The High Court of Botswana	Central Kalahari Game Reserve	Botswana (2009-2011) High Court and Court of Appeal	Water rights	Gordon Bennett, Gideon Duma Boko, Applicants, First People of the Kalahari
N≠a Jaqna Conservancy (NJC) vs 35 invading farmers and fencers	N≠a Jaqna Conservancy Won on 18 September, 2016	Namibia	Land rights, removal of fences and illegal grazers, won in High Court 20 August 2016	Legal Assistance Center and N≠a Jaqna Conservancy Management Committee
Hai//om San Jan Tsumib Applicant and Eight Others vs the Government of the Republic of Namibia and 14 Others, 2015	Etosha National Park resettlement case, on-going	Namibia	Land rights, decision pending in High Court	Legal Assistance Center, Legal Resources Foundation, Ute Dieckmann, Thomas Widlok (anthropologists)

Table 4. International, National, and Community-Based Organizations involving San and other Groups in Southern Africa

Group(s)	Organization	Founding
All minority groups in Botswana	Reteng – the Multicultural Coalition of Botswana	2002
Naro and other San in Ghanzi and Ngamiland, Botswana	Kuru Family of Organizations (KFO)	1986
Ju/'hoansi San and Herero, /Xai /Xai, Botswana	Cgae Cgae Tlhabololo Trust, 500 people, in areas NG 4, 9,293 km2 and access to NG 5, 7673 km2 (16,966 km² total)	1997
Ju/'hoansi San and Hambukushu, Tsodilo Hills, Botswana	Tsodilo Community Development Trust, 140 people, in area NG 6, 225 km²	1999
Ju/'hoansi San, Nyae Nyae and Tsumkwe, Namibia	Nyae Nyae Conservancy, 2,400 people, 8992 km²	1998
!Xun, !Kung, and Khwe San	N≠a Jaqna Conservancy, Namibia (9003 km²)	2003
Khwe San, Zambezi Region, Namibia	Kyaramacan Trust	2005
San Youth in Namibia	San Youth Network (ScyNet), //Ana-Jeh San Trust	2015
!Xóõ San and Bakgalagadi in Kgalagadi District, Botswana	Ngwaa Khobee Yaya, Community Based Conservation Trust, consisting of 3 villages (Ukhwi, Ngwatle, Ncaang), 800 people, in area KD 1, 12,180 km²	1998
G/ui, G//ana, Bakgalagadi and other San in Botswana	First Peoples of the Kalahari (FPK)	1993
Hai//om (San), Namibia	Hai//om San Development Community Trust (HSDCT)	2007
San in South Africa	South African San Institute (SASI)	1996
San in Botswana	Botswana Khwedom Council (BKC)	2008
San in Namibia	Namibia San Council (NSC)	2012
San in South Africa	National Khoe and San Council (NKC)	1999
San in Zimbabwe	Tsoro-o-tso San Development Trust (TSDT)	2013
!Xun and Khwe San	Plaatfontein, South Africa	1990 relocation to Kimberley, South Africa, 1999 moved to Plaatfontein

Group(s)	Organization	Founding
San in Southern Africa	Working Group of Indigenous Minorities in Southern Africa (WIMSA)	1996
San in Southern Africa	Khwa ttu: San Culture and Education Center, Yzerfontein, South Africa	1999-2000

Note: Some of these trusts are in the process of being reconfigured. For additional information, see Barnard (1992); Suzman (2001); LeRoux and White (2004); Hitchcock et al (2006); Dieckmann et al (2014); Sapignoli (2015, 2016). Designations such as KD and NG represent areas in Botswana which are community-controlled hunting areas (CCHAs), the former way that land zones were designated in the country for planning and management purposes; Khwa ttu means 'water pans' in the ǀXam language.

Index

About the Authors

Jeffry Gayman is Associate Professor at Hokkaido University teaching multi-cultural education and English as a foreign language. Dr. Gayman earned his Ph.D. in educational anthropology at Kyushu University where the subject of his dissertation was the Ainu.

Robert K. Hitchcock is Professor of Anthropology at Michigan State University. He earned his Ph.D. in anthropology from the University of New Mexico and is the co-author of the book, *The Ju/'hoan San of Nyae Nyae and Namibian Independence*, and numerous other publications.

Douglas W. Hume is Associate Professor of Anthropology at Northern Kentucky University. He earned his Ph.D. in anthropology from the University of Connecticut and is the author of "Anthropology: Tribal Warfare" in Nature and numerous other publications.

Xabier Irujo is Co-Director of the Center for Basque Studies at the University of Nevada at Reno. He earned a Ph.D. in history from the State University of Navarre in Spain and a Ph.D. in philosophy from the University of the Basque Country in the Basque Autonomous Community in northern Spain and is the author of the book, *Gernika, 1937: The Market Day Massacre*, and numerous other publications.

Margaret Mutu (Ngāti Kahu, Te Rarawa, Ngāti Whātua) is Professor and Head of Māori Studies at the University of Auckland. Dr. Mutu earned her Ph.D. in Māori studies and linguistics at the University of Auckland, and is the author of the book, *The State of Māori Rights*, and numerous other publications.

Sharlotte Neely is Professor of Anthropology and Director of Native American Studies at Northern Kentucky University. She earned her Ph.D. in anthropology from the University of North Carolina at Chapel Hill and is the author of the book, *Snowbird Cherokees*, and numerous other publications.

'Umi Perkins (Native Hawaiian/Kanaka Maoli) teaches Hawaiian History at the Kamehameha Schools, Kapālama and is a Lecturer at the Matsunaga Institute for Peace and Conflict Resolution at the University of Hawaii at Manoa. Dr. Perkins earned his Ph.D. in political science from the University of Hawaii at Manoa and is the author of a forthcoming book, *Reserving Native Rights: A Genealogy of Kuleana Lands in Hawai'i*, and numerous other publications.

Maria Sapignoli is a Research Fellow at the Max Planck Institute for Social Anthropology in Halle an der Saale, Germany. She earned her Ph.D. in sociology from the University of Essex in England and is the co-author of the book, *Palaces of Hope: The Anthropology of Global Organizations*, and numerous other publications.

Michael J. Simonton is Lecturer in Anthropology and Director of Celtic Studies at Northern Kentucky University. Dr. Simonton earned his Ph.D. in anthropology from the National University of Ireland, Galway and is the author of the book, *Introduction to Cultural Anthropology*, and numerous other publications

Dikka Storm is Curator and Assistant Professor in the Department of Cultural Sciences, Tromsø Museum, University of Tromsø – The Arctic University of Norway. Dr. Storm earned her Ph.D. in geography from the University of Bergen and is the author of the book, *Slettnes på Sørøya : sluttrapport, undersøkelser av Samisk kulturhistorie*, and numerous other publications.

Mark Q. Sutton is Professor Emeritus of Anthropology at California State University, Bakersfield. Dr. Sutton earned his Ph.D. in anthropology from the University of California, Riverside and is the author of the book, *Introduction to Native North America*, and numerous other publications.

Robert Tonkinson is Professor Emeritus of Anthropology at the University of Western Australia. Dr. Tonkinson earned his Ph.D. in anthropology from the University of British Columbia and is the author of the book, *The Mardu*, and numerous other publications.

Yuan-Chao Tung is Associate Professor of Anthropology at the National University of Taiwan. He earned his Ph.D. in anthropology from Southern Methodist University and is the author of the book, *An Anthropological Study of Oceania*, and numerous other publications.